Earthworms Underground

by Kevin Beals • illustrated by Debra Bandelin and Bob Dacey

Published and Distributed by

Published and Distributed by

These materials are based upon work partially supported by the National Science Foundation under grant number ESI-0242733. The Federal Government has certain rights in this material. Any opinions, findings, and conclusions or recommendations expressed in this material are those of the author(s) and do not necessarily reflect the views of the National Science Foundation.

Developed at Lawrence Hall of Science and the Graduate School of Education at the University of California at Berkeley

Seeds of Science/Roots of Reading™ is a collaboration of a science team led by Jacqueline Barber and a literacy team led by P. David Pearson and Gina Cervetti.

Delta Education LLC
PO Box 3000
Nashua, NH 03061
1-800-258-1302
www.deltaeducation.com

Earthworms Underground
594-0013
ISBN-10: 1-59821-487-X
ISBN-13: 978-1-59821-487-1
1 2 3 4 5 6 7 8 9 10   11 10 09 08 07

Contents

Introduction 4
How Earthworms Breathe 6
How Earthworms Move 8
What Earthworms Eat 10
How Earthworms Protect Themselves 14
How Earthworms Reproduce 18
Earthworm Adaptations 21
Glossary 23

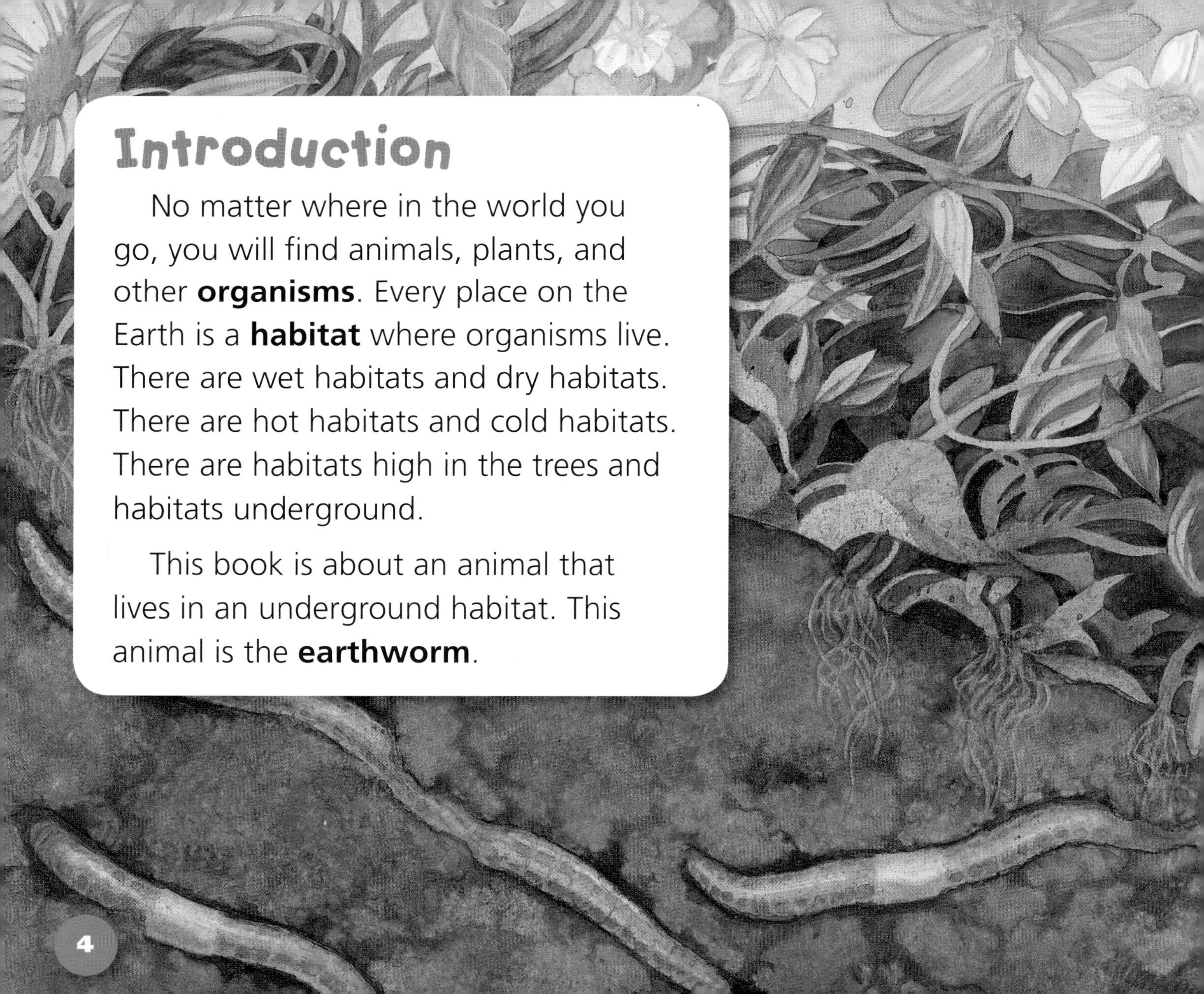

Introduction

No matter where in the world you go, you will find animals, plants, and other **organisms**. Every place on the Earth is a **habitat** where organisms live. There are wet habitats and dry habitats. There are hot habitats and cold habitats. There are habitats high in the trees and habitats underground.

This book is about an animal that lives in an underground habitat. This animal is the **earthworm**.

Can you imagine what it would be like to live underground in the **soil**? Earthworms have **adaptations** that help them **survive** in their underground habitat. What adaptations do you think earthworms have?

- How do they breathe underground?
- How do they move around?
- What do they eat?
- How do they **protect** themselves from danger?
- How do they **reproduce**?

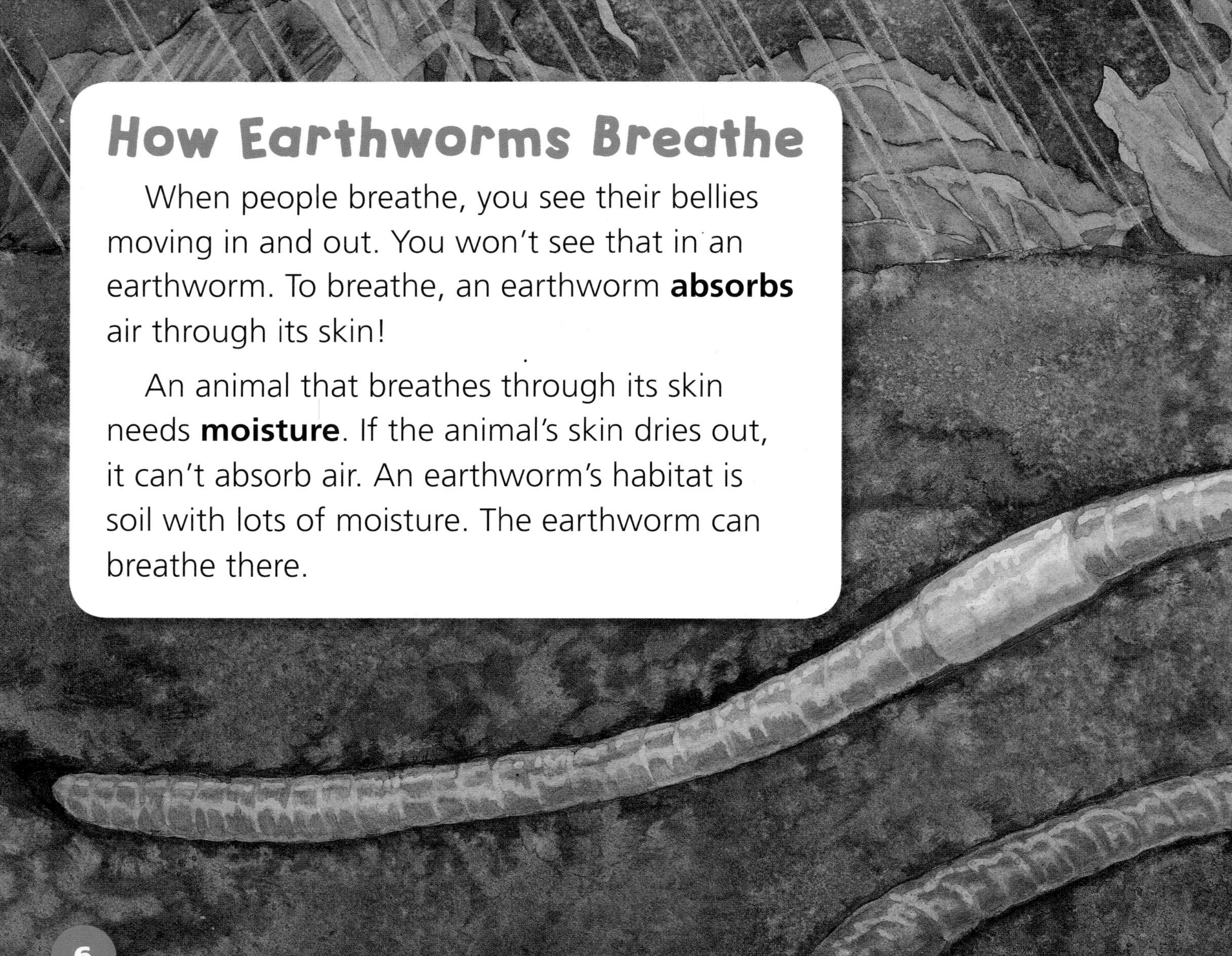

How Earthworms Breathe

When people breathe, you see their bellies moving in and out. You won't see that in an earthworm. To breathe, an earthworm **absorbs** air through its skin!

An animal that breathes through its skin needs **moisture**. If the animal's skin dries out, it can't absorb air. An earthworm's habitat is soil with lots of moisture. The earthworm can breathe there.

Earthworms don't usually come out of the soil unless it is wet above ground. They need moisture to breathe.

How Earthworms Move

Many animals move with their legs. But earthworms don't have legs! Legs would get in the way in earthworms' tiny underground **burrows**. Earthworms have different adaptations for moving through the soil. Earthworm bodies are made of **segments**. Each segment has tiny hairs on it.

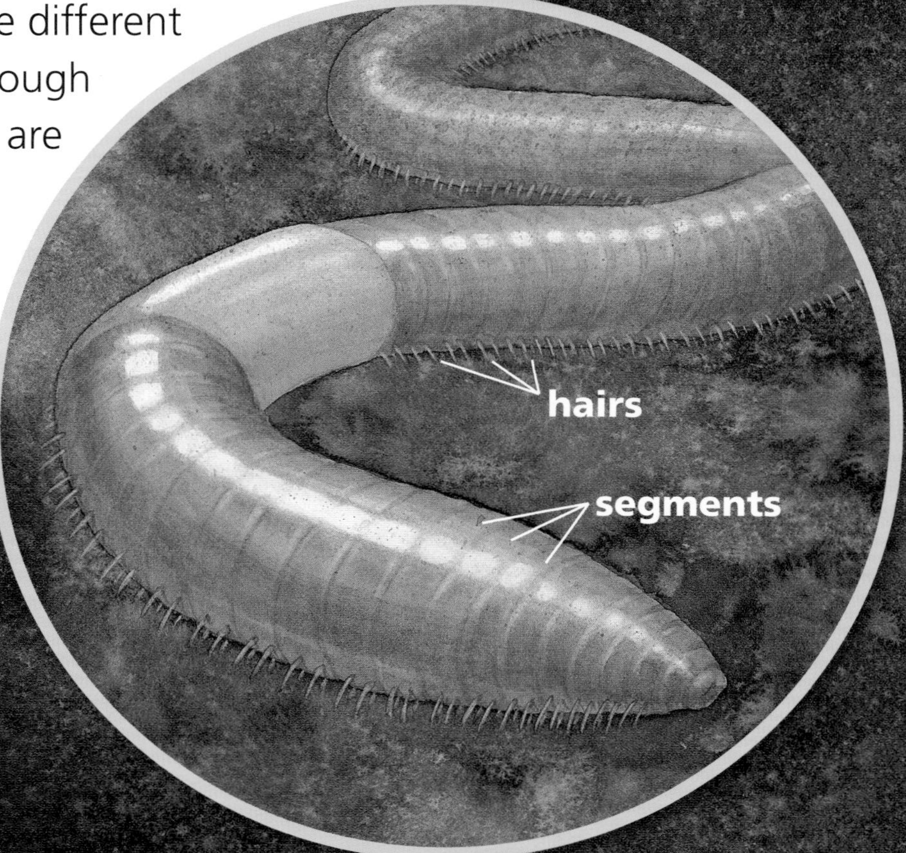

When an earthworm moves, it first reaches forward with its pointed head. The segments of its body become longer. That makes the earthworm's front end thin and long. The earthworm uses its tiny hairs to hold on to the soil.

Next the head pulls the rest of the earthworm forward. The segments pull together and become shorter. Now the earthworm is short and fat.

Then the head reaches forward again, making the front end thin and long. The earthworm reaches and pulls its way through the soil.

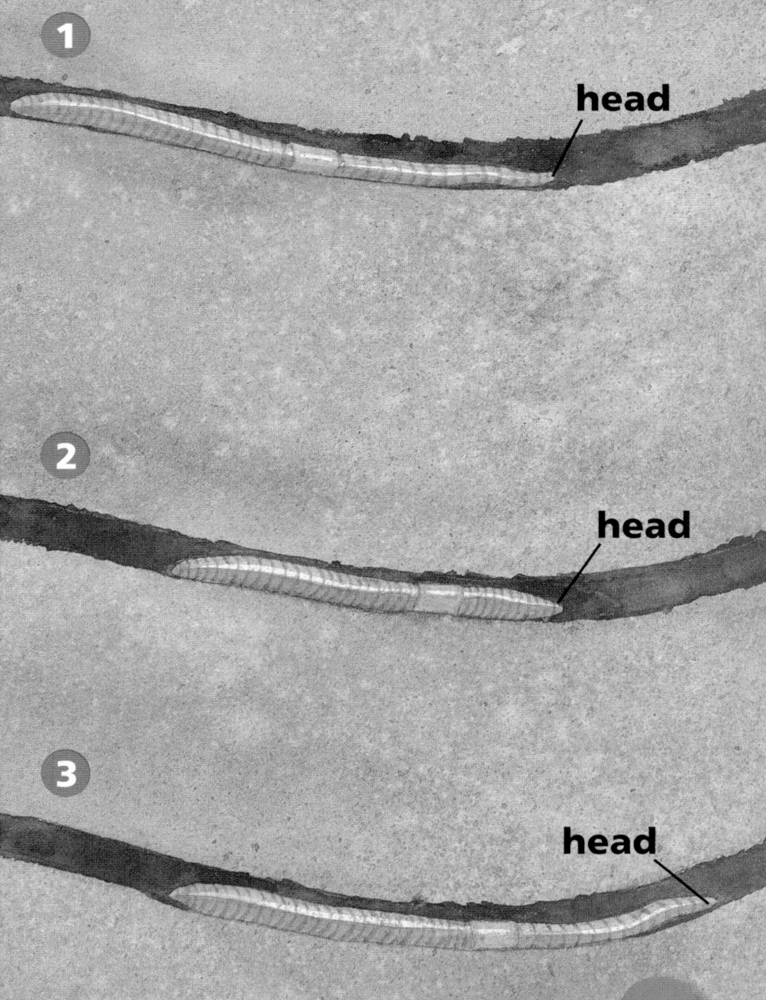

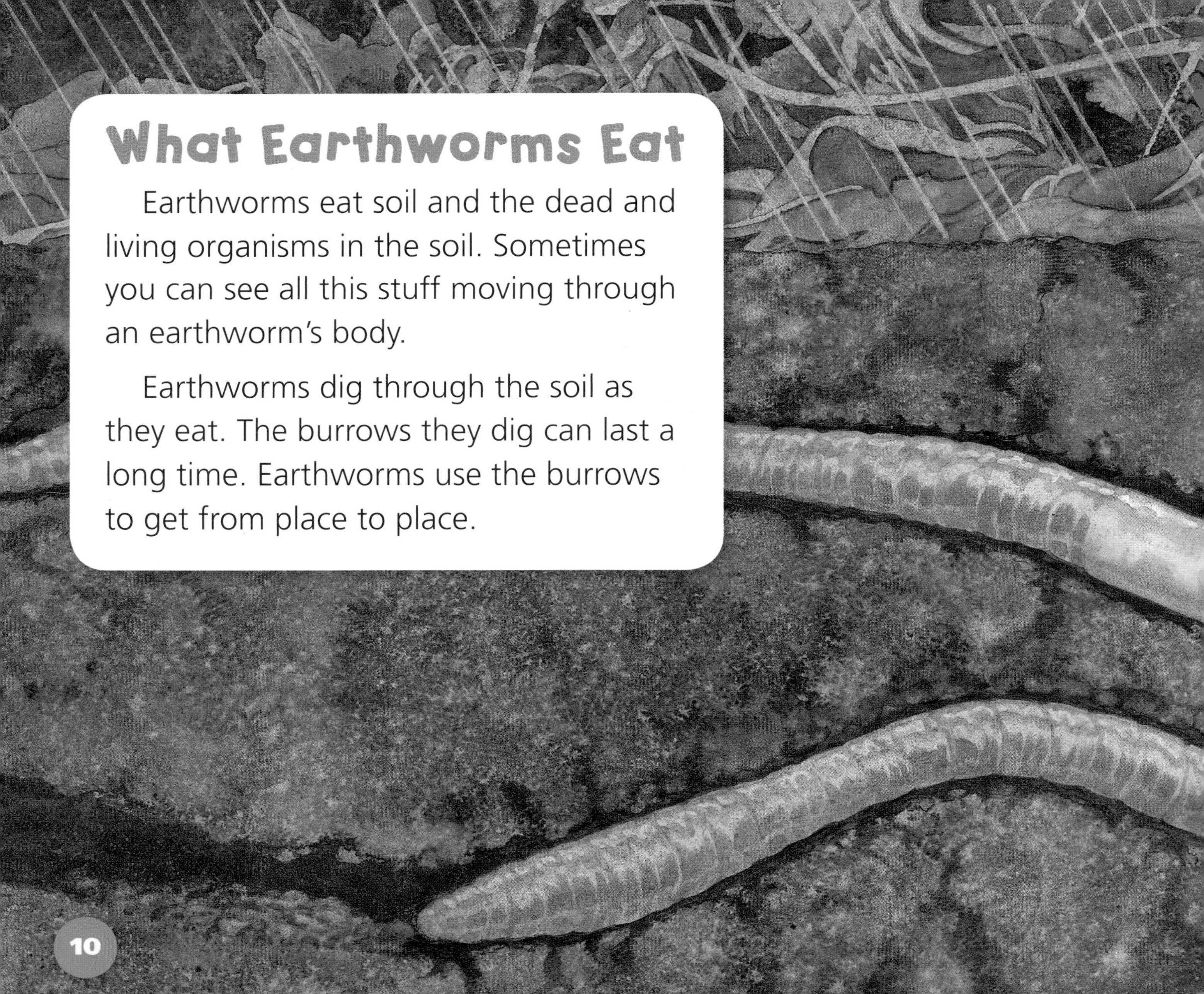

What Earthworms Eat

Earthworms eat soil and the dead and living organisms in the soil. Sometimes you can see all this stuff moving through an earthworm's body.

Earthworms dig through the soil as they eat. The burrows they dig can last a long time. Earthworms use the burrows to get from place to place.

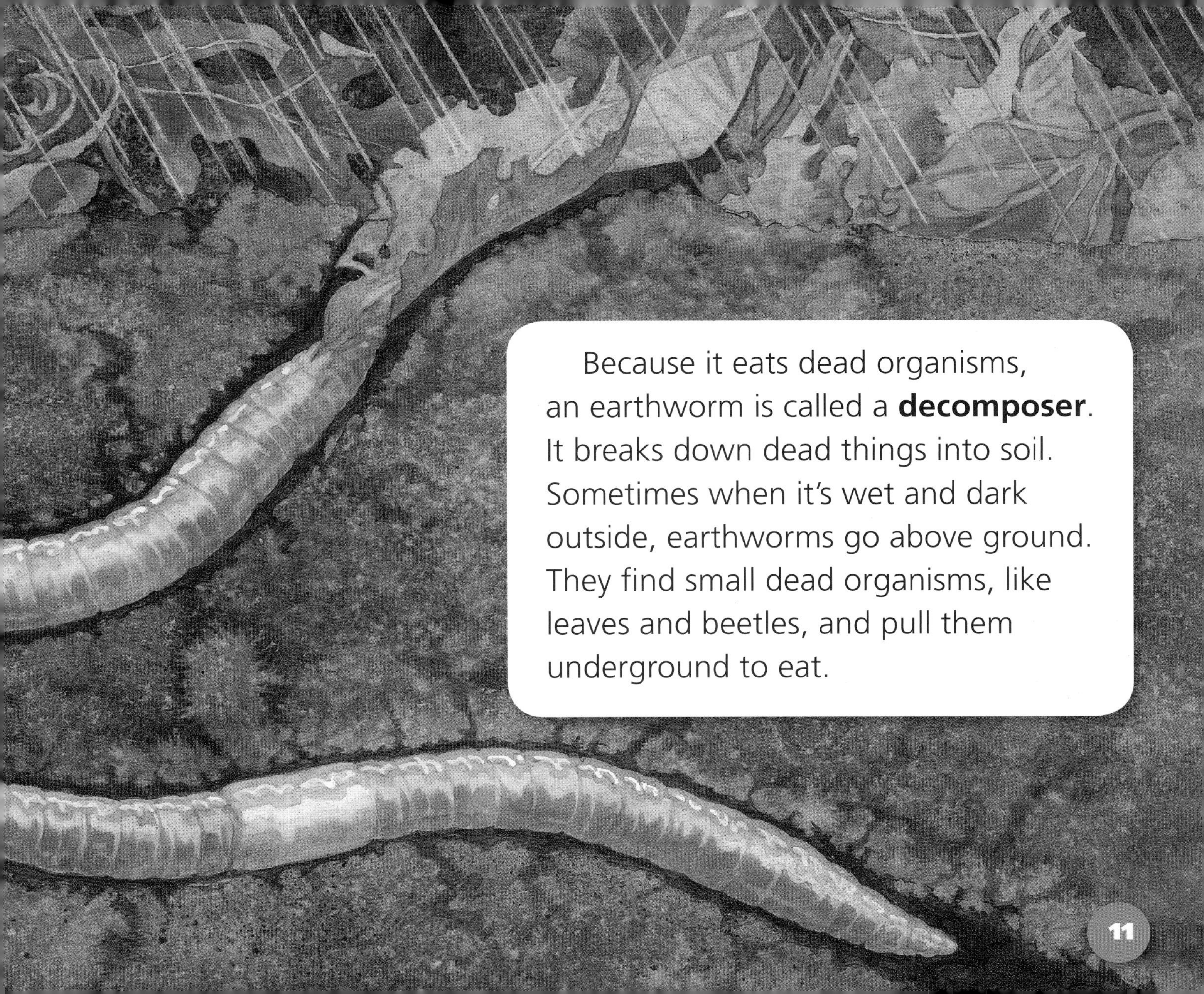

Because it eats dead organisms, an earthworm is called a **decomposer**. It breaks down dead things into soil. Sometimes when it's wet and dark outside, earthworms go above ground. They find small dead organisms, like leaves and beetles, and pull them underground to eat.

An earthworm doesn't need everything that goes into its mouth as it digs. The stuff it doesn't use comes out its other end. Earthworm **droppings** have lots of **nutrients** that mix with the soil. Plants need nutrients to grow.

An earthworm digs burrows as it eats. These burrows help let air into the soil. Plant **roots** need air. By moving around in the soil, earthworms mix up the soil's nutrients. Earthworms make the soil better for plants.

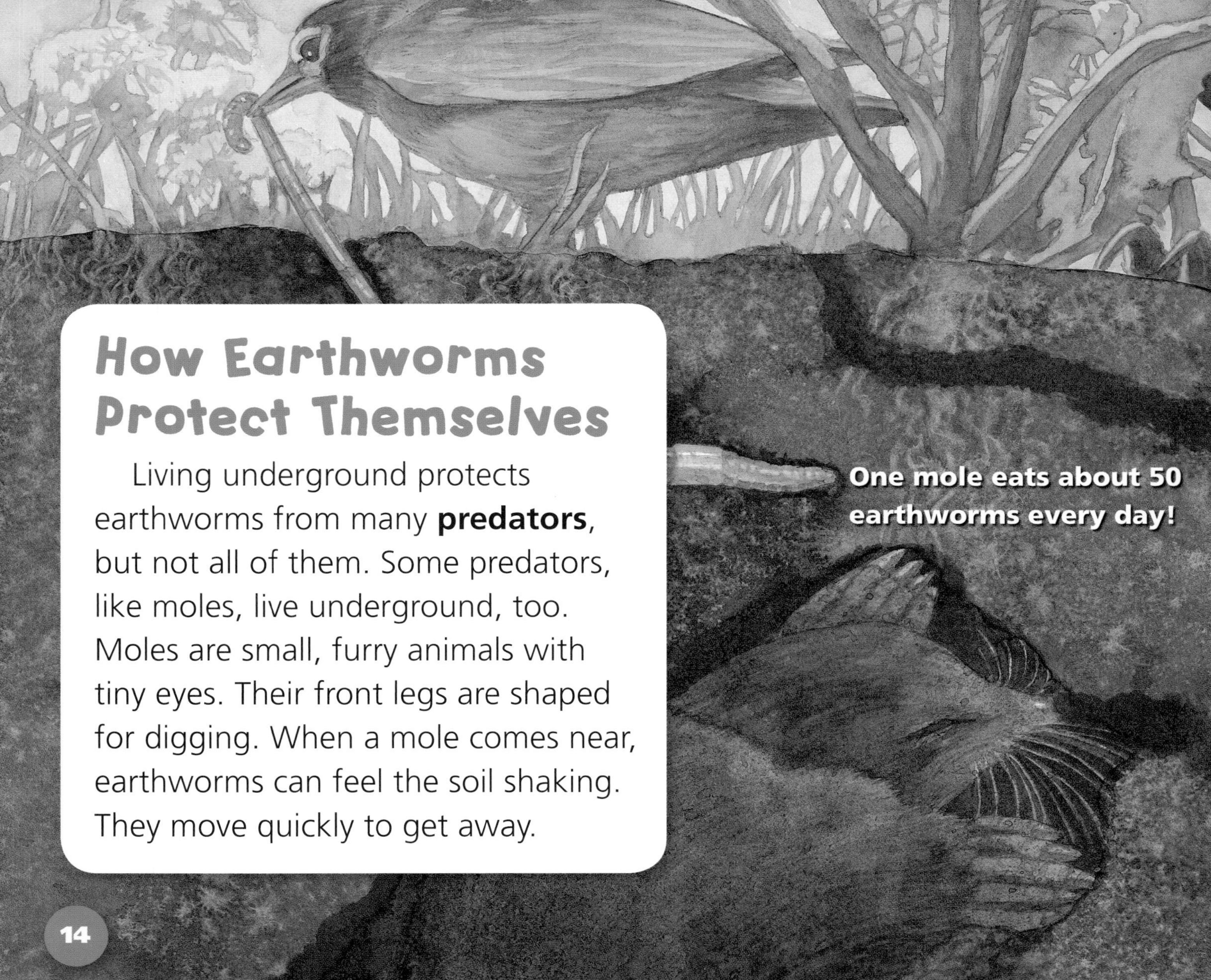

How Earthworms Protect Themselves

Living underground protects earthworms from many **predators**, but not all of them. Some predators, like moles, live underground, too. Moles are small, furry animals with tiny eyes. Their front legs are shaped for digging. When a mole comes near, earthworms can feel the soil shaking. They move quickly to get away.

Birds are also predators of earthworms. Some birds stand on the ground and listen for earthworms moving under them. The birds try to pull earthworms out of their burrows. Earthworms hold on to the soil with their tiny hairs. Sometimes the bird eats the whole earthworm. But earthworms have a strange adaptation to protect themselves.

If a bird pulls on an earthworm's tail end, sometimes it breaks off. The bird is left with just a piece of the tail. The piece keeps moving, and the bird may think it has the whole earthworm.

If only a little bit of the tail breaks off, the earthworm can move away and survive. Later the tail grows back. But if too much of the tail breaks off, the earthworm will not survive.

Something else can hurt earthworms, but it is not a predator. It is sunlight. Earthworm skin is good for breathing, but it is not good for **protection** from sunlight. Earthworms protect themselves from sunlight by staying underground. They don't usually come out unless it's dark.

How Earthworms Reproduce

When earthworms reproduce, they make more earthworms. Each earthworm is both male and female, but it can't reproduce by itself. It needs to find another earthworm to mate with. Earthworms find mates by smell.

On a wet night, lots of earthworms may come out of the ground. When there are many earthworms out, it's easier for earthworms to find mates and reproduce.

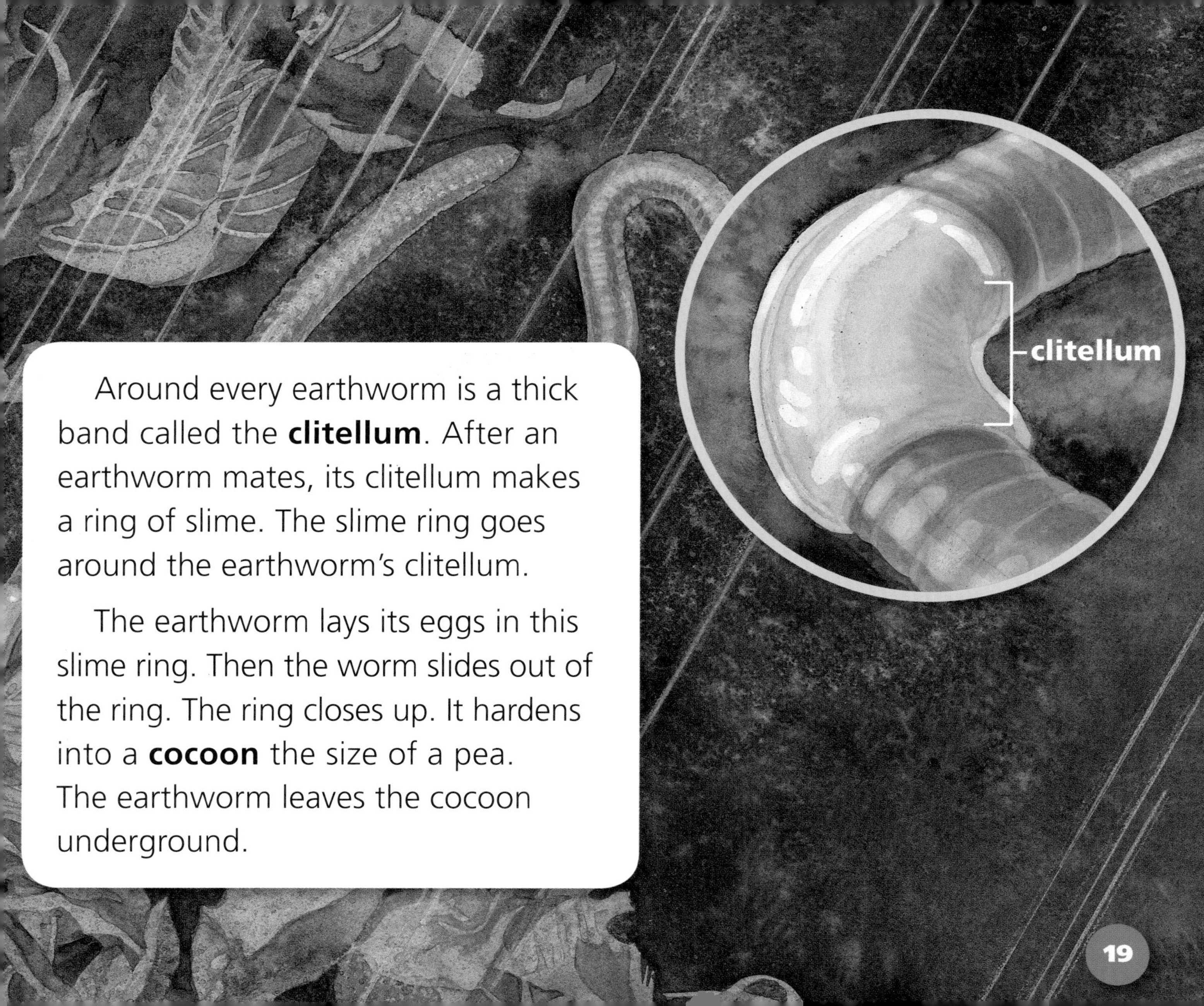

Around every earthworm is a thick band called the **clitellum**. After an earthworm mates, its clitellum makes a ring of slime. The slime ring goes around the earthworm's clitellum.

The earthworm lays its eggs in this slime ring. Then the worm slides out of the ring. The ring closes up. It hardens into a **cocoon** the size of a pea. The earthworm leaves the cocoon underground.

There may be 20 eggs inside an earthworm's cocoon. The cocoon protects the eggs, even if the soil dries out or gets very cold.

When it first **hatches** from an egg, an earthworm is tiny. It looks just like an adult earthworm but with no clitellum.

Earthworm Adaptations

An earthworm has many adaptations that help it survive underground.

- It breathes through its skin.
- It moves by pulling itself forward.
- It has tiny hairs to hold on to the soil.
- It eats dead and living things in the soil.
- Part of its tail end can break off and keep moving. Sometimes the tail end can grow back.
- It can find a mate with its sense of smell.
- Its eggs can survive weather that is very dry or cold.

Above ground in your habitat, you may not think earthworms are very special. They can't even survive above ground very long!

But they have lots of adaptations you don't have. And they can do something you can't do. They can survive in a habitat of soil. They can live underground.

absorb: to take in and hold something

adaptation: a structure or behavior that helps an organism survive in its habitat

burrow: a hole or tunnel that is made by an animal and lasts long enough for the animal to leave it and come back to it later

clitellum: a thick band around an earthworm, used for reproduction

cocoon: a protective covering for eggs or young animals

decomposer: an organism that breaks down dead plants and animals

droppings: waste that comes out of an animal

earthworm: a long animal with no bones or shell that lives in the soil and helps decompose dead things

habitat: where an organism lives and gets everything it needs to survive

hatch: to break out of an egg

moisture: wetness

nutrient: something taken in by plants and animals that helps them grow

organism: a living thing such as a plant or an animal

predator: an animal that hunts and eats other animals

protect: to keep someone or something safe

protection: keeping someone or something safe

reproduce: when an organism makes new organisms like itself

root: the part of a plant that takes in water and nutrients and helps hold the plant in place

segments: small parts of an animal's body, such as the segments of a worm

soil: a mixture of rocks, water, air, parts of dead organisms, and tiny living organisms

survive: to stay alive

SEX DISCRIMINATION

Sex Discrimination

by

D. J. WALKER,
Solicitor

A simple guide to the provisions of
THE SEX DISCRIMINATION ACT 1975

London:
Printed and published by
SHAW & SONS LTD.
Shaway House
SE26 5AE
1975

Published: November, 1975
Reprinted: March, 1976

ISBN 0 7219 0640 0 Cloth bound Edition (incorporating text of Act)

0 7219 0641 9 Paper bound Edition (without Act)

Printed in Great Britain

TABLE OF CONTENTS

PAGE

INTRODUCTION ... xi

CHAPTER 1. WHAT IS DISCRIMINATION? ... 1
- Sex Discrimination ... 1
- Marital Status Discrimination ... 6
- Anti-victimisation Provisions ... 8
- Discriminatory Practices... 10
- Exceptions... 10

CHAPTER 2. DISCRIMINATION IN EMPLOYMENT ... 14
- The Sex Discrimination Act and the Equal Pay Act... 14
- Discrimination in selecting employees and the terms of an offer ... 18
- Discrimination in terms of employment ... 21
  - Contract Workers ... 25
  - Vicarious Liability ... 26

CHAPTER 3. EXCEPTIONS TO UNLAWFUL DISCRIMINATION IN EMPLOYMENT ... 30
- Private households and small businesses ... 30
- Training facilities for a minority sex ... 31
- Particular categories of employment ... 31
- The Section 7 Exceptions ... 33

CHAPTER 4. SANCTIONS FOR DISCRIMINATION IN EMPLOYMENT ... 39
- Applications to Industrial Tribunals ... 39
  - Compensation ... 40
  - Conciliation ... 42
- Criminal Liability ... 42
- Time Limit for Applications ... 43
- Questionnaires for use prior to proceedings ... 44
- Non-Discrimination Notices ... 45
  - Power of Commission to serve Notices ... 45
  - Appeals against non-discrimination notices ... 47
- Injunctions ... 48
  - Preliminary applications by the Commission ... 51

CHAPTER 5. DISCRIMINATION IN OPPORTUNITIES FOR EMPLOYMENT AND TRAINING ... 54
- Vocational Training Bodies ... 54
  - Exception for discriminatory training ... 55
  - Exception for training involving communal accommodation ... 57
- Employment Agencies ... 58
  - Exceptions in Specific Instances ... 59
- Vicarious Liability ... 60
- Sanctions ... 61

PAGE

CHAPTER 6. DISCRIMINATION IN BUSINESS AND PROFESSIONAL ASSOCIATIONS, TRADE UNIONS AND PARTNERSHIPS, AND THE GRANTING OF QUALIFICATIONS 63
Employers' organisations, professional associations and trade unions 63
Covert Discrimination 64
Terms of membership and admission to membership 64
Discrimination during the period of membership 65
Summary 65
Exceptions to discrimination by employers' organisations and professional associations and trade unions 66
Governing bodies and qualifying bodies for professions and trades 70
Summary 72
Exceptions 73
Consideration of good character 73
Statutory appeal procedures 74
Partnerships 75
Exceptions 76
Summary 76
Partnership Contracts 78
Vicarious Liability 78

CHAPTER 7. SANCTIONS FOR BREACHES OF ACT BY BUSINESS AND PROFESSIONAL ASSOCIATIONS, TRADE UNIONS AND PARTNERSHIPS 82
Applications to Industrial Tribunals 82
Compensation 83
Conciliation 85
Criminal Liability 86
Time Limits for Applications 86
Questionnaires for use prior to proceedings 87
Non-discrimination Notices 88
Power of Commission to serve Notices 89
Appeals against non-discrimination notices ... 91
Injunctions 92
Preliminary applications by the Commission ... 93

CHAPTER 8. DISCRIMINATION IN EDUCATION 97
Unlawful discrimination under Section 22 97
Unlawful discrimination under Section 23 101
The General Duty under Section 25 102
Discrimination under Section 29 103
Vicarious liability... 104
Exceptions... 107
Physical training courses 110
Exceptions to Section 29 110
Exceptions for foreign travel 111
Charities 111
Variation of single-sex educational trusts 112

CHAPTER 9. SANCTIONS FOR DISCRIMINATION IN EDUCATION... 113
Orders giving directions by the Minister 113
County Court Proceedings 114
Time limits for proceedings in County Court ... 115
Questionnaires for use prior to proceedings 117

	PAGE
Non-discrimination Notices	118
Power of Commission to serve Notices	118
Appeals against non-discrimination notices ...	121
Injunctions	122
Injunction Applications by the Commission ...	124
CHAPTER 10. DISCRIMINATION IN THE PROVISION OF GOODS FACILITIES AND SERVICES	127
Exceptions...	128
Clubs and Private Associations	129
Non-profit making bodies	130
Political parties	132
Miscellaneous exceptions in section 35	133
Territorial Limits...	135
Discrimination in goods facilities and services defined	137
Discriminatory Contracts	139
Vicarious Liability	140
CHAPTER 11. DISCRIMINATION IN THE PROVISION OF HOUSING AND ACCOMMODATION	144
Sales and lettings...	144
Exceptions for sales and lettings	147
Treatment during occupation	148
Discrimination in the provision of accommodation under section 29	149
Exceptions to provision of accommodation under sections 29 and 30	150
Small Dwellings	151
Exemption for non-profit making associations ...	153
Communal Accommodation	154
Vicarious Liability	155
CHAPTER 12. SANCTIONS FOR DISCRIMINATION IN THE PROVISION OF GOODS, FACILITIES AND SERVICES AND ACCOMMODATION	158
County Court Proceedings	158
Time limits for proceedings	159
Questionnaires for use prior to proceedings	160
Non-discrimination Notices	162
Power of Commission to serve Notices	162
Appeals against non-discrimination notices ...	164
Injunctions	165
Injunction Applications by the Commission ...	167
CHAPTER 13. DISCRIMINATION IN ADVERTISEMENTS	171
Forms of advertising	172
Advertising for employees	174
Reliance upon statements of others	174
Sanctions	175
CHAPTER 14. THE EQUAL OPPORTUNITIES COMMISSION ...	178
Formal Investigations	178
Obtaining information in formal investigations ...	180
Non-disclosure of information obtained in formal investigations	193
Non-discrimination notices	185
Questionnaires for use prior to proceedings	188
Assistance by Commission in relation to proceedings	189

INTRODUCTION

I have to confess that I harbour an innate suspicion that, not infrequently, it is only the introduction to a book that is read, or read in full, by many people, and that this is particularly the case with text-books. I will try, therefore, to give readers some idea of what this book is about, in the hope of tempting them to read further. If I do not succeed in this, I am not likely to succeed in my main object in writing this book, which is to explain the Act in simple terms and in such a way that it can be understood, not by ordinary people, for nobody is " ordinary ", but by the average person who may have need to use the Act, and by all those in all walks of life who will play some part in administering the Act and putting its provisions into effect.

Those who are not merely skimming these lines will have noticed that, in the last paragraph, I have deliberately used the plural in order to avoid the sex-discriminatory " him " or " her ", and, although perhaps a little far-fetched, it illustrates the very basic and far-reaching effect the Act is likely to have in everyday thought and practice.

The Sex Discrimination Act is an Act which seeks not, as its name implies and its critics would have us believe, to provide for discrimination, but to prohibit **all** forms of discrimination because of a person's sex, in **all** walks of life, subject to a mixed bag of numerous specific exceptions. Nor is this all, for the Act also prohibits discrimination in employment on the grounds of " marital status ", *e.g.* an employer cannot show preference over a married man to a bachelor, or prefer a single woman to a married woman.

It is important to appreciate throughout that the Act is not a " women's charter " which merely prohibits discrimination against women. It forbids, to an equal degree, discrimination in favour of women against men. Many employers, for example, discriminate in favour of women, *e.g.* by giving them a " dowry " on marriage, or even an afternoon off before Christmas for shopping. Such practices will be unlawful under this Act, and are among the many to which changes must be made.

Much of the detail of the Act is devoted to employment and to education, but it also prohibits discrimination between the sexes, for example, in letting accommodation, in banking, insurance, mortgages, hire-purchase and other credit facilities, in professions and trade organisations, in trade unions, and in advertising such facilities or any employment.

In the following pages, I have been at pains to explain the Act in simple, everyday English and to avoid, wherever possible, not only legal phraseology and jargon, but also unnecessarily long words and phrases, together with those which, however much they may grace The Times' leaders, are not in common-or-garden use. Habits of thought and expression being what they are, I do not suppose I have always succeeded, but I can promise you that I have tried.

Bearing in mind the needs of those who are likely to read this book, I have also tried to make each subject self-contained, since the reader who is concerned with the effect of the Act in the field of employment is unlikely to be interested in the manner in which it deals with education, or housing and accommodation. Therefore, each chapter on a specific area of daily life draws together all the provisions of the Act which affect that area in any manner, no matter in which section or part of the Act they are to be found.

For the same reason, almost every chapter on a particular area of our national life is followed by a chapter dealing with all the sanctions which are applicable to a breach of the Act in that area, whether such sanctions are general in their application or relate only to the area concerned.

The direct result of this plan is a good deal of repetition, particularly in the chapters on sanctions where, I frankly admit, whole paragraphs and sections are repeated, word for word, in several chapters. I hope, however, that this will save readers turning back and forth through the pages to find the items that relate to their particular subject.

Everybody should read the first chapter, since it is the key to all the others and is **not** repeated elsewhere, and anybody who is interested in the composition and duties of the Equal Opportunities Commission should read the last chapter, although most of the **powers** of the Commission are dealt with in those other chapters to which they are relevant.

As happens with so many Acts of Parliament these days, the Act is to be brought into effect piecemeal on different dates, as and when the Home Secretary decides. Whilst this is the technical position, I understand that it is intended that most of the Act will be brought into effect on the 29th December 1975, although at one stage the Government were indicating that the provisions relating to education would be delayed until mid-1976.

To say that the Act is revolutionary is not just a platitude. If it is effective, and in this respect much will depend upon the energy and resolution of the Equal Opportunities Commission which it creates, it will indeed accomplish a revolution in the English way of life.

D. J. WALKER.

CHAPTER 1

WHAT IS DISCRIMINATION ?

Sex Discrimination

The Act employs the concept of taking a man as the standard or " norm " and providing that, if a woman with similar characteristics or of a similar standing is treated, on the grounds of her sex, less favourably than a man would be in those circumstances, that is discrimination which is unlawful. It must be understood clearly from the outset that only certain types of discrimination are unlawful. In every choice between two or more individuals, in every offer of goods, facilities, services or premises, in every promotion or relegation, there is, and must be, some element of discrimination, even if it is only on a " first come first served " basis, and the Act does not seek to outlaw or restrict discrimination as such, but only certain narrowly defined instances of it. It is, therefore, very much the case that, unless the act, omission or requirement falls clearly within one or other of the definitions contained in the Act, it is not unlawful and is not inhibited by the provisions of the Act. Since the definitions are so important, and are quite novel in English law, they are dealt with in this chapter at some length.

Because the Act applies also to discrimination against men, it then reverses the process, and provides that the definitions shall be read as applying equally to men. This " Alice through the looking-glass " treatment, whilst superficially reasonable, makes it unnecessarily difficult to appreciate the meaning and full force of many subsequent provisions of the Act and will doubtless give tribunals many headaches when attempting to construe the individual sections of the Act, and lead to anomalies.

The definition of discrimination in the Act is primarily contained in subsection (1) of section 1 and is split into two parts.

Paragraph (*a*) deals with overt or direct discrimination, that is to say, any act, rule or omission which, if one knows the full facts, is clearly and obviously discriminatory. Thus, an employer may refuse to employ a male air-line hostess, or a credit company may refuse to enter into a hire-purchase agreement with a woman unless she has a guarantor, contrary to its practice with men.

The second part of the definition clause in paragraph (*b*), deals with covert, or concealed, discrimination. That is not to say that it relates only to discrimination which there has been a deliberate attempt to hide, but to all requirements or conditions which **operate** in a discriminatory way against one sex or the other, and which cannot be shown to be justifiable irrespective of the sex.

It must be borne in mind that, in both subsections, intention and motive are quite irrelevant, and it is the **effect** of the conduct, practice or opinion which makes it unlawful. Motive may, however, be relevant to some extent in some of the exceptions to the general rule, which are referred to later, and is relevant in relation to offers of employment, and as a defence to proceedings for unlawful discrimination in the education field, and in the provision of goods, facilities or services.

The precise wording of section 1 (1) is as follows:

1.—(1) A person discriminates against a woman in any circumstances relevant for the purposes of any provision of this Act if—

(*a*) on the ground of her sex he treats her less favourably than he treats or would treat a man, or

(*b*) he applies to her a requirement or condition which applies or would apply equally to a man but—

(i) which is such that the proportion of women who can comply with it is considerably smaller than the proportion of men who can comply with it, and

(ii) which he cannot show to be justifiable irrespective of the sex of the person to whom it is applied, and

(iii) which is to her detriment because she cannot comply with it.

With this must be read subsection (3) of section 5, which reads as follows:

> (3) A comparison of the cases of persons of different sex or marital status under section 1 (1) or 3 (1) must be such that the relevant circumstances in the one case are the same, or not materially different, in the other.

Here it must be interjected that the Interpretation Act 1889 defines " person " for this purpose as including " any body of persons, corporate or incorporate ".

In addition, section 2 (the " looking glass " section) provides that:

> 2.—(1) Section 1, and the provisions of Parts II and III relating to sex discrimination against women, are to be read as applying equally to the treatment of men, and for that purpose shall have effect with such modifications as are requisite.

It will be seen that the essential factors in **overt** discrimination are:

(i) That a specific woman is treated less favourably (or a specific man is treated less favourably)

(ii) than a specific man is, or a hypothetical man would be, treated (or a specific or hypothetical woman is or would be treated)

(iii) by the person, firm or company against whom the complaint is made

(iv) on an occasion when the " relevant " circumstances are

(v) the same, or " not materially different ".

It need scarcely be said that what are the " relevant " circumstances, and whether they are " materially different ", may give rise to lengthy argument, especially when the comparison has to be made with a hypothetical person of the other sex, but the ambit of the Act is so wide that it is inevitable that these questions must be left as questions of fact, to be decided by the tribunal in every case.

Section 2 (2) provides that, in applying the above rules to discrimination against men, no account shall be taken of special treatment afforded to women in connection with pregnancy or childbirth.

It will also be seen that the essential factors in **covert** discrimination are:

(i) A requirement or condition

(ii) applied to a specific woman (or, in the " looking glass " situation, to a specific man)

(iii) by the person, firm or company against whom the complaint is made

(iv) which applies equally to a specific man or would apply equally to a hypothetical man and

(v) which is such that the ' proportion of women ' who **can** comply with it is considerably smaller than the ' proportion of men ' who **can** comply with it **and**

(vi) which he cannot show to be **justifiable** " irrespective of the sex of the person to whom it is applied ", **and**

(vii) which is to her detriment because she cannot comply with it.

It would appear that the requirement or condition need not be written, and that it can be implied or inferred as well as expressed.

The ' proportion of women ' must necessarily refer to women at large, and not merely to the proportion of those women who actually are in the situation in which they are discriminated against by the requirement or condition, or even the proportion of such women who are likely to find themselves in that situation, although, since the Act applies only to England, Scotland and Wales, women outside those areas should not be taken into account when calculating or assessing the proportion. For the purpose of this Act, even a female baby is a woman, as explained later, and must, presumably, be included when calculating the proportion. The same standard must be applied in calculating or assessing the proportion of men for the purpose of the comparison.

It must be noted that, when making the comparison, it is the proportion of each sex that **can** comply with the requirement that is to be taken into account, not the proportion who are **willing** to comply with it, or would be able to comply with it in the future, or to do so subject to some reservation. Equally, it is immaterial that compliance by either sex would involve some considerable sacrifice or hardship, or be obnoxious, providing it is physically possible. Any, or all, of these considerations may be vital in certain situations.

It will be seen that the proportion of the sex allegedly suffering discrimination has to be **considerably** smaller than the proportion of the other sex if the discrimination is to be unlawful. It will be for the tribunal dealing with the complaint or proceedings to decide whether a proportion is **considerably** smaller than another. Obviously, a requirement that all the chauffeurs employed by a particular company must sport moustaches would be possible of compliance by a considerably smaller proportion of women than of men, but a rule by a partnership that they would only offer the position of partner to persons who could drive a car might not be, depending upon current statistics of qualified drivers.

Regardless of the interpretation put upon " considerably " in this connection, the last two examples would both, on the face of it, render the respective requirements an unlawful discrimination by reason of (vi) above. One can, however, envisage circumstances in which the second requirement might be " justifiable ". It must be remarked, in passing, that it is curious that the Act does not use "*justified*", and, indeed, the phrase " cannot *show* to be justifiable " places the emphasis upon excusing the requirement after the event, whatever the original purpose may have been.

This is the appropriate point at which to mention that damages can be awarded both for overt discrimination, and for covert or concealed discrimination. Apart from this brief interjection, since the sanctions for discrimination vary according to the field in which the discrimination occurs, they will be dealt with specifically in connection with each subject.

In this book, as in the Act, the words " man " and " woman " are used for convenience, but section 5 (2) provides that " woman " means a female of **any** age, and that " man " means a male of **any** age. This has very wide implications, since it means that even babes-in-arms can suffer from unlawful discrimination, and are, presumably, entitled to the benefit of the remedies provided by the Act.

There is a qualification to the comparison with a man required in respect of both overt and covert discrimination, which is contained in subsection (2) of section 1, namely, that if a man would be treated differently according to his marital status, the treatment accorded to the woman must be compared to that which is, or would be, accorded to a man with the same marital status. Whilst this provision appears reasonable taken alone, it is extremely curious in the light of the fact that discrimination between a married person and a single person of the same sex, called " discrimination on the ground of marital status " is made unlawful throughout the Act.

Marital Status Discrimination

The concept of unlawful discrimination on the ground of " marital status " (the words used, somewhat inaccurately, by the Act) is contained in section 3 (1) which, apart from the substitution of the words " married person ", " marital status " and " unmarried person " for " woman ", " sex " and " man ", is a carbon copy of section 1 (1). As with section 1 (1), the subsection is divided into two parts, one dealing with overt discrimination and the other with covert discrimination.

It may be helpful to reproduce here the first part of the subsection (bearing in mind that there is a second part, or " leg ", which deals with covert discrimination), in order to show the general effect. The first part reads as follows:

> 3.—(1) A person discriminates against a married person of either sex in any circumstances relevant for the purposes of any provision of Part II if—
>
> (*a*) on the ground of his or her marital status he treats that person less favourably than he treats or would treat an unmarried person of the same sex.

Now, although the opening words of subsection (1) include the phrase " in any circumstances relevant for the purposes of any provision of Part II ", and Part II of the Act deals mainly with employment, subsection (1) of section 5 provides that " In this Act—(*a*) references to discrimination refer to any discrimination falling within sections 1 to 4 ", and subsection (1) of section 82 provides that " in this Act, unless the context otherwise requires, discrimination and related terms shall be construed in accordance with section 5 (1) ". It follows, therefore, that whenever the words " discriminates " and " to discriminate " are used, they mean ' discriminate on the ground of marital status ' just as much as they mean ' discriminate on the ground of sex ' and, in view of this, the reader will find that ' marital status discrimination ' is prohibited by every part of the Act, and not merely Part II.

Paragraph (*b*) of subsection (1) deals with **covert** discrimination on the ground of " marital status ", and the reader is reminded of all that has already been said about covert discrimination in respect of discrimination on the ground of sex. The paragraph is as follows:

> (*b*) he applies to that person a requirement or condition which he applies or would apply equally to an unmarried person but—
>
> (i) which is such that the proportion of married persons who can comply with it is considerably smaller than the proportion of unmarried persons of the same sex who can comply with it, and
>
> (ii) which he cannot show to be justifiable irrespective of the marital status of the person to whom it is applied, and
>
> (iii) which is to that person's detriment because he cannot comply with it.

Subsection (3) of section 5 also applies to this form of discrimination, and therefore what has been said above regarding the comparison to be made between persons of different sex applies, with equal force, to the comparison to be made between the married and the single.

It will be seen from paragraph (*a*) above that the comparison in this case must be made between persons of the **same** sex, and it is important to bear this in mind in the following chapters of this book, when the phrase " discriminate on the grounds of marital status " will not, of itself, make this apparent.

An additional, if even more obvious, point should be made, and that is that the comparison which is to be made is between **married** and **unmarried** persons; it matters not whether the latter if, for example, a woman, is a spinster, widow or divorcee.

Anti-victimisation provisions

Favouring a man who is single against one who is married cannot, by any stretch of the imagination, be brought within the phrase "sex discrimination". Nor is the short title of the Act really appropriate to section 4, which deals with victimisation, unless the section is classed as what it really is: a form of sanction. Nevertheless, since the section treats victimisation by defining it as a form of discrimination, which is forbidden by the Act, it falls to be dealt with in this chapter.

Section 4 provides that the treatment of a person " less favourably " than the treatment which is, or would be, applied to others in similar circumstances, in order to victimise that person for any one of a variety of **actual or apprehended** acts, is discrimination of the kind which is prohibited by the Act. The section refers only to overt, and not to covert, discrimination, but the use of the words " or would treat other persons " does enable comparisons to be made with hypothetical men and women.

The **acts** for which a person must not be victimised include, by subsections (1) (*a*) and (1) (*b*) of section 4, the bringing of proceedings under the Act against the person who (or body which) so discriminates (called throughout the section: " the discriminator ") and the giving of evidence or information in connection with such proceedings. Hence, there is protection, not only for someone who **suffers** discrimination because of their sex, or the fact that they are married, and seeks a remedy under the Act, but also for anyone who assists them to do so.

Subsection (1) (*c*) of section 4 makes the protection very wide indeed by extending the definition of discrimination to the unfavourable treatment of anyone who has " otherwise done **anything** under or by reference to this Act " in relation to " the discriminator ", whilst subsection (1) (*d*) of section 4 covers **allegations** that " the discriminator " has done something which would amount to a contravention of the Act (whether or not the allegation actually states that the act **is** a contravention).

It should be noted that subsection (2) of section 4 provides that unfavourable treatment of a person for any of the reasons mentioned above will **not** be discrimination if it was in respect of an **allegation** which was both false **and** not made in good faith. This could apply not only to subsection (1) (*d*) of section 4, but also to subsections (1) (*b*) and (1) (*c*) if the conduct which brought about the discrimination included a false allegation **not** made in good faith.

The precise wording of subsections (1) and (2) of section 4 is:

(1) A person (" the discriminator ") discriminates against another person (" the person victimised ") in any circumstances relevant for the purposes of any provision of this Act if he treats the person victimised less favourably than in those circumstances he treats or would treat other persons, and does so by reason that the person victimised has—

(*a*) brought proceedings against the discriminator or any other person under this Act or the Equal Pay Act 1970, or

(*b*) given evidence or information in connection with proceedings brought by any person against the discriminator or any other person under this Act or the Equal Pay Act 1970, or

(*c*) otherwise done anything under or by reference to this Act or the Equal Pay Act 1970 in relation to the discriminator or any other person, or

(*d*) alleged that the discriminator or any other person has committed an act which (whether or not the allegation so states) would amount to a contravention of this Act or give rise to a claim under the Equal Pay Act 1970,

or by reason that the discriminator knows the person victimised intends to do any of those things, or suspects the person victimised has done, or intends to do, any of them.

(2) Subsection (1) does not apply to treatment of a person by reason of any allegation made by him if the allegation was false and not made in good faith.

There are two further points that must be mentioned. The first is that the section also applies to acts and allegations which relate to the Equal Pay Act 1970. Some of the provisions of the Equal Pay Act are dealt with in the next chapter. Secondly, it is equally discrimination if the person victimised has given evidence or information in connection with, or brought proceedings, or made allegations against, **any other person.** This is to prevent any form of " blacklisting ", or collusion between a discriminator under this section and a discriminator under sections 1, 2 or 3.

Discriminatory Practices

Finally, there are the provisions relating to " discriminatory practices " contained in section 37. The wording of this section is incredibly vague and difficult to construe. Subsections (1) and (2) are as follows:

> (1) In this section " discriminatory practice " means the application of a requirement or condition which results or could result in an act of discrimination which is unlawful by virtue of any provision of Part II or III taken with section 1 (1) (*b*) or 3 (1) (*b*) or which would be likely to result in such an act of discrimination if the persons to whom it is applied were not all of one sex.
>
> (2) A person acts in contravention of this section if and so long as—
>
> (*a*) he applies a discriminatory practice, or
>
> (*b*) he operates practices or other arrangements which in any circumstances would call for the application by him of a discriminatory practice.

Apparently, it is intended that this form of words will enable the Commission to hunt around and sniff out unlawful discrimination which is apparent to no-one else, and has given rise to no complaint, much as a police dog sniffs out drugs.

It is impossible to suggest any guidelines which would enable a person, body or firm to ensure that they do not contravene the provisions of this section. Those likely to be concerned must conform to the other requirements of the Act and hope for the best.

Perhaps the only mitigating feature of this section is that, by subsection (3), it can only be enforced by the Commission in accordance with sections 67 to 71. That is to say, as will be seen later, by serving a non-discrimination notice (which is subject to many restrictions) and, if that is ignored, eventually applying to Court for an injunction.

Exceptions

Having defined the discrimination which is unlawful, one must look to the numerous exceptions scattered throughout the Act, like the currants in a cake, which provide that, in the specified circumstances, the discrimination is not, after all, unlawful. Some of these exceptions relate to a particular field or area in which discrimination may occur, and are dealt with in the appropriate Chapter; others are of a more general application, and are therefore appropriate to the question posed by this Chapter.

First, any provision to confer a benefit or benefits upon one sex only contained in the **objects** of a charity, and anything done, or any omission, in carrying out that provision, is excepted by section 43. A simple example of such a provision is the charming, if outdated, requirement in some old charities to " give £X on Michaelmas day to ten deserving widows of " such-and-such a parish.

This section applies to provisions contained in an Act of Parliament or a Charter, in a Will creating such a trust, or in a Deed. The definition is contained in subsections (3) and (4) of section 43, which are worth reproducing here:

(3) in the application of this section in England and Wales—

(*a*) " charitable instrument " means an enactment or other instrument passed or made for charitable purposes, or an enactment or other instrument so far as it relates to charitable purposes;

(*b*) " charitable purposes " means purposes which are exclusively charitable according to the law of England and Wales

(4) in the application of this section to Scotland " charitable instrument " means an enactment or instrument passed or made by or on behalf of a body of persons or trust established for charitable purposes only.

The law relating to charities is complex and the definition which the law has evolved over the centuries is designed to deal with matters totally unconnected with the objects of this Act. However, since the Act refers to the general legal definition, it may be summarised, somewhat inadequately, as follows:

1. The charity must promote a **public** benefit.
2. In addition, it must be for one or more of the following:

   (*a*) the relief of poverty

   (*b*) the advancement of education

(*c*) the advancement of religion or

(*d*) other purposes beneficial to the community.

3. It must not include a purpose outside the above.

The " other purposes beneficial to the community " are regarded in law as limited to a list contained in an Act passed during the reign of Elizabeth I which, so far as it is now relevant, is as follows:

> The relief of aged, impotent and poor people, the maintenance of sick and maimed soldiers and mariners, schools of learning, free schools and scholars in universities; the repair of bridges, ports, havens, causeways, churches, sea-banks and high-ways; the education and preferment of orphans; the marriage of poor maids; the supportation, aid and help of young tradesmen, handicraftsmen, and persons decayed; the relief or redemption of prisoners or captives.

It must be remembered that the section only exempts charities in respect of carrying out the provisions of the charity. It does not, for example, give charities any immunity in their capacity as employers.

The next exception concerns " any sport, game or other activity of a competitive nature ". Section 44 provides that participation as a competitor in events involving such an activity where the events are confined to one sex is not unlawful discrimination if the activity is of a kind in which the physical strength, stamina or physique of the **average** woman puts her at a disadvantage to the **average** man.

Any " act related to the participation of a person as a competitor " in such an event is also exempt, so that the employment of a male sprinter on better terms than a female, training arrangements confined to males, and the selection of an all-male football team, are not unlawful. The refusal, on the grounds of her sex, to choose a woman to cox a boat, however, would obviously not be excused by the section.

Since this exception refers to the **average** man and the **average** woman, it will operate to the disadvantage of exceptional women who have the strength or the skill to compete upon equal terms, or more than equal terms, with men. The " looking glass " procedure does not apply to this section, so that it exists only to preserve certain forms of discrimination against women.

The section refers only to participation or, rather, to " any act related to the participation of a person as a competitor ". It does not, therefore, excuse discrimination against women as referees, judges, linesmen, or in a similar capacity, and it is very doubtful whether the refusal to engage a woman trainer could be excused as being " related to the participation of a person as a competitor ".

The third large-scale exception is discriminatory treatment of a person in relation to an annuity life assurance policy, accident insurance policy, " or similar matter involving the assessment of risk " (section 45) if such discriminatory treatment

(*a*) was effected by reference to actuarial or other data from a source on which it was reasonable to rely and

(*b*) was reasonable having regard to the data and any other relevant factors.

In short, insurance companies may continue to charge women lower premiums for life assurance and quote them lower annual payments under annuities because, statistically, the average woman lives longer than the average man. For so long as statistics show that the average woman is less likely to be involved in an accident whilst driving a car than the average man, no doubt some insurance companies will continue to quote preferential rates for women for motor insurance. It is worth noting here that there are specific exemptions for pension arrangements both in connection with employment and in connection with membership of employers' organisations, trade and professional organisations, trade unions, and membership of a partnership.

Finally, there is a group of exceptions in sections 51 and 52 which provide that a discrimination is not unlawful if it was necessary in order to comply with a requirement of an Act of Parliament passed before the Sex Discrimination Act (*i.e.* before November 1975); or the requirement of an instrument (*e.g.* a statutory order) if the instrument was made at any time, even after the passing of the Sex Discrimination Act, by or under an Act passed before the Sex Discrimination Act; or it was done or omitted to be done for the purpose of safeguarding national security.

CHAPTER 2

DISCRIMINATION IN EMPLOYMENT

The field of employment is dealt with in the Act in a very special and particularly detailed manner. For example, the list of specific exceptions which are additional to the general exceptions in this field is a very long one. Moreover, all complaints of unlawful discrimination in employment must be made to industrial tribunals, which alone have the power to enforce the rules in this field. As will be seen, industrial tribunals have the power to impose certain sanctions which are not available for breaches of other parts of the Act.

Furthermore, the concept of unlawful discrimination on the ground of " marital status " contained in section 3 is particularly relevant to the field of employment. The wording of section 3 was quoted in full in Chapter 1, where it was discussed in detail and those comments need not be re-stated here.

Some readers may be interested to know that the section was introduced into the Act principally to deal with the " marriage bar " which, in the past, was so frequently a feature of the employment of women and some traces of which still remain. The section applies, however, equally to men, a fact which is made abundantly, if somewhat unnecessarily, clear by subsection (2) of section 3. Employers must therefore beware of overtly or covertly giving unmarried men preferential treatment over married men, or unmarried women preferential treatment over married women, **by reason of the fact that they are unmarried,** as well as avoid overtly or covertly treating a woman less favourably than a man because of her sex.

THE SEX DISCRIMINATION ACT AND THE EQUAL PAY ACT

In order to comprehend the position with regard to sex discrimination in employment, it is vital to have a grasp of the provisions of the Equal Pay Act 1970, and of both the differences and the inter-relation between that Act and the Sex Discrimination Act. This is all the more important since the Equal Pay Act does not, as its title would suggest, relate only to discrimination in pay, but deals with any term or condition of the employment which is discriminatory.

The system adopted in the Equal Pay Act to defeat discrimination is quite different to that used in the Sex Discrimination Act. By section 1, the Equal Pay Act (as amended by the Sex Discrimination Act) infers in every appropriate contract of employment a special clause, which it dubs an " equality clause ". The effect of this clause, which may also be specifically included by the parties to the contract, is to provide that **any term** of the woman's contract which at the outset, is less favourable to the woman than a term of a similar kind in a man's contract, or which subsequently becomes less favourable, is deemed to be modified so as not to be less favourable. By another " looking glass " provision (section 1 (11) of the Equal Pay Act) the same provision applies, in reverse, in favour of a man.

The last paragraph refers to every **appropriate** contract because, by section 1 (2) (*a*) of the Equal Pay Act, an " equality clause " is only implied " where a woman is employed in like work with a man in the same employment ", or, by section 1 (6), a man employed by an associated employer. It will be seen that, in this respect, the Equal Pay Act is more limited than the Sex Discrimination Act. Under the Sex Discrimination Act a woman suffering discrimination does not have to show that there is a man actually doing similar work for the same employer, but can make a comparison with a hypothetical man.

The requirements of the Equal Pay Act for making the comparison with a man are carefully set out in section 1 (4) as follows:

1.—(4) A woman is to be regarded as employed on like work with men if, but only if, her work and theirs is of the same or a broadly similar nature, and the differences (if any) between the things she does and the things they do are not of practical importance in relation to terms and conditions of employment:

and accordingly in comparing her work with theirs regard shall be had to the frequency or otherwise with which any such differences occur in practice as well as to the nature and extent of the differences.

For the sake of completeness it should be added that, by section 1 (2) (*b*) of the same Act, an equality clause can also be implied, with the same results, if a woman is employed on work " rated as equivalent " with that of a man in the same employment, but, by section 1 (5) the " rating " must be carried out " on a study undertaken with a view to evaluating in those terms the jobs to be done by all or any of the employees in an undertaking or group of undertakings ", and either her job must have been rated of an equal value " in terms of the demand made on the worker under various headings (for instance effort, skill, decision) ", or would have been given an equal value " but for the evaluation being made on a system setting different values for men and women on the same demand under any heading ".

A brief comparison of the major differences between the provisions of the two Acts relating to discrimination in the field of employment may be helpful at this point:

Sex Discrimination Act	Equal Pay Act
1. Deals with overt and covert discrimination.	Deals only with overt discrimination.
2. Deals with both discrimination in the terms of the employment contract and extra-contractual discrimination (*e.g.* in the provision of facilities).	Deals only with discrimination in the terms of the employment contract.
3. Provides for comparison with an actual **or** hypothetical man.	Provides only for comparison with a man in like work in like employment.
4. Deals with discrimination on the grounds of sex or of marriage.	Deals only with discrimination between the sexes.
5. Deals with discrimination in the advertising and offer of a job.	Deals only with discrimination after the employment has commenced.
6. Does not deal with financial discrimination after the employment has commenced.	Deals with financial and other discrimination after employment has commenced.

Sex Discrimination Act	**Equal Pay Act**
7. Claims for breach of terms of Act are dealt with by Industrial Tribunals only, save for applications for an injunction, which are heard by the County Court.	Claims for breach of terms of contract may be dealt with by courts or by industrial tribunals.
8. Sanctions for breach are: (i) injunction. (ii) declaratory order. (iii) compensation (limited to amount specified in paragraph 20 (1) (*b*) of Schedule I to the Trade Union and Labour Relations Act 1974). (iv) recommendation that the employer takes certain action to reduce the adverse effect of such discrimination, non-compliance with which may result in a compensation order (if no compensation awarded orginally) or an increase in compensation.	Sanctions for breach are: (i) Arrears of remuneration unpaid to bring rates of pay, etc., up to level required by equality clause during preceding two years. (ii) Damages. (iii) In suitable cases, injunction to prevent continuing breach.

It should be remembered that section 4 of the Sex Discrimination Act provides that if a person does one of four things in connection with the Sex Discrimination Act or the Equal Pay Act and is victimised for that reason, the victimisation is also discrimination under the Act.

The four things are as follows:

(*a*) brings proceedings against the employer or any other person under that Act or the Equal Pay Act, or

(*b*) gives evidence or information in connection with such proceedings, or

(*c*) does anything else in relation to that Act or the Equal Pay Act against the employer or any other person, or

(*d*) alleges that the employer or any other person has committed a contravention of either Act.

The words " or any other person " are used in order to make it an unlawful discrimination for employers to operate any form of black list and to refuse to employ a person who has been active in relation to a complaint or allegation against **another employer** of a contravention of either Act.

DISCRIMINATION IN SELECTING EMPLOYEES AND THE TERMS OF AN OFFER

Section 6 is the first section in the Sex Discrimination Act which makes the discrimination on the ground of sex or marital status, or by way of victimisation unlawful, whilst, at the same time, it specifies the particular occasions and manner in which such discrimination is wrong in relation to employment.

The first subsection of section 6 deals with the offer of a job, and says:

> (1) It is unlawful for a person, in relation to employment by him at an establishment in Great Britain, to discriminate against a woman:
>
> (*a*) in the arrangements he makes for the purpose of determining who should be offered that employment, or
>
> (*b*) in the terms on which he offers her that employment, or
>
> (*c*) by refusing or deliberately omitting to offer her that employment.

It is very difficult, on reading this, to conceive that it has any relation to discrimination on the ground of being married. Nevertheless, it has, because, not only does section 3 of the Act specifically (if somewhat tortuously) say " in any circumstances relevant for the purposes of any provision of Part II ", but section 5 provides that references to " discrimination " in the Act refer to any discrimination falling within sections 1 to 4, whereas references to " sex discrimination " in the Act refer only to discrimination falling within sections 1 or 2. Clauses (*a*), (*b*) and (*c*) therefore must be read as applying to discrimination against a married man or married woman in favour of a single person, as well as discrimination against a man or woman on the ground of their sex.

The first two lines of subsection (1) refer to " a person, in relation to employment by him ", *i.e.* the employer. It does not, therefore, cover employment agencies (which are subject to different provisions in section 15), or the organisations popularly known as " head-hunters ", but section 40 (2) makes the employer liable for the acts of an agent who has express or implied authority and acts in accordance with that authority, or whose acts are ratified subsequently.

The phrase " in the arrangements he makes for the purposes of determining who should be offered that employment " in paragraph (*a*) covers a multitude of sins. Indeed, the Under-Secretary of State for Employment has said that the word " arrangements " was quite deliberately used to cover even situations which could not be envisaged before the Act was passed. Whether that is a justifiable method of framing legislation is open to doubt. Certainly, " arrangements " would cover advertising or the absence of it, short-listing, announcements or circulars to existing staff, and the employment of agencies of one form or another. It is difficult to see how even any direct approach to an individual, however well qualified for the post, can avoid falling foul of this provision.

Paragraph (*b*) of section 6 (1) appears deceptively simple, and has to be approached with particular care. First, subsection (5) of section 6 excludes from its provisions any term " for the payment of money " which would, if the applicant were engaged, become a term of the contract of employment. This is, however, specifically made subject to the provisions of section 8 (3). Pausing there, subsection (5) would not affect a non-contractual term for the payment of money, *e.g.* a reference to the fact that discretionary bonuses were usually paid at certain times of the year.

Then section 8 of the Sex Discrimination Act, which deals principally with amendments to the Equal Pay Act, contains a series of subsections, intended to provide a demarcation line between the operation of the two Acts.

Subsection (2) of section 8 provides that an equality clause implied by the Equal Pay Act does not apply in determining the terms on which employment is offered (*i.e.* the employer cannot contend that his offer was discriminatory but, if the offer was accepted the equality clause was bound to be imported into the contract, thus rendering the contract, and, by implication, the offer, non-discriminatory).

Subsection (3) of section 8 reads as follows:

> (3) Where a person offers a woman employment on certain terms, and if she accepted the offer then, by virtue of an equality clause, any of those terms would fall to be modified, or any additional term would fall to be included, the offer shall be taken to contravene section 6 (1) (*b*).

This subsection appears to render only the **offer** unlawful, since the implication to be drawn from the words " and if she **accepted** the offer ", " by virtue of an equality clause " and " **would** fall to be modified " is that they apply to the situation at the moment the offer has been made, and before it has been accepted.

Subsection (4) of section 8 provides that the offer shall not, after all, be unlawful if the equality clause would not operate in respect of the variation between the woman's contract and that of the man in the same employment if the variation was genuinely due to a " material difference " between circumstances of the male and female in accordance with section 1 (3) of the Equal Pay Act. Section 1 (3) of that Act says:

> (3) An equality clause shall not operate in relation to a variation between the woman's contract and the man's contract if the employer proves that the variation is genuinely due to a material difference (other than the difference of sex) between her case and his, and such a material difference includes, for example—
>
> (*a*) the conditions under which, or the time of day when, their work is done, or any other matter relating to the carrying out by them of the duties of the job, or
>
> (*b*) their qualifications, experience, length of service, or other personal attributes (other than sex).

The ground rules for unlawful discrimination **in the terms of an offer** are, therefore:

(*a*) if a member of the opposite sex to the applicant is employed by the same employer on like work, so that an equality clause would be implied in any contract which resulted from the offer, and the offer terms are such that the equality clause would modify them, the offer is unlawful by section 8 (3), **unless** the difference between the male and female terms is due to a factor referred to in section 3 of the Equal Pay Act;

(*b*) if there is no such member of the opposite sex employed by the same employer and a term is discriminatory that is unlawful **unless** the discriminatory term is a " provision for the payment of money " which would, were the offer accepted, be included in the applicant's contract of employment;

(*c*) in any event, if the terms of the offer to a married man or married woman are less favourable than those that the employer offers to single persons (or would offer to a hypothetical single person) the offer is unlawful discrimination.

DISCRIMINATION IN TERMS OF EMPLOYMENT

As has been said, subsection (1) of section 6 deals with discrimination prior to the applicant accepting an offer of employment. The criteria changes in respect of anything done after the applicant has accepted the offer, when, by subsection (2) of section 6, it is unlawful for the employer to discriminate:

(*a*) in the way he affords her access to opportunities for promotion, transfer or training, or to any other benefits, facilities or services, or by refusing or deliberately omitting to afford her access to them, or

(*b*) by dismissing her, or subjecting her to any other detriment.

With this must be read subsection (6) of section 6, which withdraws from the orbit of subsection (2) " benefits consisting of the payment of money when the provision of those benefits is regulated by the woman's contract of employment ", and subsection (5) of section 8, which reads:

(5) An act does not contravene section 6 (2) if:

(*a*) it contravenes a term modified or included by virtue of an equality clause, or

(*b*) it would contravene such a term but for the fact that the equality clause is prevented from operating by section 1 (3) of the Equal Pay Act 1970.

Subsection (6) of section 6, like subsection (5) of section 8, is intended to draw a demarcation line between this Act and the Equal Pay Act, the principle being, apparently, that all questions of pay and other **contractual financial rewards** should be reserved exclusively to the operation of the Equal Pay Act. Unfortunately, this leaves a gaping hole in the anti-discrimination legislation, since the Equal Pay Act, it will be remembered, deals only with cases where there is a member of the opposite sex in comparable employment with the same or an associated employer.

Therefore if, for example, a woman is employed on work for which men in other firms (working the same hours, etc.) are paid more, she can do nothing about it if there is no man in her firm (or that of an ' associated employer ') employed on the same work. The Equal Pay Act would not apply, because there is no male in the same employment, and the Sex Discrimination Act is specifically excluded by section 6 (6) of that Act.

There is a curious contrast between the words " **benefits** consisting of the payment of money " used in subsection (6) and " **any provision** for the payment of money " used in subsection (5) (which deals with an offer of employment). A possible conclusion to be drawn from this difference in wording in two subsections so close together, is that " **benefits** consisting of the payment of money " is intended to refer to financial benefits **other than wages or salary**—*e.g.* a travel allowance or clothing allowance—whilst " provision for the payment of money " is intended to refer to all financial payments to the employee, including wages or salary. The word " benefit " is, after all, hardly appropriate to describe pay.

Regrettably, the Act does not attempt to define " benefit ".

If this conclusion is right, then the hole in the anti-discrimination legislation is not so large, but it still exists in respect of contractual financial rewards other than pay.

One must now turn to subsection (5) of section 8 of the Sex Discrimination Act, which reads:

> (5) An act does not contravene section 6 (2) if—
>
> (*a*) it contravenes a term modified or included by virtue of an equality clause, or
>
> (*b*) it would contravene such a term but for the fact that the equality clause is prevented from operating by section 1 (3) of the Equal Pay Act 1970.

The phraseology used in subsection (2) of section 6 of the Sex Discrimination Act is very general in nature, and is sufficient to cover virtually any contractual term. However, it will be seen that the **contravention** of any contractual term, financial or non-financial, which **can** be remedied under the

Equal Pay Act is excluded from section 6 (2) of the Sex Discrimination Act by section 8 (5) of the latter Act, unless it falls within section 8 (5) (*b*).

What remains, therefore, in subsection (2) of section 6 is what are usually loosely called " fringe benefits " which are not included in the term of an employment contract, and non-financial contractual terms which do not fall within the ambit of the Equal Pay Act, because there is no comparable person of the opposite sex employed by the same, or an associated, employer.

To sum up thus far (at the risk of repetition), discriminatory financial provisions, **once the offer has been accepted,** are not **unlawful** and can only be dealt with, if at all, under the Equal Pay Act, whilst other discriminatory **contractual** clauses are dealt with under the Equal Pay Act, if it applies, and the Sex Discrimination Act, if the Equal Pay Act does not apply, and discriminatory **non-contractual** arrangements can only be dealt with under the Sex Discrimination Act.

The next qualification to subsection (2) of section 6 is contained in subsection (7) in the following words:

> (7) Subsection (2) does not apply to benefits, facilities or services of any description if the employer is concerned with the provision (for payment or not) of benefits, facilities or services of that description to the public, or to a section of the public comprising the woman in question, unless:
>
> (*a*) that provision differs in a material respect from the provision of the benefits, facilities or services by the employer to his employees, or
>
> (*b*) the provision of the benefits, facilities or services to the woman in question is regulated by her contract of employment, or
>
> (*c*) the benefits, facilities or services relate to training.

At first sight of this (and even, perhaps, with second sight) the mind boggles. To put the subsection into some kind of perspective (although not to limit it in any way) it may be helpful to refer to the examples of facilities and services set out in section 29 (2) of the Sex Discrimination Act, which include, for example, " facilities by way of banking or insurance or for grants, loans, credit or finance ". It then appears that a bank or building society may discriminate, on the grounds of sex, in the loans it makes to employees, unless the provision of such loans to the employee concerned is regulated by the employee's contract. Similarly, a multiple store could sell goods at cost-price solely to employees of one sex (providing there was no term in the employee's contract to that effect) without such discrimination being unlawful. The reason for this exception, covering, as it does, a very wide field, is difficult to determine, but it is no more mysterious than many of the other provisions of this Act.

Notwithstanding paragraph (*c*) of subsection (7), an employer **is** permitted to discriminate in providing **access to facilities for training for employees** of one sex only, or encouraging them to take advantage of opportunities for doing certain work, if, within the preceding twelve months, either there were **no persons of that sex doing that work,** or **they were comparatively few.** This exemption is to be found in section 48 and is one example of several provisions of the Act which actively encourage discrimination.

The employer may also be held to be responsible for the actions and omissions of vocational training bodies (who are described more extensively in Chapter 5) in failing to afford access to training courses or other facilities if it can be shown that such a body was acting as an agent for the employer within the terms of subsection (2) of section 41.

It should also be observed that there is nothing in either Act to prevent an employee who has been offered a job on unequal terms, and has accepted, from making separate claims in respect both of the discriminatory offer **and** the discrimination in the employment, and that is so even if the former claim falls to be dealt with under the Sex Discrimination Act and the latter claim falls to be dealt with under the Equal Pay Act.

The reader is reminded that, in the field of employment, discrimination against a married person in favour of a single person is unlawful under the Sex Discrimination Act, although there is no similar provision in the Equal Pay Act, and that the Sex Discrimination Act (by section 4) renders the victimisation of a person who has played any part (or intends to play any part) in a claim under either Act unlawful discrimination.

Contract workers

Section 9 extends the field of unlawful discrimination to " contract workers " who are supplied to the employer by a third party. This covers not only temporary staff supplied by an employment or other agency, but also what has been known as " the lump " in the building trade and workers who are hired out with equipment—for example, crane drivers and dumper truck drivers. The discriminatory acts made unlawful by subsection (2) of section 9 however, differ from those contained in section 6 and are defined in different phraseology, whilst the Equal Pay Act does not apply as between the worker and the employer whose work they are doing, nor do the other exceptions described in this Chapter. Contract workers who contract with the employer themselves, *e.g.* outworkers in the tailoring trade, come within the provisions of section 6, and section 9 does not apply to them.

Subsection (3) of section 9 excludes discrimination against contract workers if the circumstances are such that a direct employee of that employer would not suffer unlawful discrimination because " being a man would be a genuine occupational qualification ". This phrase is dealt with at length in Chapter 3.

Section 9 is worded thus:

(1) This section applies to any work for a person (" the principal ") which is available for doing by individuals (" contract workers ") who are employed not by the principal himself but by another person, who supplies them under a contract made with the principal.

(2) It is unlawful for the principal, in relation to work to which this section applies, to discriminate against a woman who is a contract worker—

(*a*) in the terms on which he allows her to do that work, or

(*b*) by not allowing her to do it or continue to do it, or

(*c*) in the way he affords her access to any benefits, facilities or services or by refusing or deliberately omitting to afford her access to them, or

(*d*) by subjecting her to any other detriment.

(3) The principal does not contravene subsection (2) (*b*) by doing any act in relation to a woman at a time when if the work

were to be done by a person taken into his employment being a man would be a genuine occupational qualification for the job.

(4) Subsection (2) (*c*) does not apply to benefits, facilities or services of any description if the principal is concerned with the provision (for payment or not) of benefits, facilities or services of that description to the public, or to a section of the public to which the woman belongs, unless that provision differs in a material respect from the provision of the benefits, facilities or services by the principal to his contract workers.

The Act also extends to the Crown (*i.e.* the state) as an employer, by the terms of section 85. Indeed, subsection (1) of section 85 applies the Act not merely to acts done by Ministers of the Crown and government departments, but also to any act by a statutory body, or a person holding statutory office.

What is even more noteworthy, is that section 86 provides that where section 6 does not apply to an appointment to an office or post by a Minister of the Crown or government department—

(2) In making the appointment, and in making the arrangements for determining who should be offered the office or post, the Minister of the Crown or government department shall not do an act which would be unlawful under section 6 if the Crown were the employer for the purposes of this Act.

—a very far-reaching provision indeed!

Vicarious liability

This seems a suitable point at which to mention that, by section 41 of the Sex Discrimination Act, the employer is not only liable for unlawful discrimination by his employees 'in the course of their employment ' (which seems reasonable) whether or not it was with his knowledge or approval (which does not) but also for unlawful discrimination by any agent, whether the agent's authority is express or to be implied from the circumstances, and even if the discrimination was ratified by the employer after it had occurred.

The employer has a defence, by subsection (3) of section 41, if he took " such steps as were reasonably practical to prevent the employee from doing that act, or from doing in the course of his employment acts of that description " but he has no such defence in respect of any unlawful discrimination by his agents. So far as agents are concerned, therefore, it matters only that the act or omission was within their authority.

The other side of the coin is that, in the circumstances described above, both the employee and the agent may also be liable for " knowingly aiding another person " to unlawfully discriminate under section 42 of the Act, and the employee is liable even if his employer is excused because he took the steps described in subsection (3) of section 41.

Both the employee and the agent are exempted from liability by subsection (3) of section 42 if they acted in reliance on a statement made to them by the employer that, because of a provision of the Act, the discrimination would not be unlawful, and it was reasonable for them to rely upon it. This introduces a further liability on the employer who makes the statement, for if he does so knowingly or recklessly he may, by subsection (4) of section 42, be fined up to £400. This is one of the several instances of criminal liability under the Act.

Similar responsibilities for the employer are provided by sections 39 and 40 of the Sex Discrimination Act. Section 39 reads as follows:

> It is unlawful for a person—
>
> (*a*) who has authority over another person, or
>
> (*b*) in accordance with whose wishes that other person is accustomed to act,
>
> to instruct him to do any act which is unlawful by virtue of Part II or III, or procure or attempt to procure the doing by him of any such act.

Whilst Part II of the Act relates principally to employment and training for employment, Part III includes the sale of goods and the supply of facilities and services. In fact, an employer will be liable if he instructs an employee or any other person over whom he has influence to discriminate in any manner prohibited by the Act, except by publishing a discriminatory advertisement.

It will be noticed that it is not only straightforward instructions which are contrary to the section, as it refers also to " procure or attempt to procure the doing . . . of any such act ". These words can cover a very wide variety of actions and subtle pressures, and to put the matter quite beyond doubt, section 40 provides:

> (1) It is unlawful to induce, or attempt to induce, a person to do any act which contravenes Part II or III by—
>
> (*a*) providing or offering to provide him with any benefit, or
>
> (*b*) subjecting or threatening to subject him to any detriment.
>
> (2) An offer or threat is not prevented from falling within subsection (1) because it is not made directly to the person in question, if it is made in such a way that he is likely to hear of it.

Neither nods nor winks to blind horses will avoid these two sections, and the only safe course is to eschew any attempt to discriminate in a manner which is contrary to the Act.

Although sections 39 and 40 do not apply to advertisements, an employer who advertises for staff in a discriminatory manner, and informs the publisher of the advertisement that the advertisement is not unlawful because he is entitled to discriminate, whether because the discrimination is not of a kind which comes within the general prohibitions of the Act, or because it falls within an exemption to it, may be fined up to £400 if that statement is untrue. This liability is dealt with at greater length in Chapter 13.

Moreover, as will be seen in Chapter 5, an employer who falsely or misleadingly states to an employment agency that it is lawful for him to offer a job to a particular sex only (for example, because he employs only five employees) and does so knowingly or recklessly, commits a criminal offence, for which he can be fined up to £400.

One point in the definition contained in section 6 (1) of the Sex Discrimination Act has not been touched upon, namely, that it renders discrimination unlawful only if it is " in relation to employment . . . at an establishment in Great Britain ". A similar restriction is contained in section 6 (2), and in section 1 of the Equal Pay Act. A full, if complicated and, at times, abstruse, definition of ' employment at an establishment in Great Britain ' is contained in section 10 of the Sex Discrimination Act. Undoubtedly, the most difficult part of section 10 to construe is subsection (3), which is designed to deal with employees who work in premises other than their employer's (for example, maintenance engineers and construction workers) and those whose work is not carried out in any particular premises (for example, commercial travellers). It seems unlikely, however, that this subsection will often be called into question.

CHAPTER 3

EXCEPTIONS TO UNLAWFUL DISCRIMINATION IN EMPLOYMENT

PRIVATE HOUSEHOLDS AND SMALL BUSINESSES

The widest exceptions to unlawful discrimination in employment are contained in subsection (3) of section 6, which exempts " any employment for the purposes of a private household " and (disregarding persons employed by the same employer for his private household) employment by an employer who, with " associated employers " does not employ more than five people.

It is curious that the Act should refer to " any employment **for the purposes of** " a private household, and it can only be assumed that the words have a wider scope than any employment **for** a private household. It could be argued that employees of a private contractor who were sent, say, to unblock the drains or clean the windows, were employed " for the purposes of a private household ", but it is doubtful whether a tribunal would be willing to stretch the words quite so far. Probably the meaning covers such people as chauffeurs, gardeners and other permanent employees whose jobs are not so closely and obviously connected with a private household as, say, a nannie or a charwoman.

The exceptions set out in subsection (3) of section 6 do not apply if the discrimination falls within section 4, *i.e.* if it is, in fact, victimisation because the person " discriminated " against has taken, or intends to take, some part in a complaint against the employer under either the Sex Discrimination Act or the Equal Pay Act.

A further exception is contained in section 6 (4), which excludes from the provisions of section 6 (1) (*b*) and section 6 (2) provisions in relation to death or retirement. This is the exception of death benefits and retirement pensions, which is to be found elsewhere in the Act, and is necessary because insurance companies, working on actuarial statistics, quote different rates and different benefits for men and women because of the longer life expectancy of women, and it is the insurance companies who operate the pension schemes conducted by so many employers.

TRAINING FACILITIES FOR A MINORITY SEX

It has already been observed, at the very outset of this book, that the Act by no means precludes discrimination, but merely renders certain types of discrimination unlawful. In section 48, the Act actually **encourages** discrimination for if, at any time within the preceding twelve months, the employer had either no persons of a particular sex doing certain work, or the number of persons of that sex doing such work was " comparatively small ", it is **not** unlawful for him to afford access to training facilities for that work to that sex only. The subsection solemnly goes on to say that, in such circumstances, it is not unlawful for the employer to **encourage** only members of that sex to take advantage of opportunities for doing such work, but it is difficult to find anything in section 6 (or, indeed, the remainder of the Act) which would make it unlawful for an employer merely to **encourage** members of one sex to do certain work.

PARTICULAR CATEGORIES OF EMPLOYMENT

We then come to a series of exceptions which relate to certain specialised categories of employment, sub-headed in the Act " Special cases ".

The first of these, covered in section 17 at some length, relates to policemen and policewomen, and, since it is unlikely to be of general interest, and members of the police force will no doubt be capable of reading and construing the Act themselves, it need not be dealt with here.

It is necessary to interject, at this point, an exception to be found right at the end of the Act, in subsection (2) of section 85, for the armed forces. Subsection (1) of section 85 applies the Act to the Crown, and those employed by the Crown, including the Civil Service. Subsection (4) says:

> (4) Subsections (1) and (2) do not apply in relation to service in—
>
> (*a*) the naval, military or air forces of the Crown, or
>
> (*b*) any women's service administered by the Defence Council,

and subsection (6) adds:

> (6) This Act (except section 8 (1) and (6)) does not apply to employment in the case of which the employee may be required to serve in support of a force or service mentioned in subsection (4) (*a*) or (*b*).

There follows, in section 18, two provisions relating to prison officers. The first exempts from the field of unlawful discrimination any requirements which discriminate between male and female prison officers in respect of height, whilst the latter repeals section 7 (2) of the Prison Act, 1952, in order to permit a man to be the Governor of a women's prison.

Curiously enough, prior to the Sex Discrimination Act, there was no statutory bar on a woman becoming the Governor of a men's prison, so that it was not necessary to provide for the reverse case.

Section 19 contains an exemption for organised religion and is phrased thus:

> (1) Nothing in this Part applies to employment for purposes of an organised religion where the employment is limited to one sex so as to comply with the doctrines of the religion or avoid offending the religious susceptibilities of a significant number of its followers.

This section only permits discrimination in an employment which is limited to one sex. If the organised religion employs both sexes in any area of employment, whether as ministers or in any other capacity, it must not discriminate between them save in the ordination or qualification of ministers.

Moreover, the exception only applies if the discrimination is either to comply with the doctrines of the religion or to avoid offending the religious susceptibilities of a significant number of the followers. This does not excuse discrimination which is based on sheer prejudice.

Section 20 renders lawful any discrimination in the employment, promotion, transfer or training of a midwife, whether under subsections (1) and (2) (*a*) of section 6, or section 14 (which is dealt with in detail in Chapter IV). This is not to say that the vocation remains closed to men, however, as subsection (4) amends the Midwives' Act 1951 to make it possible for men to qualify and practice as midwives. The situation is therefore that a man can be a midwife, but he cannot complain if he suffers discrimination.

Women will now be able to be employed in mines on work which requires them to go underground, provided that either the mine is not being worked, or they do not ordinarily have to spend a " significant proportion " of their time underground, by virtue of the amendment to the Mines and Quarries Act 1954 and the Coal Mines Regulation Act 1908, contained in section 21. This is curious, since it forms an exception to the general rule in section 51 (the principal object of which is to preserve the protective legislation which is contained in the Factories Acts and elsewhere to safeguard women) that discrimination which is necessary to comply with an Act which preceded the Sex Discrimination Act is not unlawful.

THE SECTION 7 EXCEPTIONS

Section 7 contains a long list of categories of jobs and circumstances in which it is not unlawful to discriminate in arrangements for selecting employees, for offering them employment (section 6 (1)) and in opportunities for promotion, transfer or training for employment, and in dismissing or subjecting the employee to any detriment (section 6 (2)) if, in that employment, being of a specific sex is a " genuine occupational qualification " for the job.

In passing, the word " genuine " does not seem to add much to the requirement, but it was apparently included to cover the case of Danny La Rue! The draughtsman of the Act presumably had not read, or did not believe, Danny La Rue's declaration that he had retired.

These exceptions do not apply to discrimination on the ground of " marital status " nor to the anti-victimisation provisions of section 4.

By subsection (2) of section 7, " being a man is a genuine occupational qualification for a job " only in eight specific instances, the first seven of which do not apply to filling a vacancy (as opposed, for example, to promotion or training) if the employer already has suitable employees of the other sex for such a job. By subsection (4) of section 7, for existing employees to be suitable they must be capable of doing the job, sufficiently numerous " to meet the employer's likely requirements . . . without undue inconvenience ", and it must be reasonable to employ them on the job in question.

The eight instances are set out below, followed by comments, where appropriate, but in reading the quotations from the Act it should be remembered that the " looking glass " provisions apply to these exceptions also, so that, for example, men can be barred from women's toilets, just as women can be barred from men's toilets.

> **(a) the essential nature of the job calls for a man for reasons of physiology (excluding physical strength or stamina) or, in dramatic performances or other entertainment, for reasons of authenticity, so that the essential nature of the job would be materially different if carried out by a woman.**

The second half of this paragraph is clear and applies to readily identifiable situations. Unfortunately, this cannot be said of the first half, despite the fact that it is the Mark II version, the Mark I version having been dropped by the Government when the Bill came before the Lords. A short dictionary definition of " physiology " is: " the science of the processes of life in animals and plants ", and the use of this word, therefore, is of little assistance to those who are genuinely seeking to ensure that their actions and activities are not unlawful.

> **(b) the job needs to be held by a man to preserve decency or privacy because—**
>
> **(i) it is likely to involve physical contact with men in circumstances where they might reasonably object to it being carried out by a woman, or**
>
> **(ii) the holder of the job is likely to do his work in circumstances where men might reasonably object to the presence of a woman because they are in a state of undress or are using sanitary facilities.**

It should be noted that, in each case, the phrase is " might reasonably object ". This does not call for a specific objection, but the hypothetical objection put forward by the employer must not be such that it is unreasonable.

> (c) **the nature or location of the establishment makes it impracticable for the holder of the job to live elsewhere than in premises provided by the employer, and—**
>
> (i) **the only such premises which are available for persons holding that kind of job are lived in or normally lived in by men and are not equipped with separate sleeping accommodation for women and sanitary facilities which could be used by women in privacy from men, and**
>
> (ii) **it is not reasonable to expect the employer either to equip those premises with such accommodation and facilities or to provide other premises for women.**

The obvious example of such an establishment is a lighthouse at sea, or an oil rig but it will also afford exemption to ships and to some remote construction sites.

Indeed, the words " or normally lived in " in sub-paragraph (i) were added to cover the position of ships signing-on a crew for the first time after being launched, a refit or being laid-up. The General Council of British Shipping pointed out that, in these circumstances, if a woman were first in the queue to sign-on, she could not be turned away on the ground that the only accommodation was " lived in " by men. Whether the words quoted above will preserve the discrimination against women in such circumstances would seem to depend upon whether the words " normally lived in by men " are interpreted as meaning " according to custom lived in by men ", or " have been used to being lived in by men ". The same point may apply to other " establishments ".

It will be noticed that it must be **impracticable** for the employee to live elsewhere, and that it must be **unreasonable** to expect the employer to re-equip the premises or provide other accommodation. Taken together, these two adjectives impose a very stringent test.

A rather lengthy reference to another section must be made at this point, as it is closely related to the provisions of paragraph (*c*). This is section 46, which provides exemptions where communal accommodation is provided.

Exception for employment necessitating communal accommodation

Communal accommodation is defined by subsection (1) of section 46 as meaning residential accommodation which includes dormitories, or " other shared sleeping accommodation which, for reasons of privacy or decency, should be used by men only or by women only ". The subsection goes on to say that, for this purpose, it may **include** some **shared** sleeping accommodation for men, and some for women, or " some ordinary sleeping accommodation " (*i.e.* bedrooms or cabins) and still be within the definition.

Subsection (2) adds that " communal accommodation " also includes residential accommodation " all or part of which should be used by men only, or women only, because of the nature of the sanitary facilities serving the accommodation ". It seems rather extraordinary that residential accommodation should be given exemption merely because of the type of toilets which are provided, but the later provisions of this section must be considered in conjunction with subsection (2).

The section goes on to give exemption from the provisions of the Act relating to employment in the following words:

> (3) Nothing in Part II or III shall render unlawful sex discrimination in the admission of persons to communal accommodation if the accommodation is managed in a way which, given the exigencies of the situation, comes as near as may be to fair and equitable treatment of men and women.
>
> (4) In applying subsection (3) account shall be taken of—
>
> (*a*) whether and how far it is reasonable to expect that the accommodation should be altered or extended, or that further alternative accommodation should be provided; and
>
> (*b*) the frequency of the demand or need for use of the accommodation by men as compared with women,

Subsection (5) of section 46 then declares:

> (5) Nothing in Part II or III shall render unlawful sex discrimination against a woman or against a man as respects the provision of any benefit, facility or service if—
>
> (*a*) the benefit, facility or service cannot properly and effectively be provided except for those using communal accommodation, and

(*b*) in the relevant circumstances the woman or, as the case may be, the man could lawfully be refused the use of the accommodation by virtue of subsection (3).

This is followed by a requirement for compensation (not necessarily financial compensation) in subsection (6) in these words:

(6) Neither subsection (3) nor subsection (5) is a defence to an act of sex discrimination under Part II unless such arrangements as are reasonably practicable are made to compensate for the detriment caused by the discrimination; but in considering under subsection (5) (*b*) whether the use of communal accommodation could lawfully be refused (in a case based on Part II), it shall be assumed that the requirements of this subsection have been complied with as respects subsection (3).

It will be seen that the latter part of this subsection puts the burden of proving that the accommodation is **not** managed fairly and equitably firmly on the employee.

To return to section 7, paragraph (*d*) of subsection (2) is by no means unconnected with the provisions of section 46 just referred to, and provides that being a man is a genuine occupational qualification where—

(d) the nature of the establishment, or of the part of it within which the work is done, requires the job to be held by a man because—

(i) it is, or is part of, a hospital, prison or other establishment for persons requiring special care, supervision or attention, and

(ii) those persons are all men (disregarding any woman whose presence is exceptional), and

(iii) it is reasonable, having regard to the essential character of the establishment or that part, that the job should not be held by a woman.

The third paragraph of this subsection leaves it very much to the tribunal whether, for example, it would be **reasonable** to refuse to employ a woman as governor of a men's prison.

(e) the holder of the job provides individuals with personal services promoting their welfare or education, or similar personal services, and those services can most effectively be provided by a man.

This subsection, which is extremely puzzling at first sight, is said to have been inserted to permit the continuance of discrimination in the probation service, although whether the continuance of such discrimination is justified or reasonable is open to considerable doubt. It is certainly in very general, not to say delightfully vague, terms, and may well be used for purposes beyond the contemplation of the legislators.

(f) the job needs to be held by a man because of restrictions imposed by the laws regulating the employment of women.

This clause exists solely to preserve the position with regard to protective legislation which is beneficial to women, such as that contained in the Factories Acts.

(g) the job needs to be held by a man because it is likely to involve the performance of duties outside the United Kingdom in a country whose laws or customs are such that the duties could not, or could not effectively, be performed by a woman.

(h) the job is one of two to be held by a married couple.

This exclusion applies principally, of course, to the management of public houses, but would also apply to resident caretakers. It is the one exception which applies to filling a vacancy whether or not the employer already has suitable employees of the other sex.

It is sufficient if only some of the duties fall within one of the exceptions set out above.

CHAPTER 4

SANCTIONS FOR DISCRIMINATION IN EMPLOYMENT

Although discrimination falling within the various definitions set out at the beginning of the Act is made "unlawful" by section 6, it is not criminal, and, generally speaking, it does not even give the employee a right of action in a court of law. It is otherwise with the Equal Pay Act, which does not debar the employee from suing for damages for breach of contract in the High Court or the County Courts.

The bar on court proceedings is, in effect, contained jointly in section 62, which provides that a breach of the Act shall incur no penalty, criminal or civil, unless the Act specifically provides, and is followed by section 63, which provides that a complaint of unlawful discrimination may be presented to an industrial tribunal.

APPLICATIONS TO INDUSTRIAL TRIBUNALS

The employee who has suffered unlawful discrimination can complain to an industrial tribunal, in accordance with section 63, and this will obviously be the simplest and most common remedy. Indeed, since the industrial tribunals also have jurisdiction under the Equal Pay Act, it will be far the most convenient course where it is desired to pursue claims under both Acts; for example, where the offer of employment is a breach of the Sex Discrimination Act and the conditions of employment which are operated after engagement are a breach of the Equal Pay Act.

A complaint against an employer alleging unlawful discrimination by an employee or agent of his, for which he is liable under section 41, can also be made to an industrial tribunal under the provisions of subsection (1) (*b*) of section 63.

By subsection (1) of section 65, an industrial tribunal has power to make—

(*a*) an order declaring the rights of the complainant and the respondent in relation to the act to which the complaint relates;

(*b*) an order requiring the respondent to pay to the complainant compensation of an amount corresponding to any damages he could have been ordered by a county court or by a sheriff court to pay to the complainant if the complaint had fallen to be dealt with under section 66;

(*c*) a recommendation that the respondent take within a specified period action appearing to the tribunal to be practicable for the purpose of obviating or reducing the adverse effect on the complainant of any act of discrimination to which the complaint relates.

Compensation

The total compensation which the industrial tribunal can award under paragraph (*b*) above is limited, by subsection (2), to " the amount for the time being specified in paragraph 20 (1) (*b*) of Schedule 1 to the Trade Union and Labour Relations Act 1974 " which amount is currently £5,200.

Such compensation is defined by paragraph (*b*) as " an amount corresponding to any damages he could have been ordered by a county court . . . to pay to the complainant . . . under section 66 ", and it should not be overlooked that subsection (4) of section 66 specifically provides that such damages may include compensation for injury to feelings, in addition to compensation under any other head.

There is one point of difficulty in this respect, and that is that the county courts have no jurisdiction to entertain an action in tort in which the claim exceeds £1,000. In an ordinary action, if the plaintiff simply claims damages, without quantifying the amount, it is customary for the formal Particulars of Claim to specify that the plaintiff abandons any amount by which his damages may be found to exceed £1,000, in order to ensure that the county court judge has jurisdiction to hear the action.

As will be seen later, a claim in respect of an act of discrimination which is unlawful under Part III of the Act can be made the subject of civil proceedings " in like manner as any other claim in tort " by subsection (1) of section 66 and, by subsection (2), must be brought in the county court. The Act contains no specific provision to enable county courts to entertain claims for more than £1,000, and if the county court judge cannot award damages of more than £1,000 to a claimant under the Act, neither can an industrial tribunal.

It may be that the words at the end of subsection (2) " but all such remedies shall be obtainable in such proceedings as, apart from this subsection, would be obtainable in the High Court " can be construed as not only extending the county court jurisdiction in respect of the **kind** of remedies, but also in respect of the financial limits on them. However, until the point has been decided by the courts, it cannot be regarded as free from doubt.

It is clear that by subsection (3) of section 66, no damages for **covert** discrimination (either under subsection (1) (*b*) of section 1 or under subsection (1) (*b*) of section 3), can be awarded if the employer **proves** that the requirement or condition in question was **not** applied with the intention of treating the individual discriminated against unfavourably on the ground of sex or marital status. It follows, therefore, that the industrial tribunal could not award compensation in those circumstances either, since the amount of damages which a county court could award would be nil.

As will be seen hereafter, the Commission can apply to an industrial tribunal under the power contained in subsection (1) of section 73, and obtain orders in the terms of paragraphs (*a*) and (*c*) of subsection (1) of section 65, quoted above, but in such an application the Commission cannot obtain an order for compensation.

One should not be deceived by the fact that paragraph (*c*) of subsection (1) of section 65 refers merely to " a recommendation " into thinking that it provides no effective sanction, since, by subsection (3) of section 65, if the employer fails to carry out such a recommendation **without reasonable justification,** the industrial tribunal may increase the compensation awarded under paragraph (*b*) (even, apparently, beyond the limit already mentioned, since the restriction in subsection (2) applies only to subsection (1) (*b*) and not to subsection (3) (*a*), which authorises the increase) or may order compensation under paragraph (*b*) if they did not do so originally.

Conciliation

It may be, however, that the majority of applications to industrial tribunals will never result in an order containing, or leading to, a penalty on the employer. This is because subsection (1) of section 64 provides that if a copy of the application, or ' complaint ', is sent to a conciliation officer, he has a duty to endeavour to promote a settlement of the dispute without its being determined by the industrial tribunal if either **both** the parties request him to do so, **or** he considers he could act with a reasonable chance of success. The latter part of this provision entitles a conciliation officer to impose an attempt at conciliation upon the parties against their will, if he sees fit so to do.

There is also provision, in subsection (2) of section 64, for the conciliation officer to act **before** any application or complaint is presented to the tribunal, if he is requested so to do by either party. Notwithstanding section 64, the Act imposes no obligation upon industrial tribunals to send copies of complaints to a conciliation officer.

Whether acting under subsection (1) or subsection (2), the conciliation officer (who will be one of the officers appointed under paragraph 26 (1) of the First Schedule to the Trade Union and Labour Relations Act 1974) is charged by subsection (3) to have regard to the " desirability of encouraging the use of other procedures available for the settlement of grievances ", and, by subsection (4), anything communicated to him is not admissible in evidence except with the consent of the person from whom the information was obtained.

CRIMINAL LIABILITY

For employers the only criminal liability under the Act is not for discriminating unlawfully, but for knowingly or recklessly making a misleading or false statement to an employee or agent, a third party or the publisher of an advertisement, to the effect that a certain act or omission or the publication of an advertisement is not unlawful under the Act. For such a statement an employer can be fined up to £400 under sections 15, 38 or 42, whichever may be appropriate.

TIME LIMIT FOR APPLICATIONS

Again, it is **extremely** important to remember that, by subsection (1) of section 76, a complaint to an industrial tribunal under section 63 (which deals with complaints of discrimination in the field of employment) **must be presented within three months of the act or omission to which it refers.** Similarly, subsection (4) of section 76 requires that an application by the Commission itself under subsection (1) of section 73 must be made **within six months** of the act or omission to which it refers.

Although by subsection (5) of section 76 the industrial tribunal has power to hear the complaint or application even if these periods have passed, obviously this enabling power should not be relied upon unnecessarily.

The periods are not necessarily as short as they seem, however, since subsection (6) of section 76 provides that—

> (*a*) where the inclusion of any term in a contract renders the making of the contract an unlawful act that act shall be treated as extending throughout the duration of the contract, and
>
> (*b*) any act extending over a period shall be treated as done at the end of that period, and
>
> (*c*) a deliberate omission shall be treated as done when the person in question decided upon it,

and continues, for good measure:

> and in the absence of evidence establishing the contrary a person shall be taken for the purposes of this section to decide upon an omission when he does an act inconsistent with doing the omitted act or, if he has done no such inconsistent act, when the period expires within which he might reasonably have been expected to do the omitted act if it was to be done.

QUESTIONNAIRES FOR USE PRIOR TO PROCEEDINGS

It should, perhaps, be mentioned at this juncture that the Act specifically authorises the Secretary of State by order to prescribe:

(*a*) forms by which the person aggrieved may question the respondent on his reasons for doing any relevant act, or on any other matter which is or may be relevant;

(*b*) forms by which the respondent may if he so wishes reply to any questions,

by subsection (1) of section 74. The purpose of such forms is described by the same subsection as being:

> With a view to helping a person ("the person aggrieved") who considers he may have been discriminated against in contravention of this Act to decide whether to institute proceedings and, if he does so, to formulate and present his case in the most effective manner.

What is far more important is subsection (2), which provides:

> (2) Where the person aggrieved questions the respondent (whether in accordance with an order under subsection (1) or not)—
>
> (*a*) the question and any reply by the respondent subject to the following provisions of this section shall be admissible as evidence in the proceedings;
>
> (*b*) if it appears to the court or tribunal that the respondent deliberately and without reasonable excuse omitted to reply within a reasonable period or that his reply is evasive or equivocal, the court or tribunal may draw any inference from that fact that it considers it just and equitable to draw, including an inference that he committed an unlawful act.

Paragraph (*a*) does not enlarge the law at all, as the county courts have always had ample provision for communications between the parties to be admissible in evidence, but paragraph (*b*) certainly does extend the existing law. Prior to the passing of the Act, it would have been impossible for any reasonable and rational court or industrial tribunal to draw, merely from the respondent's failure to reply to questions or his equivocal or evasive reply, the inference that he had committed an unlawful act.

Subsection (3) of section 74 adds:

(3) The Secretary of State may by order—

(*a*) prescribe the period within which questions must be duly served in order to be admissible under subsection (2) (*a*), and

(*b*) prescribe the manner in which a question, and any reply by the respondent, may be duly served.

NON-DISCRIMINATION NOTICES

At this point, it becomes necessary to explain the procedure for a non-discrimination notice, especially since the issue of such notices (which, in practice, establish without a judicial enquiry that a breach of the Act has taken place) by any body other than a local authority or government department, is somewhat of an innovation in English law.

Power of Commission to serve Notices

By subsection (2) of section 67, the Commission can **only** issue a non-discrimination notice in the course of a formal investigation. The procedure for a formal investigation is set out at greater length in Chapter 14, but it would seem that it is not primarily intended to be a mere routine process to be invoked whenever a complaint of unlawful discrimination is received which appears to merit investigation, but a far more substantial inquiry for the purpose of investigating, for example, specific areas of discrimination, certain parts of the country, or even individual large firms or trade organisations.

As will be seen, this appears from the fact that a formal investigation may be initiated by the Secretary of State (section 57), that if it is initiated by the Commission they must first lay down terms of reference and either give general notice of it or notice to the persons named in the terms of reference (section 58), that a Commissioner may be nominated to conduct the formal investigation and the Commission's functions delegated to him (section 57 (3)) and that the Commission may appoint **one or more** additional Commissioners for the purposes of a formal investigation.

Of course, it is true that subsection (2) (*b*) of section 59 contemplates a formal investigation for the purpose of establishing whether a person specified in the terms of reference has been or is discriminating unlawfully, but, in view of the formalities attendant upon a formal investigation, it would seem unlikely that such investigations are to be an everyday occurrence.

It follows from this that non-discrimination notices are normally by-products of a substantial inquiry of a general nature, and not a common-or-garden method of enforcing the provisions of the Act. Moreover, the requirements for a non-discrimination notice in subsection (5) of section 67 include prior notice to the person who is to be the object of it, specifying the grounds on which the Commission contemplate serving it, an opportunity for such person to make written or oral representations, and the consideration of such representations.

A non-discrimination notice will require the employer not to commit (or omit) certain acts which contravene sections 6 and 9, or one or other of them, to inform the Commission of changes in his arrangements to give effect to that requirement, and to inform other persons concerned of such changes. All these provisions are contained in subsection (2) of section 67, which is worded thus:

> (2) If in the course of a formal investigation the Commission becomes satisfied that a person is committing, or has committed, any such acts, the Commission may in the prescribed manner serve on him a notice in the prescribed form (" a non-discrimination notice ") requiring him—
>
> (*a*) not to commit any such acts, and
>
> (*b*) where compliance with paragraph (*a*) involves changes in any of his practices or other arrangements,
>
> (i) to inform the Commission that he has effected those changes and what the changes are, and
>
> (ii) to take such steps as may be reasonably required by the notice for the purpose of affording that information to other persons concerned.

Subsections (3) and (4) continue:

> (3) A non-discrimination notice may also require the person on whom it is served to furnish the Commission with such other information as may be reasonably required by the notice in order to verify that the notice has been complied with.
>
> (4) The notice may specify the time at which, and the manner and form in which, any information is to be furnished to the

Commission, but the time at which any information is to be furnished in compliance with the notice shall not be later than five years after the notice has become final.

In addition to being one of the two grounds on which the Commission can apply to the County Court for an injunction, by the combined effect of subsection (7) of section 67 and subsection (4) of section 59, failure to comply with a requirement in a non-discrimination notice regarding making known changes in practices or other arrangements, once the notice has become final, entitles the Commission to apply to the County Court for an order to enforce compliance. Even if the Commission has " reasonable cause to believe " that the person served with the notice intends not to comply with part of it, they may apply for such an order. Failure " without reasonable excuse " to comply with the county court order renders the person served with the non-discrimination notice liable to a fine in a sum not exceeding £10. What is far more important is that it gives the Commission the right to apply to Court for an injunction, as explained in the next few pages.

Appeals against non-discrimination notices

In view of the contents of the last paragraph, it may be some comfort to know that an employer can appeal to an industrial tribunal against any requirement of a non-discrimination notice which he has received, under subsection (1) of section 68, providing he does so within six weeks of being served with the notice.

If, on hearing such an appeal, the tribunal considers the requirement appealed against to be unreasonable, whether because it is based on an incorrect finding of fact, or for any other reason, it must quash the requirement. In most legal processes to " quash " means to annul or extinguish, but the word is given a new dimension by the Act, which permits the tribunal, under subsection (3) of section 68, to insert some other requirement in the notice in place of the requirement quashed. In effect, therefore, the tribunal can **amend** the requirement in any way it pleases.

Indeed, the industrial tribunal is completely unfettered. The words in subsection (2) of section 68 " because it is based on an incorrect finding of fact or for **any** other reason " mean that the tribunal can approach the matter afresh and reject the requirement for any reason, even a reason unconnected with the issue of the non-discrimination notice and the circumstances preceding the issue, whilst there is equally no restriction upon the nature of the requirement which the tribunal may impose in place of one quashed, and it is perfectly possible for it to have nothing whatever to do with the original requirement and still be within the authority given to the tribunal by subsection (3) of section 68.

Clearly, in view of the very serious potential situation which a non-discrimination notice produces, an employer should appeal against the requirements of such a notice if at all possible. By subsection (4) of section 68, a requirement inserted in a non-discrimination notice by an industrial tribunal in place of one quashed cannot, in turn, be the subject of an appeal to the tribunal.

INJUNCTIONS

The exception to the bar on court actions (there has to be an exception, of course) is that, by subsection (2), section 62 does not prevent the Courts from making the somewhat exotically-named orders of " certiorari, mandamus and prohibition ". These orders are made by the High Court when hearing appeals from inferior courts and tribunals and are discussed later.

The Equal Opportunities Commission, which is established by the Act, is specifically empowered under section 71 to apply to the County Court for an injunction in certain circumstances (or, in those circumstances, to take the equivalent action in Scotland).

The fact that section 85 provides that the Act applies to the Crown (that is to say, to all Government departments and bodies) has already been noticed. The **enforcement** provisions are, however, subject to the Crown Proceedings Act 1947, and therefore, since the latter Act specifically does not extend the remedy of an injunction to the Crown, no injunction can be obtained against the Crown under the Sex Discrimination Act.

As indicated above, the Equal Opportunities Commission is empowered, by section 71, to apply to the County Court in two cases, namely, where they have served the employer with a non-discrimination notice, or where a court or tribunal has made a finding that the employer has committed an act of unlawful discrimination, or has contravened the Equal Pay Act.

In each case, the Commission may apply for an injunction (the wording is permissive and places no obligation on the Commission to do so) if they believe that, unless restrained, the employer is likely to commit another unlawful discriminatory act or a breach of the Equal Pay Act.

The application by the Commission must be made within five years of the finding against the employer by the Court or tribunal, or if it is based upon service of a non-discrimination notice, of the notice becoming " final ". Subsection (4) of section 82 defines " final ", in this context, as being when the time for appeal against the finding of the Court, or against the non-discrimination notice, has expired without an appeal being lodged or, if an appeal is lodged, when that appeal is dismissed, withdrawn or abandoned.

It is worth noting that subsection (2) of section 71 prohibits the Commission from **alleging,** when applying to the County Court for an injunction, that the employer against whom the injunction is sought has to quote the subsection " done an act which is within the jurisdiction of an industrial tribunal ", unless a finding by an industrial tribunal that they have done that act has become final. This may inhibit the Commission in attempting to prove that the " responsible body " is **likely** to contravene one or other of these Acts unless restrained, as is required by section 71 (1); in other words, it may be necessary to have two or more adverse findings by industrial tribunals or County Courts against an employer, which have become final, before an injunction can be obtained under section 71.

The somewhat inelegant phrase " done an act which is within the jurisdiction of an industrial tribunal " is explained by subsection (4) of section 73. If the references to other parts of the Act, and to section 2 of the Equal Pay Act, are followed through, the act is seen to be:

either—

(*a*) an act of discrimination which is unlawful by virtue of Part II of the Sex Discrimination Act (*i.e.* the unlawful acts described in Chapters 1, 2, 5 and 6) or

(*b*) an act of discrimination which is unlawful by virtue of sections 38, 39 or 40 (*i.e.* a discriminatory advertisement, an instruction to another person to discriminate, or an inducement to or pressure upon another person to discriminate) or

(*c*) an act contravening a term which is deemed to be included in an employee's contract, or a term in such a contract which is deemed to be modified, by an " equality clause " under the Equal Pay Act.

Preliminary applications by the Commission

The Commission is specifically authorised, by subsection (1) of section 73, to apply to an industrial tribunal for a finding that the employer has unlawfully discriminated against an individual. On such an application, the Commission may obtain an order, similar to the order which can be made under subsection (1) (*a*) of section 65 (which is dealt with at the beginning of this Chapter) declaring the rights of the employer and employee and also a recommendation by the tribunal under subsection (1) (*c*) of section 65, that the employer take specific action within a limited period to obviate or reduce the adverse effect of such discrimination. The industrial tribunal cannot make an order for the payment of compensation under subsection (1) (*b*) of section 65 if the application is made by the Commission.

Once an order or recommendation such as is referred to in the preceding paragraph has become final, it enables the Commission to apply to the County Court for an injunction in exactly the same way as if a finding that the employer had unlawfully discriminated had been made by an industrial tribunal on the complaint of the employee. Furthermore, by subsection (3) of section 73, such an order or recommendation, when it has become final, must be treated as conclusive by the Court hearing the application for an injunction, and also by any industrial tribunal which hears a complaint of unlawful discrimination by the employee. This is the first time that the decision of one industrial tribunal has been made binding upon other industrial tribunals.

It is worth noting that subsection (2) of section 71 and subsection (5) of section 72 prohibit the Commission from **alleging,** when applying to the County Court for an injunction, that the person against whom the injunction is sought has contravened the Sex Discrimination Act or the Equal Pay Act, unless a finding that there has been such a contravention, made by an industrial tribunal has become final. This may inhibit the Commission in attempting to prove that the person is **likely** to contravene one or other of those Acts unless restrained, as is required by section 71; in other words, it may be necessary to have two or more adverse findings by industrial tribunals against an employer, which have become final, before an injunction can be obtained. This would seem to stretch the old adage of " one dog, one bite " considerably!

The somewhat inelegant phrase " done an act which is within the jurisdiction of an industrial tribunal " is explained by subsection (4) of section 73. If the references to other parts of the Act, and to section 2 of the Equal Pay Act, are followed through, the act is seen to be:

either—

(*a*) an act of discrimination which is unlawful by virtue of Part II of the Sex Discrimination Act (*i.e.* the unlawful acts described in Chapters 1, 2, 5 and 6) or

(*b*) an act of discrimination which is unlawful by virtue of sections 38, 39 or 40 (*i.e.* a discriminatory advertisement, an instruction to another person to discriminate, or an inducement to or pressure upon another person to discriminate) or

(*c*) an act contravening a term which is deemed to be included in an employee's contract, or a term in such a contract which is deemed to be modified, by an " equality clause " under the Equal Pay Act.

CERTIORARI, MANDAMUS AND PROHIBITION

A short explanation of these exotically-named High Court Orders is necessary, since they are, in fact, forms of appeal from inferior courts, tribunals and public bodies.

The ramifications and limitations of these procedures are far too extensive and complex to be dealt with in a book such as this, and the present exposition is inadequate to the point of being misleading in many respects, but it will, it is hoped, be sufficient to indicate where such appeal procedures may be relevant to the matters covered by the Act, and where they are inappropriate.

Certiorari is a High Court Order which quashes (and here the word **really** means annuls) the proceedings of an inferior court or body having the legal right to determine questions affecting the right of subjects. It is therefore suitable as a method of appeal from some of the bodies to whom sections 12 and 13 apply, if it is desired to completely extinguish any decisions made by them. The order will not, however, be made by the High Court if it is to quash proceedings in an area of jurisdiction which the High Court does not itself possess, and therefore certiorari would not be a suitable method of appeal from decisions of the county courts and industrial tribunals made under the powers conferred solely upon them by this Act.

Mandamus is an order made by the High Court directing an inferior court, tribunal or public body to do something which is in the nature of a public duty and appertains to their office. In general, it is used to enforce statutory rights and duties, to require public officials and public bodies to carry out their duties, and to command inferior tribunals to exercise their jurisdiction. It cannot be used if the official or body has a discretion in the matter, as opposed to a strict obligation or duty. Hence, it could be used against both county courts and industrial tribunals in the event of the latter refusing to exercise a non-discretionary power conferred upon them by this Act.

An order of prohibition by the High Court is the opposite of an order of mandamus and, as the name suggests, forbids an inferior court or tribunal to continue proceedings if it is attempting to exceed its jurisdiction. In view of the complexity of this Act, that is a situation which could well arise.

CHAPTER 5

DISCRIMINATION IN OPPORTUNITIES FOR EMPLOYMENT AND TRAINING

VOCATIONAL TRAINING BODIES

There is an area of training which falls between that which is provided by the employers individually, on the one hand, and by education authorities, on the other. That is the training which is provided by the bodies referred to in subsection (2) of section 14. This subsection specifically refers to the industrial training boards established under the Industrial Training Act 1964, the Manpower Services Commission, the Employment Service Agency and the Training Service Agency. The subsection also refers to any association comprising employers with the principal object of affording their employees access to training facilities, and to such other persons providing facilities for training for employment as may be designated by the Secretary of State.

Subsection (1) of section 14 renders it unlawful to discriminate in the **terms** on which such bodies afford access to training courses, or other facilities, to a man or woman seeking or undergoing **training which would help to fit them for any employment,** or by refusing or deliberately omitting to afford such access. To avoid overlapping, subsection (3) of section 14 takes out of the effect of the section discrimination which is rendered unlawful by the sections relating to education.

The precise terms of subsection (1) of section 14 are as follows:

> (1) It is unlawful for a person to whom this subsection applies, in the case of a woman seeking or undergoing training which would help to fit her for any employment, to discriminate against her—
>
> (*a*) in the terms on which that person affords her access to any training courses or other facilities, or
>
> (*b*) by refusing or deliberately omitting to afford her such access.

Exception for discriminatory training

Despite this, it is not unlawful for the bodies mentioned to afford access to facilities for training to men only, or to women only, for work of a kind in which either no-one of that sex at all was employed during the preceding twelve months, or the members of that sex employed during that time were comparatively small. This exception is to be found in section 47, subsection (1) of which reads:

(1) Nothing in Parts II to IV shall render unlawful any act done in relation to particular work by a training body in, or in connection with—

(i) affording women only, or men only, access to facilities for training which would help to fit them for that work or

(ii) encouraging women only, or men only, to take advantage of opportunities for doing that work,

where it appears to the training body that at any time within the twelve months immediately preceding the doing of the act there were no persons of the sex in question doing that work in Great Britain or the number of persons of that sex doing the work in Great Britain was comparatively small.

As with subsection (1) of section 48, which, it will be recalled, applies the same exemption to employers, this applies equally to encouraging members of only one sex to take up such work.

Subsection (1) of section 47 refers to the position with regard to such work in the whole of Great Britain, but by subsection (2) of section 47 the same principle applies to individual areas of Great Britain, even if the conditions are not met for Great Britain as a whole, if the training is for such work in the area concerned, or the encouragement relates to opportunities for such work in that area. The terms of subsection (2) are:

(2) Where in relation to particular work it appears to a training body that although the condition for the operation of subsection (1) is not met for the whole of Great Britain it is met for an area within Great Britain nothing in Parts II to IV shall render unlawful any act done by the training body in, or in connection with—

(*a*) affording persons who are of the sex in question and who appear likely to take up that work in that area access to facilities for training which would help to fit them for that work, or (*b*) encouraging persons of that sex to take advantage of opportunities in the area for doing that work.

The section then makes special provision for women who have been away from work for some time in order to have and bring up a family, although the terms of the subsection are wide enough to cover those who simply give up their jobs on marriage to look after the home, those who stay at home to care for elderly or disabled relatives, and, of course, men. This provision is in subsection (3), the text of which is as follows:

> (3) Nothing in Parts II to IV shall render unlawful any act done by a training body in, or in connection with, affording persons access to facilities for training which would help to fit them for employment, where it appears to the training body that those persons are in special need of training by reason of the period for which they have been discharging domestic or family responsibilities to the exclusion of regular full-time employment.
>
> The discrimination in relation to which this subsection applies may result from confining the training to persons who have been discharging domestic or family responsibilities, or from the way persons are selected for training, or both.

The section applies not only to the bodies specified at the beginning of this Chapter, but also to any person or body designated for this specific purpose by the Secretary of State under subsection (4), and any such person or body can be designated in respect of the entire section, or merely for subsections (1) and (2), or, conversely, merely for subsection (3).

Both the prohibition provided by section 14 and the exemption from it provided by section 47 are specifically extended to cases where the actual facilities are provided by third parties, and not the bodies referred to in section 14, by section 50.

Section 16 renders it equally unlawful for the Manpower Services Commission, the Employment Service Agency or the Training Services Agency to discriminate in the provision of facilities and services under section 2 of the Employment and Training Act 1973 (which deals with the functions of the Manpower Services Commission and the Agencies). But for section 16, these bodies would have been protected in respect of such functions, by the terms of section 51, which exempts all acts which are necessary in order to comply with an Act passed before the Sex Discrimination Act. But this section does not apply in a case when they are acting as an employment agency under the Employment and Training Act 1973, or carrying out functions under that Act to which section 14 of the Sex Discrimination Act applies, as subsection (2) of section 16 (another demarcation subsection) provides.

Exception for training involving communal accommodation

Another exemption which may affect the bodies to which this Chapter relates is to be found in section 46, which deals with communal accommodation. References to the full provision of this section, as it affects the field of employment, have already been made in Chapter 3, and, in particular, the definition of communal accommodation need not be repeated here. Attention is drawn to the fact that an exemption for **admission** to communal accommodation (and, hence, to some training courses) is provided by subsections (3) and (4) in the following terms:

> (3) Nothing in Part II or III shall render unlawful sex discrimination in the admission of persons to communal accommodation if the accommodation is managed in a way which, given the exigencies of the situation, comes as near as may be to fair and equitable treatment of men and women.
>
> (4) In applying subsection (3) account shall be taken of—
>
> (*a*) whether and how far it is reasonable to expect that the accommodation should be altered or extended, or that further alternative accommodation should be provided; and
>
> (*b*) the frequency of the demand or need for use of the accommodation by men as compared with women.

These provisions are enlarged, to some extent, by subsection (5) which reads:

> (5) Nothing in Part II or III shall render unlawful sex discrimination against a woman or against a man as respects the provision of any benefit, facility or service if—
>
> (*a*) the benefit, facility or service cannot properly and effectively be provided except for those using communal accommodation, and
>
> (*b*) in the relevant circumstances the woman or, as the case may be, the man could lawfully be refused the use of the accommodation by virtue of subsection (3).

In applying these subsections, however, regard must be had to subsection (6) which provides:

> (6) Neither subsection (3) nor subsection (5) is a defence to an act of sex discrimination under Part II unless such arrangements as are reasonably practicable are made to compensate for the detriment caused by the discrimination; but in considering under subsection (5) whether the use of communal accommodation could lawfully be refused (in a case based on Part II), it shall be assumed that the requirements of this subsection have been complied with as respects subsection (3).

The two points to note about this last subsection are that the compensation arrangements are not **primarily** financial, and that the second half of the subsection effectively puts the burden of proving that the accommodation is **not** managed in a fair and equitable manner, as between the sexes, upon the individual who suffers the discrimination.

EMPLOYMENT AGENCIES

An employment agency is defined in subsection (1) of section 82 as someone who provides services for the purpose of finding employment for workers, or supplying employers with workers, whether or not they do so for profit. It matters not, therefore, for the purpose of this Act, whether the agency obtains its fee from the employer or from the worker, nor whether it is a bureau operated by a professional body for its members.

The definition is certainly wide enough to cover the Government-operated employment exchanges, now the Employment Service Agency, and the Manpower Services Commission, and the Training Services Agency in respect of their employment agency functions, and those organisations are subject to all the provisions of this section when carrying out their functions as employment agencies under the Employment and Training Act 1973.

Three forms of discrimination in the employment agencies' operations are covered by subsection (1) of section 15, and each is made unlawful by the subsection. The first is in the terms on which the agency **offers** to provide any of its services; the second is discrimination by refusing or deliberately omitting to **provide** such services; and the third is **in the way** it provides them. By subsection (3) of section 15 the word " services " includes " guidance on careers and any other services related to employment ". Subsection (1) reads as follows:

> (1) It is unlawful for an employment agency to discriminate against a woman—
>
> (*a*) in the terms on which the agency offers to provide any of its services, or
>
> (*b*) by refusing or deliberately omitting to provide any of its services, or
>
> (*c*) in the way it provides any of its services.

Subsection (2) of section 15 renders it unlawful for a local education authority to discriminate when carrying out its functions under section 8 of the Employment and Training Act 1973. But for this section, local authorities would have also been exempt when carrying out those functions, under the provisions of section 51 relating to prior statutory authority.

When dealing with all the types of employment agencies mentioned above, it must be remembered that, in addition to the prohibitions in respect of their services referred to above, they will be responsible, under section 6, as employers if they discriminate in respect of their employees, both interviewing, managerial and ancillary staff **and** the staff whom they employ for hiring-out to employers.

Exceptions in specific instances

Employment agencies and local authorities will not, of course, be liable if the employment was such that the employer could lawfully offer it to a person of one sex only (*e.g.* the post of midwife), and subsection (4) provides that section 15 does not apply to such a case.

Moreover, by subsection (5) of Section 15, an employment agency or local authority will not be liable for unlawful discrimination if it acted in reliance upon a statement made to it by an employer to the effect that the discrimination would not be unlawful because of the provisions of subsection (4), provided that it was reasonable for it to rely upon that statement.

VICARIOUS LIABILITY

Employment agencies may also be liable (*e.g.* for discrimination in the offer of employment) by section 42 for knowingly aiding the employer to discriminate. This section could also apply, of course, to the vocational training bodies mentioned above, in certain circumstances, and certainly applies to the associations of employers referred to in this Chapter. Subsection (3) of section 42 reproduces the exemption contained in subsection (5) of section 15 in respect of agents who rely upon a statement by the employer that the discrimination is not unlawful, if it was reasonable to rely upon it. Conversely, by section 41, they may render the employer liable for their acts of unlawful discrimination, even if the employer had no knowledge of such acts.

There are other instances of vicarious liability which affect the firms and organisations to which this Chapter relates. Section 39, which has already been noticed in Chapter 2 in connection with employment, renders it unlawful to instruct someone to do an act, or to procure or attempt to procure the doing of an act, which is unlawful under Part II or Part III of the Act if the person instructed or procured is subject to the authority of the firm or organisation, or " accustomed to act " in accordance with its wishes.

Section 40 goes further, and provides that:

> (1) It is unlawful to induce, or attempt to induce, a person to do any act which contravenes Part II or III by—
>
> (*a*) providing or offering to provide him with any benefit, or
>
> (*b*) subjecting or threatening to subject him to any detriment.
>
> (2) An offer or threat is not prevented from falling within subsection (1) because it is not made directly to the person in question, if it is made in such a way that he is likely to hear of it.

As was said in a previous chapter, neither nods nor winks to blind horses will avoid these two sections, and the only safe course is to eschew any attempt to discriminate in a manner which is contrary to the Act.

Yet another provision which affects the firms and organisations referred to in this Chapter is the liability of an advertiser who untruthfully informs the publisher of an advertisement which indicates, " or might reasonably be understood as indicating " an intention to contravene the Act, that what is proposed in the advertisement is not unlawful. Unlawful advertisements are dealt with at greater length in Chapter 13, but it should be noted here that the penalty for knowingly or recklessly making such a statement to a publisher is a fine of up to £400.

SANCTIONS

The sanctions for unlawful discrimination both by the vocational training bodies referred to in this Chapter, and by employment agencies, are, with one exception, identical with those for such discrimination by employers, which are discussed in Chapter 3, substituting the appropriate body or employment agency for the employer, and the reader is referred to page 39 on this aspect.

The one sanction that is peculiar to the provisions relating to employment agencies is another of the rare criminal penalties in the Act. This is that an employer who knowingly or recklessly informs an employment agency or local authority that the circumstances are such that it is lawful for him to offer the position in question to one sex only, commits an offence under subsection (6) of section 15 if the information was false or misleading in a material respect. For that offence the employer can be fined up to £400. Section 42 which, as has already been mentioned, makes it unlawful to knowingly aid an employer to discriminate unlawfully, contains, in subsection (4), an identical provision.

Complaints that a third party has knowingly aided the employer to discriminate unlawfully, or that the employer is liable for discrimination by an employee or agent, under sections 42 and 41, as mentioned above, are also made to an industrial tribunal, in accordance with subsection (1) (*b*) of section 63.

Vocational training bodies and employment agencies must also have regard to the provisions of section 77. Subsection (1) of section 77 renders the term of a contract void if:

(*a*) its inclusion renders the making of the contract unlawful by virtue of this Act, or

(*b*) it is included in furtherance of an act rendered unlawful by this Act, or

(*c*) it provides for the doing of an act which would be rendered unlawful by this Act.

Paragraph (*b*), in particular, could apply to contracts, written or unwritten, between employment agencies and employers, and certainly some terms of arrangements between individual employers and employer-organised vocational training bodies could fall within the wording of paragraphs (*a*) and (*b*).

Subsection (3) of section 77 renders a term unenforceable by the party in whose favour the term would operate if it purports to exclude or limit any provision of the Act or the Equal Pay Act.

CHAPTER 6

DISCRIMINATION IN BUSINESS AND PROFESSIONAL ASSOCIATIONS, TRADE UNIONS AND PARTNERSHIPS, AND THE GRANTING OF QUALIFICATIONS

EMPLOYERS' ORGANISATIONS, PROFESSIONAL ASSOCIATIONS AND TRADE UNIONS

A very broad spectrum of associations and organisations is covered by section 12, subsection (1) of which reads:

> (1) This section applies to an organisation of workers, an organisation of employers, or any other organisation whose members carry on a particular profession or trade for the purposes of which the organisation exists.

Obviously, this wording covers trade unions, the Confederation of British Industry, and, for example, the Chartered Accountants' Institute, but the list is virtually endless. On the other hand, the definition would not appear to cover chambers of commerce, the members of which are not necessarily employers and certainly do not carry on a common trade. Subsection (1) of section 82 defines " profession " as including any vocation or occupation and " trade " as including any business, so that such bodies as a stock exchange or Lloyds would be covered by section 12.

Subsection (2) of section 12 makes it unlawful for any such association or organisation to discriminate against non-members in the terms on which it is willing to admit them to membership, or by refusing or deliberately omitting to accept their application for membership.

It is important to recall, at this stage, that (apart from victimisation) the " discrimination " to which the Act relates is discrimination on the grounds of sex or marital status. Therefore, subsection (2) does not make it unlawful to offer different terms to would-be members who, for example, have different qualifications, or live in different areas, **provided such differentiation applies to men and women, the married and the unmarried, alike.**

Covert Discrimination

To the general rule just stated must be made an equally general exception, concerning what is referred to in Chapter 1 as " covert discrimination ". If a trade union, professional association or trade organisation operates a restriction on membership, or preferential terms for membership, under a rule which, although it applies equally to both sexes (or to the married and the unmarried), **is such that the proportion of one sex who can comply with it is considerably smaller than the proportion of the other sex** (or the proportion of the married of one sex is considerably smaller than the proportion of the unmarried of that sex) **AND** it cannot be shown to be justifiable **irrespective** of sex (or marital status), it is discriminating unlawfully, and will be subject to all the sanctions which are discussed in the next Chapter.

The provisions of the Act relating to covert discrimination have been dealt with in considerable detail in Chapter 1, and any reader who has not read that Chapter, or has skimmed through it, should now read it with some care, applying all that is said there to trade unions, professional associations and trade organisations in place of a person, firm or company, since it may obviously be of very considerable importance to the organisation and conduct of such bodies.

Terms of membership and admission to membership

There is a subtle distinction between the terms of paragraph (*a*) of subsection (2), which reads:

> (*a*) in the terms on which it is prepared to admit her to membership.

(it will be recalled that, under the " looking-glass " provisions, this applies in reverse, to men and, by virtue of section 3, to the married as opposed to the single), and paragraph (*b*) of subsection (2), which reads:

> (*b*) by refusing, or deliberately omitting to accept, her application for membership,

inasmuch as the former deals with what the organisation is **prepared** to do, and the latter with what it actually **does** when it receives an application for membership. It is possible, therefore, to make a complaint of unlawful discrimination in respect of the membership terms of an organisation without applying to join it, but a complaint under paragraph (*b*) can only be made **after** an unsuccessful application for membership.

Discrimination during the period of membership

The prohibition on discriminating against the member of a trade union, professional association or trade organisation, contained in subsection (3) of section 12, is in very broad terms, and makes it unlawful for such a body to discriminate:

> (*a*) in the way it affords [the member] access to any benefits, facilities or services, or by refusing or deliberately omitting to afford [the member] access to them, or
>
> (*b*) by depriving [the member] of membership, or varying the terms on which [he or] she is a member, or
>
> (*c*) by subjecting [the member] to any other detriment.

A moment's thought will reveal that these words, especially "any other detriment", cover every incident of membership of such a body. Once a body falls within the definition contained in subsection (1), therefore, it must ensure that in everything that it does, or holds itself out to do, it does not discriminate between one member and another because of a member's sex or because a member is married.

Summary

The test for unlawful discrimination by the bodies referred to in section 12 is, therefore:

Discrimination:

(*a*) in the terms on which it is prepared to admit a person to membership or—

(*b*) by refusing, or deliberately omitting, to accept that person's application for membership or—

(*c*) in the way it affords to a member access to any benefits, facilities or services, or by refusing or deliberately omitting to afford the member access to them (other than death or retirement benefits) or—

(*d*) by depriving the member of membership, or varying the terms of membership for that member or—

(*e*) subjecting the member to any other detriment

in every case either:

(*f*) on the ground of the sex, or married status of the applicant or member or—

(*g*) by applying to the applicant an " unfavourable requirement " which the trade union, employers' organisation, professional or trade association applies or would apply, equally to both sexes, or to the married and unmarried alike but which:

(i) is such that the proportion of married persons of the same sex, or persons of the applicant's, or member's, sex (as the case may be), who can comply with the requirement is considerably smaller than the proportion of unmarried persons of the same sex, or persons of the other sex (as the case may be), who can comply with it, **and**

(ii) which the trade union, employers' organisation, professional or trade association cannot show to be justifiable irrespective of the marital status, or the sex (as the case may be) of the applicant or member to whom it is applied

(*h*) always provided that the comparison of the cases of persons of different marital status, or different sex, for this purpose is such that the relevant circumstances in the one case are the same, or not materially different, in the other.

Exceptions to discrimination by employers' organisations and professional associations and trade unions

The only specific exceptions to the provisions of section 12 are threefold, the first of which is very limited in its scope. One is the exception which occurs repeatedly throughout the Act in respect of death and retirement benefits, and it is worth pointing out here that subsection (1) of section 82 defines retirement as being voluntary or involuntary, and on grounds of age, length of service or incapacity.

The second specific exception is contained in section 48, and relates to training for posts in the body concerned, and to soliciting additional members, where it is desirable to redress an imbalance. This is, of course, one of the sections in the Act which **encourages** discrimination in favour of one sex, in order to redress the effects of discrimination suffered by that sex in the past, and, needless to say, its most common application will be in favour of women, since they have been the chief sufferers in the past.

By subsection (2) of section 48, anything done by an organisation which comes within section 12 in connection with:

> (*a*) affording female members of the organisation only, or male members of the organisation only, access to facilities for training which would help to fit them for holding a post of any kind in the organisation, or
>
> (*b*) encouraging female members only, or male members only, to take advantage of opportunities for holding such posts in the organisation,

is not unlawful if, within the preceding twelve months, there were either no persons, or a " comparatively small " number of persons of the sex in question holding such posts.

In the same way, by subsection (3) of section 48, any step taken by an organisation within section 12 to encourage women only, or men only, to become members is not unlawful if, during the preceding twelve months, either the organisation had no members of that sex, or the members of that sex were in comparatively small proportion to the total membership.

There is also an exception, to be found in paragraph 1 of Schedule 4, which is solely to enable the organisations to which section 12 applies to re-arrange their rules and procedures regarding contributions and benefits to conform to the requirements of the Act. The paragraph is, therefore, transitional, as the heading to Schedule 4 suggests. It reads as follows:

> 1. Section 12 does not apply, as respects any organisation—
>
> (*a*) to contributions or other payments falling to be made to the organisation by its members or by persons seeking membership, or

(*b*) to financial benefits accruing to members of the organisation by reason of their membership,

where the payment falls to be made, or the benefit accrues, before 1st January 1978 under rules of the organisation made before the passing of this Act.

The third specific exception is to be found in section 49 and relates to membership of committees, sub-committees, councils and similar bodies within organisations to which section 12 applies, **the members of which, or the majority of members of which, are elected.** Organisations and bodies within section 12 will not be discriminating unlawfully if they make special arrangements to ensure a minimum number of members of one sex on such committees or councils, or in the organisation as a whole if membership is by election.

The wording of subsection (1) of section 49 is:

(1) If an organisation to which section 12 applies comprises a body the membership of which is wholly or mainly elected, nothing in section 12 shall render unlawful provision which ensures that a minimum number of persons of one sex are members of the body—

(*a*) by reserving seats on the body for persons of that sex, or

(*b*) by making extra seats on the body available (by election or co-option or otherwise) for persons of that sex on occasions when the number of persons of that sex in the other seats is below the minimum,

where in the opinion of the organisation the provision is in the circumstances needed to secure a reasonable lower limit to the number of members of that sex serving on the body, and nothing in Parts II to IV shall render unlawful any act done in order to give effect to such a provision.

The word " comprises " used in the beginning of this subsection can mean either " includes " or " consists of ", but it is only the **former** meaning which is intended here, as is clear from subsection (2), which says:

(2) This section shall not be taken as making lawful—

(*a*) discrimination in the arrangements for determining the persons entitled to vote in an election of members of the body, or otherwise to choose the persons to serve on the body, or (*b*) discrimination in any arrangements concerning membership of the organisation itself.

Another exemption which may affect the bodies to which this Chapter relates is to be found in section 46, which deals with communal accommodation. References to the full provision of this section, as it affects the field of employment, have already been made in Chapter 3, and, in particular, the definition of communal accommodation need not be repeated here. Attention is drawn to the fact that an exemption for **admission** to communal accommodation (and, hence, to some training courses) is provided by subsections (3) and (4) in the following terms:

(3) Nothing in Part II or III shall render unlawful sex discrimination in the admission of persons to communal accommodation if the accommodation is managed in a way which, given the exigencies of the situation, comes as near as may be to fair and equitable treatment of men and women.

(4) In applying subsection (3) account shall be taken of—

(*a*) whether and how far it is reasonable to expect that the accommodation should be altered or extended, or that further alternative accommodation should be provided; and

(*b*) the frequency of the demand or need for use of the accommodation by men as compared with women.

These provisions are enlarged, to some extent, by subsection (5) which reads:

(5) Nothing in Part II or III shall render unlawful sex discrimination against a woman, or against a man, as respects the provision of any benefit, facility or service if—

(*a*) the benefit, facility or service cannot properly and effectively be provided except for those using communal accommodation, and

(*b*) in the relevant circumstances the woman or, as the case may be, the man could lawfully be refused the use of the accommodation by virtue of subsection (3).

This is followed by a requirement for compensation (not necessarily financial compensation) in subsection (6) in these words:

(6) Neither subsection (3) nor subsection (5) is a defence to an act of sex discrimination under Part II unless such arrangements as are reasonably practicable are made to compensate for

the detriment caused by the discrimination; but in considering under subsection (5) (*b*) whether the use of communal accommodation could lawfully be refused (in a case based on Part II), it shall be assumed that the requirements of this subsection have been complied with as respects subsection (3).

It will be seen that the latter part of this subsection puts the burden of proving that the accommodation is **not** managed fairly and equitably firmly on the employee.

GOVERNING BODIES AND QUALIFYING BODIES FOR PROFESSIONS AND TRADES

Section 13 legislates against discrimination by those bodies which confer professional qualifications or control entry to a profession, vocation, occupation, trade or business. Once again, the wording used in subsection (1) of section 13 is very comprehensive, and is worth reproducing:

> (1) It is unlawful for an authority or body which can confer an authorisation or qualification which is needed for, or facilitates, engagement in a particular profession or trade to discriminate against a woman.

As already mentioned, by subsection (1) of section 82, " profession " includes any vocation or occupation and " trade " includes any business.

In addition to such obvious targets as the British Medical Association and the Law Society, which exercise monopoly control over entry into their respective professions by statutory authority, the section, by its use of the words " or facilitates engagement in " applies to the Institute of Chartered Accountants, and other accountancy bodies which have no monopoly powers, and to such bodies as the General Council of the Stock Exchange, of Lloyds, and of the Jockey Club, whose authorisation is, in practice, a pre-requisite to carrying on business by an individual in London as a stockbroker or insurance underwriter, or the vocation throughout England of a jockey, respectively. The wording also extends to licensing justices, local authorities with power to license employment agencies and places of entertainment, and many other statutory authorities. What may be a little less evident, although nonetheless true, is that the section also covers trade unions, membership of which is, in practice, often a pre-requisite to engaging in employment in a particular trade, certainly where a " closed shop " is operated.

It will be noticed that many of the bodies which fall within the scope of section 13 in respect of the qualifications or authorisations they confer in their particular field are also within the provisions of section 12 in respect of the terms on which they admit members or the facilities which they afford to members once they have been admitted.

The terms on which members are admitted to such bodies, and the qualification or authorisation which they confer may be synonymous, but it should not be assumed that this is always the case. For example, the Law Society is basically a club, membership of which is open only to qualified solicitors, but is not incumbent upon them, and its jurisdiction to confer and withdraw the qualification of solicitor is a completely separate function, whilst many professional bodies have two, or even more, **classes** or **grades** of members with different terms of membership, and even different professional functions applying to each class or grade.

The discrimination rendered unlawful by section 13 is:

(*a*) in the terms on which it is prepared to confer on [him or] her that authorisation or qualification, or

(*b*) by refusing or deliberately omitting to grant [him or] her application for it, or

(*c*) by withdrawing it from [him or] her or varying the terms on which [he or] she holds it.

These stipulations are amplified by subsection (3) of section 13, which explains that " authorisation or qualification " includes recognition, registration, enrolment, approval and certification, whilst " confer " includes renew or extend.

The reader is again reminded that, by definition, " discrimination " is discrimination because of sex or because the person is married. Discrimination for any other reason is **not** unlawful. Having said that, it must be added, once more, that the Act applies to covert discrimination, as described in Chapter 1, and therefore, in many instances, there may be unlawful discrimination where no such discrimination was intended.

At the same time, it should be recalled that subsection (3) of section 5 provides that any comparison between the position with regard to one sex and the position with regard to another, or the position of the married as against the unmarried, must be such that the relevant circumstances in the one case are the same as, or not materially different from, those in the other. To state an obvious example, the Law Society is not expected, therefore, to apply to a female would-be articled clerk with the degree of Bachelor of Law (itself a triumph of non-discrimination, at least in nomenclature!) the same requirements that it would apply to her male counterpart with no law degree.

Summary

The specification for unlawful discrimination by such governing bodies can, therefore, be summarised as follows:

It must be:

(*a*) in the terms on which it is prepared to confer, renew or extend an authorisation or qualification, or—

(*b*) by refusing, or deliberately omitting to grant an application for authorisation or qualification, or—

(*c*) by withdrawing authorisation or qualification from a person, or varying the terms on which he or she holds it,

either—

(*d*) on the ground of the sex or married status of the person under consideration or—

(*e*) by applying to the person under consideration an " unfavourable requirement " which the governing body applies or would apply equally to both sexes, or to the married and unmarried alike, but which:

(i) is such that the proportion of persons of that person's sex who can comply with the requirement is considerably smaller than the proportion of the other sex or, if the person be married, is such that the proportion of married persons who can comply with it is considerably smaller than the proportion of unmarried persons of the same sex who can comply with it, **and**

(ii) which the governing body cannot show to be justifiable, irrespective of the sex, or the married status, as the case may be, of the person under consideration

(*f*) always provided that the comparison of the cases of persons of different sex, or marital status, for this purpose must be such that the relevant circumstances in the one case are the same, or not materially different, in the other.

Exceptions

By subsection (4) of section 13, these provisions do not apply to educational establishments falling within the province of sections 22 and 23 of the Act, which includes local authority schools, independent schools and universities. It follows that universities will be able to continue to confer degrees, even where such degrees effectively control entrance to a profession or vocation, in a manner which discriminates between the sexes.

Furthermore, religious bodies are exempt from the provisions of section 13, by subsection (2) of section 19, in the following circumstances—

> (2) Nothing in section 13 applies to an authorisation or qualification (as defined in that section) for purposes of an organised religion where the authorisation or qualification is limited to one sex so as to comply with the doctrines of the religion or avoid offending the religious susceptibilities of a significant number of its followers.

Consideration of good character

Section 13 also contains a subsection (subsection (2)) which appears to widen the scope of the Act considerably:

> (2) Where an authority or body is required by law to satisfy itself as to his good character before conferring on a person an authorisation or qualification which is needed for, or facilitates, his engagement in any profession or trade then, without prejudice to any other duty to which it is subject, that requirement shall be taken to impose on the authority or body a duty to have regard to any evidence tending to show that he, or any of his employees, or agents (whether past or present), has practised unlawful discrimination in, or in connection with, the carrying on of any profession or trade.

The sting in this subsection is that the authority or body must have regard to **" any evidence tending to show "** that the applicant, " his employees or agents " (whether past or present) " has practised unlawful discrimination in . . . connection with the carrying on of any profession or trade ".

It will be noticed that the unlawful discrimination need not have been practised in the profession or trade for which the applicant is being considered, and can have apparently taken place at any time in the past. Moreover, the unlawful discrimination may have been carried out by someone over whom the applicant had no real control, namely a mere agent, and in respect of a different profession or trade to that which the applicant was, at the time of the unlawful discrimination, engaged upon.

What is worse, however, is that the authority or body is required to have regard, not to any **finding** of unlawful discrimination, but to " any evidence tending to show " that such discrimination was practised. This seems to open the gates to a veritable Tom Tiddler's ground of spies, informers and purveyors of tittle-tattle. It is devoutly to be hoped that the authorities and bodies concerned will give very little weight to such evidence, unless it is of nothing less than a finding of unlawful discrimination by a court or industrial tribunal.

Statutory appeal procedures

Although strictly a point in connection with sanctions, it is convenient to note here that, where any Act of Parliament prescribes an appeal procedure in respect of the refusal to grant, or the withdrawal of, an authorisation or qualification by an authority or body to which section 13 applies, that appeal procedure is preserved by subsection (2) of section 63, and any act or omission which gives rise to such an appeal cannot form the subject of a complaint to an industrial tribunal. To give two concrete examples: appeals from an order of the Law Society's Disciplinary Committee striking-off a solicitor for misconduct will continue to go to the Court of Appeal, whilst appeals from similar orders of the General Medical Council will continue to be taken before the Privy Council.

PARTNERSHIPS

First, it should be clearly stated that the provisions relating to partnerships are confined, by subsection (1) of section 11, to those with six or more partners, and, in the somewhat rare case nowadays of a limited partnership under the Limited Partnership Act 1907, what would commonly be called "sleeping partners" are not counted for this purpose. The Secretary of State has power, by subsection (1) (*c*) of section 80, to amend this figure of six by statutory order.

By subsection (2) of section 11, the prohibitions contained in the section are extended to "persons proposing to form themselves into a partnership", and it should be remembered, in these days when some small companies are reverting to partnerships for tax and similar reasons, that this would apply to the directors of the company in such circumstances.

In these cases, the forbidden conduct, in relation to a position as partner in the firm, is, by subsection (1), to discriminate:

(*a*) in the arrangements they make for the purpose of determining who should be offered that position, or

(*b*) in the terms on which they offer her that position, or

(*c*) by refusing or deliberately omitting to offer her that position, or

(*d*) in a case where the woman already holds that position:

- (i) in the way they afford her access to any benefits, facilities or services, or by refusing or deliberately omitting to afford her access to them, or
- (ii) by expelling her from that position, or subjecting her to any other detriment.

It will be remembered that, in this respect, the female includes the male, and *vice versa.*

There is, of course, a great deal of discrimination in partnerships, most of which reflects the inequality of the partners in financial contribution, experience, extent of following amongst the clients or customers, amount or importance of work done, and even general ability. It is right that, where the contribution to the business is not equal, the rewards should not be equal, and it is worth reiterating here that, by the first "leg" of subsection (1) of section 1, and of subsection (1) of section 3, the discrimination must be on the grounds of sex or status as a married person. There is also, however, the prohibition on covert discrimination contained in the second " leg " of those two subsections, and that is likely to be of particular importance to partnerships. The avid reader (if one exists) will need no reminding that both overt and covert discrimination have been dealt with at length in Chapter 1.

In connection with partnerships, it should not be overlooked that victimisation of a partner who has played a part, or intends to play a part, in proceedings under the Equal Pay Act, or who alleges a contravention of that Act, is, by section 4, also unlawful discrimination, particularly as many partners are remunerated by salary only.

Exceptions

The specific exceptions in the case of partnerships are two-fold, and may be stated shortly. First, there is the common exception, found repeatedly in the Act, in respect of death benefits and retirement pensions, which is the necessary consequence of differences in actuarial statistics. Secondly, by subsection (3) of section 11, paragraphs (*a*) and (*c*) do not apply where, if the position were that of an employee and not a partner, being of one or other sex would be a " genuine occupational qualification " for the job. The precise extent of " genuine occupational qualification " is, of course, dealt with in pages 33 to 38.

Summary

It will no doubt be at least as useful to partners as to others who read this work, and probably even more useful, to draw together the threads of discrimination as it affects them, so that the picture on the tapestry can be discerned. Unlawful discrimination, therefore, as it applies to partners and prospective partners, is discrimination:

(*a*) by a partnership of six or more partners

(*b*) in relation to a position as a partner in the firm, whether—

(*c*) in the arrangements they make for the purpose of determining who should be offered that position, or—

(*d*) by refusing or deliberately omitting to offer that position (unless being of the opposite sex to the prospective partner is a "genuine occupational qualification") or—

(*e*) in the terms (financial or otherwise) on which they offer that position to the prospective partner, or, if the person concerned is already a partner:

(*f*) in the way they afford him or her access to any benefits, facilities or services, or by refusing or deliberately omitting to afford him or her access to them or

(*g*) by expelling him or her from the partnership or subjecting him or her to any other detriment either—

(*h*) on the ground of the sex or married status of the partner or prospective partner or—

(*i*) by applying to the partner or prospective partner an "unfavourable requirement" which they apply or would apply equally to both sexes, or to the married and the unmarried, alike, but which

(*j*) is such that the proportion of married persons of the same sex, or members of that person's sex (as the case may be) who can comply with the requirement is considerably smaller than the proportion of unmarried persons of the same sex, or persons of the opposite sex (as the case may be) who can comply with it and

(*k*) which the partners cannot show to be justifiable, irrespective of the marital status, or the sex (as the case may be) of the partner or prospective partner, always provided:

(*l*) that the comparison of the cases of persons of different marital status, or different sex, for this purpose, is such that the relevant circumstances in the one case are the same, or not materially different, in the other, and

(*m*) in the case of limited partnerships, the person under consideration is not, or is not to be, a limited partner under the provisions of the Limited Partnerships Act 1907.

Partnership Contracts

The provisions of section 77 may be particularly apposite to partnerships. This invalidates a term in a contract if:

(*a*) its inclusion renders the making of the contract unlawful by virtue of this Act, or

(*b*) it is included in furtherance of an act rendered unlawful by this Act, or

(*c*) it provides for the doing of an act which would be rendered unlawful by this Act.

Similarly, by subsection (2) of section 77, if the inclusion of a term in a contract constitutes unlawful discrimination, or is in furtherance of, or provides for, such discrimination against a party to the contract, it is **unenforceable against that party.** This is very different to the term being void because, of course, it could be enforced by **that** party against other parties to the contract—a particularly useful advantage if the term in question contains both obligations upon **and** benefits to the party discriminated against.

Subsection (4) of section 77 authorises an application to the County Court to remove or modify a contractual term to which subsection (2) applies.

Further, a term in a contract which would exclude or limit any provision of the Act is, by subsection (3) of section 77 **unenforceable by any person in whose favour the term would operate,** although the subsection does not apply to an agreement settling a complaint to an industrial tribunal with the assistance of a conciliation officer. This subsection is less favourable to the person who suffers the discrimination than subsection (2), since, if the term were sufficiently extensive to confer a benefit on that person, the benefit would be lost.

Vicarious Liability

As has been pointed out already, employers are made specifically responsible for the discriminatory acts of their employees by subsection (1) of section 41 if the acts are done by the employees " in the course of their employment " (a phrase which has been the subject of judicial definition in the course of so many cases in the law of negligence that to attempt an explanation here would overburden this book). This vicarious responsibility could be of importance to the larger partnerships where, for example, staff supervisors have jurisdiction over partners, at least junior partners, in many day-to-day matters.

It is, of course, a defence to any proceedings brought against the partnership for the discriminatory act of an employee, to prove that they took such steps as were reasonably practicable to prevent the employee from doing that act, or from doing acts of that description in the course of his or her employment, in accordance with subsection (3) of section 41.

A similar vicarious responsibility exists for principals in relation to their agents under subsection (2) of section 41. Some partnerships will employ third parties to conduct the negotiations leading to the admission of a new partner, particularly in the case of a salaried partner or an amalgamation, and it should be remembered that the agent may go beyond his (or her) brief. Moreover, accountants, brokers, solicitors, and a whole range of service-providing third parties may, in law, constitute agents of the partnership and may, advertently or inadvertently, discriminate against a partner in providing those services. There is, however, in the case of agents, no defence corresponding to the provisions of subsection (3).

Since so many partnerships are providers of services, often in a confidential and advisory capacity, it is as well to remind them that they may also be liable for knowingly aiding another person to discriminate unlawfully, under the provisions of section 42. Additionally, if their principal is liable for an act of theirs by virtue of the provisions of subsection (1) of section 41, they are '**deemed to aid**' the principal in that act of discrimination by subsection (2) of section 42, although it may still be possible for them to show that they did not do so knowingly, under the terms of subsection (3) of section 42, if—

> (*a*) he acts in reliance on a statement made to him by that other person that, by reason of any provision of this Act, the act which he aids would not be unlawful, and
>
> (*b*) it is reasonable for him to rely on the statement.

If, on the other hand, they are guilty of making to someone else a statement such as is described in (*a*) above, they render themselves liable to a fine of up to £400.

This is one of several instances of criminal liability under the Act.

Similar responsibilities are provided by sections 39 and 40. Section 39 reads as follows:

> It is unlawful for a person—
>
> (*a*) who has authority over another person, or
>
> (*b*) in accordance with whose wishes that other person is accustomed to act,
>
> to instruct him to do any act which is unlawful by virtue of Part II or III, or procure or attempt to procure the doing by him of any such act.

Whilst Part II of the Act relates principally to employment and training for employment, Part III includes the sale of goods and the supply of facilities and services. In fact, a party will be liable if he instructs an employee or any other person over whom he has influence to discriminate in any manner prohibited by the Act, except, by publishing a discriminatory advertisement.

It will be noticed that it is not only straightforward instructions which are contrary to the section, as it refers also to " procure or attempt to procure the doing . . . of any such act ". These words can cover a very wide variety of actions and subtle pressures, and to put the matter quite beyond doubt, section 40 provides—

> (1) It is unlawful to induce, or attempt to induce, a person to do any act which contravenes Part II or III by—
>
> (*a*) providing or offering to provide him with any benefit, or
>
> (*b*) subjecting or threatening to subject him to any detriment.
>
> (2) An offer or threat is not prevented from falling within subsection (1) because it is not made directly to the person in question, if it is made in such a way that he is likely to hear of it.

Neither nods nor winks to blind horses will avoid these two sections, and the only safe course is to eschew any attempt to discriminate in a manner which is contrary to the Act.

Although sections 39 and 40 do not apply to advertisements, a body or firm which advertises in a discriminatory manner, and informs the publisher of the advertisement that the advertisement is not unlawful because they are entitled to discriminate, whether because the discrimination is not of a kind which comes within the general prohibitions of the Act, or because it falls within an exemption to it, may be fined up to £400 if that statement is untrue. This liability is dealt with at greater length in Chapter 13.

Moreover, as was seen in Chapter 5, an employer who falsely or misleadingly states to an employment agency that it is lawful for him to offer a job to a particular sex only (for example, because he employs only five employees) and does so knowingly or recklessly, commits a criminal offence, for which he can be fined up to £400.

CHAPTER 7

SANCTIONS FOR BREACHES OF ACT BY BUSINESS AND PROFESSIONAL ASSOCIATIONS, TRADE UNIONS AND PARTNERSHIPS

As explained in connection with employment, the discrimination which is made " unlawful " by the Act is not criminal, and usually does not even give the person suffering from it a right to sue in the courts. This is because section 62 excludes all penalties, both criminal and civil, save for those specifically provided by the Act. The Act provides a variety of penalties which are examined again in this Chapter in relation to the bodies, and the **instances** of discrimination, dealt with in the last Chapter.

APPLICATIONS TO INDUSTRIAL TRIBUNALS

An individual who has suffered unlawful discrimination can complain to an industrial tribunal, under the provisions of section 63, and this may well be the simplest and most common remedy.

A complaint against a partnership alleging unlawful discrimination by their employee or agent, for which they are liable under section 41, can also be made to an industrial tribunal under the provisions of subsection (1) (*b*) of section 63.

By subsection (1) of section 65, an industrial tribunal has the power to make—

(*a*) an order declaring the rights of the complainant and the respondent in relation to the act to which the complaint relates;

(*b*) an order requiring the respondent to pay to the complainant compensation of an amount corresponding to any damages he could have been ordered by a county court or by a sheriff court to pay to the complainant if the complaint had fallen to be dealt with under section 66;

(*c*) a recommendation that the respondent take within a specified period action appearing to the tribunal to be practicable for the purpose of obviating or reducing the adverse effect on the complainant of any act of discrimination to which the complaint relates.

In many cases an order under paragraph (*a*) will be all that is necessary, for most of the bodies to which this Chapter relates will act upon the decision of the tribunal and carry it out to its fullest extent. There are certainly some bodies and partnerships, however, which will try to get round a declaratory order by the tribunal, or to adjust the position by taking measures which are not caught, or not clearly caught, by the Act, and there will be cases in which the complainant will prefer to obtain compensation under paragraph (*b*) and turn their back on the body or partnership which has abused them.

Compensation

In view of the large sums of money that may be involved for a person, for example, debarred from admission to or following a profession, or being a partner in a substantial firm, such individuals must remember that the total compensation which the industrial tribunal can award under paragraph (*b*) above is limited, by subsection (2), to " the amount for the time being specified in paragraph 20 (1) (*b*) of Schedule 1 to the Trade Union and Labour Relations Act 1974 " which amount is currently £5,200.

As we have seen, the compensation which can be awarded by an industrial tribunal under paragraph (*b*) is defined by that paragraph as " an amount corresponding to any damages he could have been ordered by a county court . . . to pay to the complainant . . . under section 66 ", and it should not be overlooked that subsection (4) of section 66 specifically provides that such damages may include compensation for injury to feelings, in addition to compensation under any other head.

There is one point of difficulty in this respect, and that is that the county courts have no jurisdiction to entertain an action in tort in which the claim exceeds £1,000. In an ordinary action, if the plaintiff simply claims damages, without quantifying the amount, it is customary for the formal Particulars of Claim to specify that the plaintiff abandons any amount by which his damages may be found to exceed £1,000, in order to ensure that the county court judge has jurisdiction to hear the action.

As will be seen later, a claim in respect of an act of discrimination which is unlawful under Part III of the Act can be made the subject of civil proceedings " in like manner as any other claim in tort " by subsection (1) of section 66 and, by subsection (2), must be brought in the county court. The Act contains no specific provision to enable county courts to entertain claims for more than £1,000, and if the county court judge cannot award damages of more than £1,000 to a claimant under the Act, neither can an industrial tribunal.

It may be that the words at the end of subsection (2) " but all such remedies shall be obtainable in such proceedings as, apart from this subsection, would be obtainable in the High Court " can be construed as not only extending the county court jurisdiction in respect of the **kind** of remedies, but also in respect of the financial limits on them. However, until the point has been decided by the courts, it cannot be regarded as free from doubt.

As we have also seen, by subsection (3) of section 66, no damages for **covert** discrimination (either under subsection (1) (*b*) of section 1 or under subsection (1) (*b*) of section 3), can be awarded if the body or partnership **proves** that the requirement or condition in question was **not** applied with the intention of treating the individual discriminated against unfavourably on the ground of sex or marital status. It follows, therefore, that the industrial tribunal could not award compensation in those circumstances either, since the amount of damages which a county court could award would be nil.

The Commission can also apply to an industrial tribunal under the power contained in subsection (1) of section 73, and obtain orders in the terms of paragraphs (*a*) and (*c*) quoted above, but in such an application the Commission cannot obtain an order for compensation.

So far as the bodies referred to in this Chapter are concerned, including partnerships, declaratory orders under paragraph (*a*) above, and recommendations under paragraph (*c*) above, may be more important and more common in practice than orders for compensation.

This is as true of paragraph (*c*) as of paragraph (*a*), because, as has been said before, one should not be deceived by the fact that it refers merely to " a recommendation " into thinking that it provides no effective sanction. By subsection (3) of section 65, if the body in respect of which the recommendation is made fails to carry out such a recommendation **without reasonable justification,** the industrial tribunal may increase the compensation awarded under paragraph (*b*) (even, apparently, beyond the limit already mentioned, since the restriction in subsection (2) applies only to subsection (1) (*b*) and not to the subsection, subsection (3) (*a*), which authorises the increase), or may order compensation under paragraph (*b*) if they did not do so originally.

Conciliation

As has also been said before, the majority of applications to industrial tribunals may never result in an order containing, or leading to, a penalty. This is because subsection (1) of section 64 provides that if a copy of the application, or ' complaint ', is sent to a conciliation officer, he has a duty to endeavour to promote a settlement of the dispute without its being determined by the industrial tribunal, if either **both** the parties request him to do so, **or** he considers he could act with a reasonable chance of success. The latter part of this provision entitles a conciliation officer to impose an attempt at conciliation upon the parties against their will, if he sees fit so to do.

There is also provision, in subsection (2) of section 64, for the conciliation officer to act **before** any application or complaint is presented to the tribunal if he is requested so to do by either party. Notwithstanding section 64, the Act imposes no obligation upon industrial tribunals to send copies of complaints to a conciliation officer.

Whether acting under subsection (1) or subsection (2), the conciliation officer (who will be one of the officers appointed under paragraph 26 (1) of the First Schedule to the Trade Union and Labour Relations Act 1974) is charged by subsection (3) to have regard to the " desirability of encouraging the use of other procedures available for the settlement of grievances ", and, by subsection (4), anything communicated to him is not admissible in evidence except with the consent of the person from whom the information was obtained.

CRIMINAL LIABILITY

It will be recalled that the only criminal liability under the Act is not for discriminating unlawfully, but for knowingly or recklessly making a misleading or false statement to an employee or agent, a third party or the publisher of an advertisement, to the effect that a certain act or omission or the publication of an advertisement is not unlawful under the Act. For such a statement a body or partnership can be fined up to £400, under sections 15, 38 or 42, whichever may be appropriate.

TIME LIMITS FOR APPLICATIONS

Again, it is **extremely** important to remember that, by subsection (1) of section 76, a complaint to an industrial tribunal under section 63 (which deals with complaints of discrimination in the field of employment) **must be presented within three months of the act or omission to which it refers.** Similarly, subsection (4) of section 76 requires that an application by the Commission itself under subsection (1) of section 73 must be made within **six** months of the act or omission to which it refers.

Although by subsection (5) of section 76, the industrial tribunal has power to hear the complaint or application even if these periods have passed, if it considers that " it was not reasonably practicable to comply " with them, obviously this enabling power should not be relied upon unnecessarily.

As with employers, so with the bodies which are the subject of this Chapter, such periods are not always as short as they seem, because subsection (6) of section 76 provides that—

> (*a*) where the inclusion of any term in a contract renders the making of the contract an unlawful act that act shall be treated as extending throughout the duration of the contract, and
>
> (*b*) any act extending over a period shall be treated as done at the end of that period, and
>
> (*c*) a deliberate omission shall be treated as done when the person in question decided upon it,

and continues, for good measure:

> and in the absence of evidence establishing the contrary a person shall be taken for the purposes of this section to decide upon an omission when he does an act inconsistent with doing the omitted act, or, if he has done no such inconsistent act, when the period expires within which he might reasonably have been expected to do the omitted act if it was to be done.

QUESTIONNAIRES FOR USE PRIOR TO PROCEEDINGS

It should, perhaps, be mentioned at this juncture that the Act specifically authorises the Secretary of State by order to prescribe:

> (*a*) forms by which the person aggrieved may question the respondent on his reasons for doing any relevant act, or on any other matter which is or may be relevant;
>
> (*b*) forms by which the respondent may if he so wishes reply to any questions,

by subsection (1) of section 74. The purpose of such forms is described by the same subsection as being:

> With a view to helping a person (" the person aggrieved ") who considers he may have been discriminated against in contravention of this Act to decide whether to institute proceedings and, if he does so, to formulate and present his case in the most effective manner.

What is far more important is subsection (2), which provides:

> (2) Where the person aggrieved questions the respondent (whether in accordance with an order under subsection (1) or not)—
>
> (*a*) the question and any reply by the respondent subject to the following provisions of this section shall be admissible as evidence in the proceedings;

(*b*) if it appears to the court or tribunal that the respondent deliberately and without reasonable cause omitted to reply within a reasonable period or that his reply is evasive or equivocal, the court or tribunal may draw any inference from that fact that it considers it just and equitable to draw, including an inference that he committed an unlawful act.

Paragraph (*a*) does not enlarge the law at all, as the county courts have always had ample provision for communications between the parties to be admissible in evidence, but paragraph (*b*) certainly does extend the existing law. Prior to the passing of the Act, it would have been impossible for any reasonable and rational court or industrial tribunal to draw, merely from the respondent's failure to reply to questions or his equivocal or evasive reply, the inference that he had committed an unlawful act.

Subsection (3) of section 74 adds:

(3) The Secretary of State may by order—

(*a*) prescribe the period within which questions must be duly served in order to be admissible under subsection (2) (*a*), and

(*b*) prescribe the manner in which a question, and any reply by the respondent, may be duly served.

NON-DISCRIMINATION NOTICES

The position with regard to non-discrimination notices and injunctions against partnerships and the bodies and associations dealt with in this Chapter is identical with the position with regard to such measures against employers, but what was said upon those matters in Chapter 4 is reproduced here for the convenience of those who are primarily interested in this Chapter.

At this point, it becomes necessary to explain the procedure for a non-discrimination notice, especially since the issue of such notices (which, in practice, establish without a judicial inquiry that a breach of the Act has taken place) by any body other than a local authority or government department, is somewhat of an innovation in English law.

Power of Commission to serve Notices

By subsection (2) of section 67, the Commission can **only** serve a non-discrimination notice in the course of a formal investigation. The procedure for a formal investigation is set out at greater length in Chapter 14, but it would seem that it is not primarily intended to be a mere routine process to be invoked whenever a complaint of unlawful discrimination is received which appears to merit investigation, but a far more substantial inquiry for the purpose of investigating, for example, specific areas of discrimination, certain parts of the country, or even individual large firms or trade organisations.

As has been said before, this appears from the fact that a formal investigation may be initiated by the Secretary of State (section 57), that if it is initiated by the Commission they must first lay down terms of reference and either give general notice of it or notice to the persons named in the terms of reference (section 58), that a Commissioner may be nominated to conduct the formal investigation and the Commission's functions delegated to him (section 57 (3)) and that the Commission may appoint **one or more** additional Commissioners for the purposes of a formal investigation.

As already observed, it is true that subsection (2) (*b*) of section 59 contemplates a formal investigation for the purpose of establishing whether a person specified in the terms of reference has been or is discriminating unlawfully, but, in view of the formalities attendant upon a formal investigation, it would seem unlikely that such investigations are to be an everyday occurrence.

It follows from this that non-discrimination notices are normally by-products of a substantial inquiry of a general nature, and not a common-or-garden method of enforcing the provisions of the Act. Moreover, the requirements for a non-discrimination notice in subsection (5) of section 67 include prior notice to the person who is to be the object of it, specifying the grounds on which the Commission contemplate serving it, an opportunity for such person to make written or oral representations, and the consideration of such representations.

A non-discrimination notice requires the person served with it not to commit (or omit) certain acts which contravene sections 11, 12 and 13, or one or other of them, to inform the Comission of changes in his arrangements to give effect to that requirement, and to inform other persons concerned of such changes. All these provisions are contained in subsection (2) of section 67, which is worded thus:

> (2) If in the course of a formal investigation the Commission becomes satisfied that a person is committing, or has committed, any such acts, the Commission may in the prescribed manner serve on him a notice in the prescribed form (" a non-discrimination notice ") requiring him—
>
> (*a*) not to commit any such acts, and
>
> (*b*) where compliance with paragraph (*a*) involves changes in any of his practices or other arrangements,
>
> (i) to inform the Commission that he has effected those changes and what the changes are, and
>
> (ii) to take such steps as may reasonably be required by the notice for the purpose of affording that information to other persons concerned.

Subsections (3) and (4) continue:

> (3) A non-discrimination notice may also require the person on whom it is served to furnish the Commission with such other information as may be reasonably required by the notice in order to verify that the notice has been complied with.
>
> (4) The notice may specify the time at which, and the manner and form in which, any information is to be furnished to the Commission, but the time at which any information is to be furnished in compliance with the notice shall not be later than five years after the notice has become final.

In addition to being one of the two grounds on which the Commission can apply to the County Court for an injunction, by the combined effect of subsection (7) of section 67 and subsection (4) of section 59, failure to comply with a requirement in a non-discrimination notice regarding making known changes in practices or other arrangements, once the notice has become final, entitles the Commission to apply to the County Court for an order to enforce compliance. Even if the Commission has " reasonable cause to believe " that the person served with the notice intends not to comply with part of it, they may apply for such an order. Failure " without reasonable excuse " to comply with the county court order renders the person served with the non-discrimination notice liable to a fine in a sum not exceeding £10. What is far more important is that it gives the Commission the right to apply to Court for an injunction, as explained in the next few pages.

Appeals against non-discrimination notices

In view of the contents of the last paragraph, it may be some comfort to know that a body or partnership can appeal to an industrial tribunal against **any** requirement of a non-discrimination notice which they have received, under subsection (1) of section 68, providing they do so within six weeks of being served with the notice.

If, on hearing such an appeal, the tribunal considers the requirement appealed against unreasonable, whether because it is based on an incorrect finding of fact, or for any other reason, it must quash the requirement. In most legal processes to " quash " means to annul or extinguish, but the word is given a new dimension by the Act, which permits the tribunal, under subsection (3) of section 68, to insert some **other** requirement in the notice in place of the requirement quashed. In effect, therefore, the tribunal can **amend** the requirement in any way it pleases.

Indeed, the industrial tribunal is completely unfettered. The words in subsection (2) of section 68 " because it is based on an incorrect finding of fact or for **any** other reason " mean that the tribunal can approach the matter afresh and reject the requirement for any reason, even a reason unconnected with the issue of the non-discrimination notice and the circumstances preceding the issue, whilst there is equally no restriction upon the nature of the requirement which the tribunal may impose in place of one quashed, and it is perfectly possible for it to have nothing whatever to do with the original requirement and still be within the authority given to the tribunal by subsection (3) of section 68.

Clearly, in view of the very serious potential situation which a non-discrimination notice produces, any organisation or partnership should appeal against the requirements of such a notice if at all possible. By subsection (4) of section 68, a requirement inserted in a non-discrimination notice by an industrial tribunal in place of one quashed cannot, in turn, be the subject of an appeal to the tribunal.

INJUNCTIONS

The exception to the bar on court actions (there has to be an exception, of course) is that, by subsection (2), section 62 does not prevent the Courts from making the somewhat exotically-named orders for " certiorari, mandamus and prohibition ". These orders are made by the High Court when hearing appeals from inferior courts and tribunals and are discussed later.

The Equal Opportunities Commission, which is established by the Act, is specifically empowered, under section 71, to apply to the County Court for an injunction in certain circumstances (or, in those circumstances, to take the equivalent action in Scotland).

Any individual who is suffering unlawful discrimination and hopes the Commission will seek an injunction, however, should be warned that injunctions are not granted lightly, since they are considered to interfere with the freedom of the citizen (using the word here to encompass firms, limited companies and other bodies). The injustice suffered by the individual will have to be substantial, not trivial, it must be incapable of being adequately compensated by such a sum of money as an industrial tribunal would award, and the ' balance of convenience ' (*i.e.* inconvenience) must lie with making the injunction, as opposed to leaving things as they are.

The fact that section 85 provides that the Act applies to the Crown (that is to say, to all Government departments and bodies) has already been noticed. The enforcement provisions are, however, subject to the Crown Proceedings Act 1947, and therefore, since the latter Act specifically does not extend the remedy of an injunction to the Crown, no injunction can be obtained against the Crown under the Sex Discrimination Act.

As indicated above, the Equal Opportunities Commission is empowered, by section 71, to apply to the County Court in two cases, namely, where they have served the body or partnership with a non-discrimination notice, or where a court or tribunal has made a finding that the body or partnership has committed an act of unlawful discrimination, or has contravened the Equal Pay Act.

It is particularly important to notice the last few words since the " persistent discrimination " (as it is termed by the Act) to which section 71 relates, need not take place in only one field covered by the Act, and a finding that, say, a trade association had contravened the Equal Pay Act in respect of an **employee,** coupled with a non-discrimination notice relating to a practice *vis-a-vis* its **members,** would be quite sufficient to found an application for an injunction. In each case, the Commission may apply for an injunction (the wording is permissive and places no obligation on the Commission to do so) if they believe that, unless restrained, the body or partnership is likely to commit another unlawful discriminatory act, or a breach of the Equal Pay Act.

The application by the Commission must be made within five years of the finding against the body or the partnership by the Court or tribunal, or if it is based upon service of a non-discrimination notice, of the notice becoming " final ". Subsection (4) of section 82 defines " final ", in this context, as being when the time for appeal against the finding of the Court, or against the non-discrimination notice, has expired without an appeal being lodged or, if an appeal is lodged, when that appeal is dismissed, withdrawn or abandoned.

Preliminary applications by the Commission

The Commission is specifically authorised, by subsection (1) of section 73, to apply to an industrial tribunal for a finding that a body or partnership has unlawfully discriminated against an individual. On such an application, the Commission may obtain an order, similar to the order which can be made under subsection (1) (*a*) of section 65 (which is dealt with at the beginning of this Chapter) declaring the rights of the body or partnership and the individual respectively and also a recommendation by the tribunal under subsection (1) (*c*) of section 65, that the body or partnership take specific action within a limited period to obviate or reduce the adverse effect of such discrimination. The industrial tribunal cannot, however, make an order for the payment of compensation under subsection (1) (*b*) of section 65 if the application is made by the Commission.

Once an order or recommendation such as is referred to in the preceding paragraph has become final, it enables the Commission to apply to the County Court for an injunction in exactly the same way as if a finding that the body or partnership had unlawfully discriminated had been made by an industrial tribunal on the complaint of an individual. Furthermore, by subsection (3) of section 73, such an order or recommendation, when it has become final, must be treated as conclusive by the Court hearing the application for an injunction, and also by any industrial tribunal which hears a complaint of unlawful discrimination by an individual. This is the first time that the decision of one industrial tribunal has been made binding upon other industrial tribunals.

It is worth noting that subsection (2) of section 71 and subsection (5) of section 72 prohibit the Commission from **alleging,** when applying to the County Court for an injunction, that the body or partnership against whom the injunction is sought has (to quote the subsection) " done an act which is within the jurisdiction of an industrial tribunal ", unless a finding by an industrial tribunal that they have done that act, has become final. This may inhibit the Commission in attempting to prove that the body or partnership is **likely** to contravene one or other of these Acts unless restrained, as is required by section 71; in other words, it may be necessary to have two or more adverse findings by industrial tribunals against a body or partnership which have become final, before an injunction can be obtained. This would seem to stretch the old adage of " one dog, one bite " considerably!

The somewhat inelegant phrase " done an act which is within the jurisdiction of an industrial tribunal " is explained by subsection (4) of section 73. If the references to other parts of the Act, and to section 2 of the Equal Pay Act, are followed through, the act is seen to be:

either—

(*a*) an act of discrimination which is unlawful by virtue of Part II of the Sex Discrimination Act (*i.e.* the unlawful acts described in Chapters 1, 2, 5 and 6) or

(*b*) an act of discrimination which is unlawful by virtue of sections 38, 39 or 40 (*i.e.* a discriminatory advertisement, an instruction to another person to discriminate, or an inducement to or pressure upon another person to discriminate) or

(*c*) an act contravening a term which is deemed to be included in an employee's contract, or a term in such a contract which is deemed to be modified, by an " equality clause " under the Equal Pay Act.

CERTIORARI, MANDAMUS AND PROHIBITION

A short explanation of these exotically-named High Court Orders is necessary since they are, in fact, forms of appeal from inferior courts, tribunals and public bodies.

The ramifications and limitations of these procedures are far too extensive and complex to be dealt with in a book such as this, and the present exposition is inadequate to the point of being misleading in many respects, but it will, it is hoped, be sufficient to indicate where such appeal procedures may be relevant to the matters covered by the Act, and where they are inappropriate.

Certiorari is a High Court Order which quashes (and here the word **really** means annuls) the proceedings of an inferior court or body having the legal right to determine questions affecting the right of subjects. It is therefore suitable as a method of appeal from some of the bodies to whom sections 12 and 13 apply, if it is desired to completely extinguish any decisions made by them. The order will not, however, be made by the High Court if it is to quash proceedings in an area of jurisdiction which the High Court does not itself possess, and therefore certiorari would not be a suitable method of appeal from decisions of the county courts and industrial tribunals made under the powers conferred solely upon them by this Act.

Mandamus is an order made by the High Court directing an inferior court, tribunal or public body to do something which is in the nature of a public duty and appertains to their office. In general, it is used to enforce statutory rights and duties, to require public officials and public bodies to carry out their duties, and to command inferior tribunals to exercise their jurisdiction. It cannot be used if the official or body has a discretion in the matter, as opposed to a strict obligation or duty. Hence, it could be used both against some of the bodies to whom sections 13 and 14 apply and against county courts and industrial tribunals in the event of the latter refusing to exercise a non-discretionary power conferred upon them by this Act.

An order of prohibition by the High Court is the opposite of an order of mandamus and, as the name suggests, forbids an inferior court or tribunal to continue proceedings if it is attempting to exceed its jurisdiction. In view of the complexity of this Act, that is a situation which could well arise.

CHAPTER 8

DISCRIMINATION IN EDUCATION

For reasons known, perhaps, only to the Government draftsman who drafted the Act, there are four separate, but overlapping, anti-discrimination provisions in Part III of the Act dealing with the field of education.

The first of these, in section 22, describes certain specific instances of discrimination (albeit covering a very wide range of matters) which it characterises as unlawful discrimination; the second, in section 23, is a sweeping-up provision but relates only to local education authorities; whilst the third, in section 25, creates a general duty to provide facilities and benefits without sex discrimination. The fourth is contained in section 29, and renders unlawful certain specific instances of discrimination in the provision of goods, facilities and services, subsection (2) of section 29 making it clear beyond peradventure that " facilities " includes facilities for education.

To add to the confusion, each provision relates to a different, but overlapping, range of educational bodies, only local education authorities being common to all four. The latter, therefore, have the unenviable task of having to consider four different definitions in order to discover whether they err!

UNLAWFUL DISCRIMINATION UNDER SECTION 22

By section 22 it is unlawful for the " responsible body " of an " educational establishment " (both of which terms are defined in a table to the subsection which is reproduced below) to discriminate against a female in certain respects. These are as follows:

(*a*) in the terms on which it offers to admit her to the establishment as a pupil, or

(*b*) by refusing or deliberately omitting to accept an application for her admission to the establishment as a pupil, or (*c*) where she is a pupil of the establishment—

(i) in the way it affords her access to any benefits, facilities or services, or by refusing or deliberately omitting to afford her access to them, or

(ii) by excluding her from the establishment or subjecting her to any other detriment.

By the combined operation, no less, of subsection (1) of section 82 and subsection (1) (*a*) of section 5, " to discriminate " imports to discriminate on the ground of sex under sections 1 and 2, to discriminate on the ground of " marital status " under section 3, and by way of victimisation under section 4.

So far as " marital status " is concerned, it is true that subsection (1) of section 3 uses the words " in any circumstances relevant for the purposes of Part II ", which would lead one to suppose that it applied only to the fields of employment, trade associations and trade unions, qualifying bodies and partnerships. This is not so, however, as the subsections of section 82 and section 5 quoted above, taken together, extend the concepts of discrimination on the ground of " marital status " to the whole Act, wherever the word " discrimination " is used by itself.

A complete, but necessarily tedious, definition of the discrimination made unlawful by section 22, therefore, is that it is:

(A) By a body to which the section applies (as defined below)

(B) discriminating—

(i) by treating an individual on the ground of that individual's sex, less favourably than it would treat a member of the opposite sex, or—

(ii) by applying to an individual a requirement or condition which it applies or would apply equally to a member of the opposite sex, but which

(*a*) is such that the proportion of members of the individual's sex who can comply with it is considerably smaller than the proportion of members of the opposite sex who can comply with it, **and**

(*b*) it cannot show to be justifiable irrespective of the sex of the person to whom it is applied, or—

(iii) by treating an individual, on the ground of that individual's marital status, less favourably than it treats or would treat an **unmarried** person **of the same sex,** or—

(iv) by applying to an individual an unfavourable requirement or condition which, although in those circumstances, or circumstances as nearly as may be resembling those circumstances, they apply or would apply it equally to an unmarried person

(*a*) is such that the proportion of married persons who can comply with it is considerably smaller than the proportion of unmarried persons who can comply with it, **and**

(*b*) which they cannot show to be justifiable irrespective of the marital status of the person to whom it is applied

provided that the comparison between persons of different sex or marital status (as the case may be) is such that the **relevant circumstances** in the one case are the same, or not materially different, in the other) or—

(vi) by treating an individual less favourably than in those circumstances it treats or would treat other persons by reason—

(*a*) that the individual has brought proceedings, given evidence or information in connection with proceedings against it, or done anything else against it, in respect of the Act or the Equal Pay Act, or alleged that it is in contravention of either Act, or (*b*) that it knows or suspects the individual intends so to do

(unless, in the case of such an allegation, it was false **and** not made in good faith)

(C) in respect of the terms on which it offers to admit that individual as a pupil, or by omitting or deliberately refusing to accept that individual's application for admission as a pupil to " the establishment " (as defined below) or—

(D) if the individual is already a pupil of " the establishment " in the way it affords that individual access to any benefits, facilities or services, or by refusing or deliberately omitting to afford such access or—

(E) by excluding the individual from " the establishment " or subjecting that individual to any other detriment.

It is appreciated that this definition is indigestible to the point of biliousness, but it will serve as a useful check list both for specific situations and for any reconsideration of procedures.

Discrimination on the ground of marital status or victimisation may seem a little misplaced at first sight, but both forms of discrimination may have particular relevance to universities.

Section 22 contains a table which is in reasonably clear and comprehensive terms, and is worth reproducing here—

TABLE

Establishment	**Responsible body**
England and Wales	
1. Educational establishment maintained by a local education authority.	Local education authority or managers or governors, according to which of them has the function in question.
2. Independent school not being a special school.	Proprietor.
3. Special school not maintained by a local education authority.	Proprietor.
4. University.	Governing body.

5. Establishment (not falling within paragraphs 1 to 4) providing full-time or part-time education, being an establishment designated under section 24 (1).	Governing body.
Scotland	
6. Educational establishment managed by an education authority.	Education authority.
7. Educational establishment in respect of which the managers are for the time being receiving grants under section 75 (*c*) or (*d*) of the Education (Scotland) Act 1962.	Managers of the educational establishment.
8. University.	Governing body.
9. Independent school.	Proprietor.
10. Any other educational establishment (not falling within paragraphs 6, 7 and 9) providing full or part-time school education or further education.	Managers of the educational establishment.

When reading this table, it must be remembered that by subsection (1) of section 82 " school " has the meaning given to it in the Education Act 1944, namely:

> an institution for providing primary or secondary education or both primary and secondary education, being a school maintained by a local education authority, an independent school or a school in respect of which grants are made by the Minister to the proprietor of the school; and the expression " school " where used without qualification includes any such school or all such schools as the context may require,

and " proprietor " has the meaning attributed to it by the same Act, namely: " the person or body of persons responsible for the management of the school ".

UNLAWFUL DISCRIMINATION UNDER SECTION 23

The next provision, in section 23, makes it unlawful for a local education authority, in the carrying out of such of its functions under the Education Acts 1944 to 1975 as do not fall under section 22, to do any act which constitutes **sex discrimination.**

This extends section 22 in two ways: First, it renders the local education authority liable in respect of **functions** not within the Table to section 22. Secondly, it makes the local education authority liable for **any** sex discrimination by it in the exercise of those functions, even if it does not fall within paragraphs (*a*) to (*c*) of section 22.

THE GENERAL DUTY (UNDER SECTION 25)

We now come to the fact that certain bodies concerned with education (broadly those responsible for local education authority establishments and for special schools not maintained by the local education authority), have a " general duty ", under section 25, to secure that the facilities for education which they provide, and any ancillary benefits or services, are provided **without sex discrimination.**

It is difficult to see in what manner (if at all) the general duty goes beyond the **range** of discrimination covered by section 22, although certainly it applies to other **bodies,** since subsection (6) of section 25 reads:

> (6) Subsection (1) applies to—
>
> (*a*) local education authorities in England and Wales;
>
> (*b*) education authorities in Scotland;
>
> (*c*) any other body which is a responsible body in relation to—
>
> (i) an establishment falling within paragraph 1, 3 or 7 of the Table in section 22;
>
> (ii) an establishment designated under section 24 (1) as falling within paragraph (*a*) or (*c*) of section 24 (2);
>
> (iii) an establishment designated under section 24 (1) as falling within paragraph (*b*) of section 24 (2) where the grants in question are payable under section 100 of the Education Act 1944;

thus, in effect, extending the liability for the discrimination outlawed by section 23 to the managers and governors of local education authority schools, to the proprietors of special schools not maintained by the local education authority, and to the governing body of any establishment designated by the

Secretary of State under section 24. The proprietors of independent schools and the governing bodies of universities are conspicuously absent from the list.

Although the " general duty " is to provide educational facilities and ancillary benefits and services without sex discrimination, a breach of the duty is not made unlawful, and subsection (4) of section 25 specifically states that there shall be no sanction for a breach of the general duty, other than as provided by that section. These are dealt with under the heading of " Sanctions " in Chapter 9.

DISCRIMINATION UNDER SECTION 29

Section 29, which appears in the Act immediately beneath a sub-heading " Goods, facilities, services and premises ", renders it unlawful for any body " concerned with the provision (for payment or not) of goods, facilities or services to the public or a section of the public " to discriminate in certain specific ways against one who seeks to obtain or use those goods, facilities or services. One might be forgiven for not immediately connecting this prohibition with education, but subsection (2) of section 29, which gives some examples of the kind of facilities and services covered by the section, refers, at (*d*), to " facilities for education ", and at (*g*) to " the services of . . . any local or other public authority ".

With such an abundance of other anti-discrimination provi-ions relating to education, one might question whether section 29 is of any real importance to bodies dealing with the main stream of education. The answer to that question is that section 29 differs from section 22 in some of the special forms of discrimination which are prohibited; it differs from section 23 in applying to every body in the field of education and to discrimination on the grounds of marital status and victimisation as well as sex; and it differs from section 25 first, in that it applies to bodies and establishments not covered by the latter section, in particular to independent schools and universities, and, secondly, in that the person who has suffered the discrimination may enforce it in the County Courts.

A " demarcation provision " is to be found in subsection (3) of section 35, which provides that section 29 does not apply to any discrimination which is rendered unlawful by sections 22 or 23 or which is excluded from those sections by sections 26 and 27 (which deal with single-sex establishments) and section 28 (which deals with physical training courses). Hence, in relation to those two sections, section 29 is only effective to the extent that it exceeds their provisions.

The forms of discrimination prohibited by section 29 in the provision of goods, facilities or services, again using the male as the standard or " norm " are:

(*a*) by refusing or deliberately omitting to provide her with any of them, or

(*b*) by refusing or deliberately omitting to provide her with goods, facilities or services of the like quality, in the like manner and on the like terms as are normal in his case in relation to male members of the public or (where she belongs to a section of the public) to male members of that section.

Of course, the " looking-glass " provisions apply to these words, and " discrimination " in **this** section means any discrimination described in sections 1, 3 and 4, and not merely discrimination on the ground of sex.

If, therefore, the reader will refer back to the lengthy definitions of discrimination on page 98 and replace (C), (D) and (E) with (*a*) and (*b*) above, the full area of the prohibition contained in section 29 will be seen. Particular attention should be paid to the difference in wording between (*b*) above and (D) in the earlier definition, when it will be seen that the latter makes no reference to quality. There may also be a distinction, in some instances, between—

" in the way it affords . . . access to any services "

and—

" refusing . . . . to provide . . . services . . . in the like manner ".

Vicarious Liability

This seems a suitable point at which to mention that, by section 41, educational bodies and authorities are not only liable for unlawful discrimination by their employees ' in the course of their employment ' (which seems reasonable) whether or not it was with their knowledge or approval (which does not), but also for unlawful discrimination by any agent, whether the agent's authority is express or to be implied from the circumstances, and even if the discrimination was ratified by the body after it had occurred.

The body or authority has a defence, by subsection (3) of section 41, if they took " such steps as were reasonably practical to prevent the employee from doing that act, or from doing in the course of his employment acts of that description " but they have no such defence in respect of any unlawful discrimination by their agents. So far as agents are concerned, therefore, it matters only that the act or omission was within their authority.

The other side of the coin is that, in the circumstances described above, both the employee and the agent may also be liable for " knowingly aiding another person " to unlawfully discriminate under section 42, and the employee is liable even if his employers are excused because they took the steps described in subsection (3) of section 41.

Both the employee and the agent are exempted from liability by subsection (3) of section 42 if they acted in reliance on a statement made to them by the body or authority that, because of a provision of the Act, the discrimination would not be unlawful, and it was reasonable for them to rely upon it. This introduces a further liability on the body or authority that makes the statement, for if they do so knowingly or recklessly, they may, by subsection (4) of section 42, be fined up to £400. This is one of the several instances of criminal liability under the Act.

Similar responsibilities for the educational bodies are provided by sections 39 and 40. Section 39 reads as follows:

It is unlawful for a person—

(*a*) who has authority over another person, or

(*b*) in accordance with whose wishes that other person is accustomed to act, to instruct him to do any act which is unlawful by virtue of Part II or III, or procure or attempt to procure the doing by him of any such act.

Whilst Part II of the Act relates principally to employment and training for employment, Part III covers not only education but also the sale of goods and the supply of facilities and services. In fact, an educational body will be liable if it instructs an employee or any other person over whom it has influence to discriminate in any manner prohibited by the Act, except by publishing a discriminatory advertisement.

It will be noticed that it is not only straightforward instructions which are contrary to the section, as it refers also to " procure or attempt to procure the doing . . . of any such act ". These words can cover a very wide variety of actions and subtle pressures, and to put the matter quite beyond doubt, section 40 provides—

(1) It is unlawful to induce, or attempt to induce, a person to do any act which contravenes Part II or III by—

(*a*) providing or offering to provide him with any benefit, or

(*b*) subjecting or threatening to subject him to any detriment.

(2) An offer or threat is not prevented from falling within subsection (1) because it is not made directly to the person in question, if it is made in such a way that he is likely to hear of it.

Neither nods nor winks to blind horses will avoid these two sections, and the only safe course is to eschew any attempt to discriminate in a manner which is contrary to the Act.

Although sections 39 and 40 do not apply to advertisements, an educational body that advertises in a discriminatory manner, whether for staff or for pupils, and informs the publisher of the advertisement that the advertisement is not unlawful because it is entitled to discriminate, either because the discrimination is not of a kind which comes within the general prohibitions of the Act, or because it falls within an exemption to it, may be fined up to £400 if that statement is untrue. This liability is dealt with at greater length in Chapter 13.

Moreover, as was seen in Chapter 5, employers who falsely or misleadingly state to an employment agency that it is lawful for them to offer a job to a particular sex only (for example, because they employ only five employees) and does so knowingly or recklessly, commits a criminal offence, for which he can be fined up to £400.

Before going on to set out the exceptions to unlawful discrimination in the field of education, it is worth referring again to the provisions of section 85, which applies the Act to the Crown. Subsection (1) of section 85 reads:

> (1) This Act applies—
>
> (*a*) to an act done by or for purposes of a Minister of the Crown or government department, or
>
> (*b*) to an act done on behalf of the Crown by a statutory body or a person holding a statutory office,
>
> as it applies to an act done by a private person.

Section 85 may bring within the purview of section 29 (insofar as it applies to the provision of facilities for education) educational facilities provided by the Civil Service, and by other emanations of the Crown. It is well to note, however, that the armed forces are specifically excluded from the operation of subsection (1) of section 85 by subsection (4).

EXCEPTIONS

The most far-reaching exceptions to the sections of the Act relating to employment concern what the Act chooses to call " single-sex establishments ". The phrase proves to include a goodly number of schools which are not limited solely to pupils of one sex.

First, by subsection (1) of section 26, there are exempted from paragraphs (*a*) and (*b*) of section 22 (those dealing with discrimination in relation to admitting pupils) establishments which admit pupils of one sex only, or would be taken to do so " if there were disregarded pupils of the opposite sex whose admission is exceptional, or, alternatively, whose numbers are ' comparatively small ' and whose admission is confined to particular courses of instruction or teaching classes ".

Moreover, in the case of such establishments as would be "taken to admit pupils of one sex only", under subsection (1) of section 26 the fact that pupils of one sex are confined to particular courses of instruction or teaching classes is, by subsection (3), not to be taken to contravene either paragraph (*c*) (i) of section 22 (which deals, it will be recalled, with affording pupils access to benefits, facilities or services), or the general duty imposed by section 25.

Secondly, by subsection (2) of section 26, the caveat in respect of the admission of pupils in paragraphs (*a*) and (*b*) of section 22, and the general duty under section 25, do not apply to the admission of boarders—

> Where a school which is **not** a single-sex establishment has some pupils as boarders and others as non-boarders, and admits as boarders pupils of one sex only (or would be taken to admit as boarders pupils of one sex only if there were disregarded boarders of the opposite sex whose numbers are comparatively small)

nor, in such cases, do the provisions of subsection (*c*) (i) of section 22 (which deals with affording pupils access to benefits, facilities or services) apply to boarding facilities.

Whilst subsection (2) of section 26 provides this exemption for co-educational schools which take boarders of only one sex, section 46 contains a more limited exemption for co-educational schools which board both sexes. The first part of the section is as follows:

> (1) In this section "communal accommodation" means residential accommodation which includes dormitories or other shared sleeping accommodation which for reasons of privacy or decency should be used by men only, or by women only (but which may include some shared sleeping accommodation for men, and some for women, or some ordinary sleeping accommodation).
>
> (2) In this section "communal accommodation" also includes residential accommodation all or part of which should be used by men only, or by women only, because of the nature of the sanitary facilities serving the accommodation.

This may well excuse some co-educational schools which restrict their intake of boarders of one sex because of shortage of dormitory accommodation.

Subsection (5) ensures that co-educational schools which have some dormitory accommodation of a standard lower or less convenient than the remainder of their dormitories are not necessarily acting unlawfully if they are forced to allocate the lower standard or less convenient accommodation to one sex.

The subsection reads:

> (5) Nothing in Part II or III shall render unlawful sex discrimination against a woman as respects the provision of any benefit, facility or service if—
>
> (*a*) the benefit, facility or service cannot properly and effectively be provided except for those using communal accommodation, and
>
> (*b*) in the relevant circumstances, the woman could lawfully be refused the use of the accommodation by virtue of subsection (3).

Whilst subsection (3) and the first part of subsection (4) say:

> (3) Nothing in Part II or III shall render unlawful sex discrimination in the admission of persons to communal accommodation if the accommodation is managed in a way which, given the exigencies of the situation, comes as near as may be to fair and equitable treatment of men and women.
>
> (4) In applying subsection (3) account shall be taken of—
>
> (*a*) whether and how far it is reasonable to expect that the accommodation should be altered or extended, or that further alternative accommodation should be provided;

The application of the section also to the general duty is put beyond doubt by subsection (7) in the following terms:

> (7) Section 25 shall not apply to sex discrimination within subsection (3) or (5).

The remaining two exceptions for single-sex establishments are contained in section 27, and are both transitional provisions for establishments which decide to turn co-educational. They follow the pattern set by section 26 of dealing first with schools in general, and then with boarding schools. In each case, the responsible body, as defined in column (1) of the Table to section 22, may apply for an exemption order, authorising discriminatory admissions during the transitional period specified in the order. To the limited extent of admission or non-admission in accordance with the terms of such an order, and of refusals to admit whilst the application for such an order (apparently, whether granted or not) is pending, the body will not be in contravention of the Act.

Physical training courses

A minor exception to the provisions of sections 22, 23 and 25 is contained in section 28, and relates to further education courses being—

" (*a*) a course of physical training, or

(*b*) a course designed for teachers of physical training ".

Exceptions to section 29

For those who may be inclined to remedy unlawful discrimination in education by the use of section 29, instead of (or in addition to) sections 22, 23 or 25, it is worth noting that, by subsection (1) of section 35, section 29 does not apply to an " establishment for persons requiring special care, supervision or attention "; or to a place " occupied or used for the purposes of an organised religion " if the sex discrimination there practised is " to comply with the doctrines of that religion or avoid offending the religious susceptibilities of any of its followers " (both being exceptions which one might have expected to find in relation to the three earlier sections).

However, there is a further exemption from section 29 for non-profit making bodies under section 34. The full details of this section are to be found in Chapter 10, but, put briefly, it applies to non-profit making bodies which were not established by statute and which either have as their **main object** the provision of benefits for one sex only, or restrict their **membership** to one sex.

By subsections (3) and (4) of section 34, such non-profit making organisations as have the provision of benefits for one sex only as their main object may provide benefits in accordance with that object without contravening section 29.

Similarly, by subsection (2) of section 34, such non-profit making organisations as limit their membership to one sex only can provide benefits, facilities or services of any kind **to their members,** despite section 29.

This reference to section 34 would not be complete without mention of the fact that sections 78 and 79 (which are dealt with in detail below) permit the Secretary of State, upon application by the trustees or " responsible body ", to amend the terms of certain educational trusts which are limited to one sex, so as to extend them to both sexes.

Exceptions for foreign travel

There is also an exception for educational facilities in respect of foreign travel, which is now such a prominent feature of most school curricula. This is to be found in subsection (5) of section 36, and is limited to accommodation in foreign establishments and travel on transport other than ships registered in British ports. The full subsection is in these terms:

> (5) Sections 22, 23 and 25 do not apply to benefits, facilities or services outside Great Britain except—
>
> (*a*) Travel on a ship registered at a port of registry in Great Britain and
>
> (*b*) benefits, facilities or services provided on a ship so registered.

There is a transitional exemption to be found in paragraph 2 of Schedule 4, in the following terms:

> 2.—(1) If the responsible body for any educational establishment which (apart from this subparagraph) would be required to comply with the provisions of section 22 (*b*), and of section 25 so far as they apply to acts to which section 22 (*b*) relates, from the commencement of those provisions, is of the opinion that it would be impracticable for it to do so, it may before that commencement apply for an order authorising discriminatory admissions during the transitional period specified in the order.
>
> (2) Section 27 (2) to (5) and Schedule 2 shall apply for the purposes of sub-paragraph (1) as they apply in relation to transitional exemption orders.

Charities

The exemption for charities is contained in section 43 and covers acts done in order to give effect to a provision contained in a charitable instrument for conferring benefits on persons of one sex only. This exemption, being an exemption from all the provisions of the Act, was discussed at length in Chapter 1.

VARIATION OF SINGLE-SEX EDUCATIONAL TRUSTS

There is a special provision for educational trusts in section 78, which will be of interest to all educationalists. This allows the Secretary of State to amend the terms of certain trusts which are restricted to benefits to one sex, or which do not benefit the sexes equally, upon the application of the trustees or the " responsible body ", so as to extend the benefits equally to both sexes. Subsection (2) of section 78 is in the following terms:

> (2) If on the application of the trustees, or of the responsible body (as defined in section 22), the Secretary of State is satisfied that the removal or modification of the restriction would conduce to the advancement of education without sex discrimination, he may by order make such modifications of the instrument as appear to him expedient for removing or modifying the restrictions, and for any supplemental or incidental purposes.

By subsection (1), this applies to any trust deed or other instrument:

> (*a*) which concerns property applicable for or in connection with the provision of education in any establishment in paragraphs 1 to 5 of the Table in section 22, and
>
> (*b*) which in any way restricts the benefits available under the instrument to persons of one sex.

The powers of the Secretary of State are subject to a twenty-five years rule by subsection (3), which reads as follows:

> (3) If the trust was created by gift or bequest, no order shall be made until twenty-five years after the date on which the gift or bequest took effect, unless the donor or his personal representatives, or the personal representatives of the testator, have consented in writing to the making of the application for the order.

The section goes on to provide for the applicant for such an order to publish a notice giving particulars of the proposed order and requiring any representations to be made to the Secretary of State within the period (not less than one month) fixed by him; and for the Secretary of State to take into account such representations before making the order.

There is a separate provision for Scotland in section 79.

CHAPTER 9

SANCTIONS FOR DISCRIMINATION IN EDUCATION

ORDERS GIVING DIRECTIONS BY THE MINISTER

So far as sanctions in the field of education are concerned, it may well make for greater clarity to proceed from the particular to the general. In pursuit of this objective, the first sanctions to be discussed are those which are peculiar to section 25.

As we have seen, subsection (4) of section 25 precludes all sanctions other than those for which the section specifically provides. These are that, first, if the Minister for Education is satisfied that a body to which section 25 applies has acted, or is proposing to act, unreasonably in respect of the general duty, he can give directions as to the exercise by it of any power, or the performance by it of any duty, in a similar manner to the directions which he can give under section 68 of the Education Act 1944.

Secondly, if the Minister is satisfied that a body to which section 25 applies has failed to discharge the general duty imposed upon it, he can make an order declaring the body to be in default in respect of the general duty, and giving such directions for the purpose of enforcing the execution of that duty as appear to him to be expedient. This power is identical to that given to the Secretary of State by section 99 of the Education Act 1944, and, like it, on the application of the Secretary of State to the High Court, it can be enforced by an order of mandamus. Orders of mandamus, are explained (at least superficially) at the end of this Chapter.

The powers of the Secretary of State under sections 68 and 99 of the Education Act 1944 can also be exercised in respect of any failure to perform the duties imposed by sections 22 and 23, but only, oddly enough, against the **bodies** mentioned in subsection (6) of section 25, *i.e.* **not** against the proprietors of independent schools or the governing bodies of universities.

COUNTY COURT PROCEEDINGS

Any sufferer from such discrimination as is made unlawful by sections 22, 23 and 29 may sue the person or body which is guilty of that discrimination in the County Court (or the sheriff court in Scotland) " in like manner as any other claim in tort " (or in Scotland ' in reparation for breach of statutory duty '), by virtue of section 66. Whilst the section appears to align unlawful discrimination with torts such as negligence or defamation for the purpose of County Court procedure and jurisdiction, it is doubtful whether it actually **constitutes** such discrimination a tort for all purposes known to the law.

It is clear from the terms of subsections (3) and (4) that damages are a remedy which can be obtained in any such proceedings in the County Court. What is far from clear is whether the County Court can grant an injunction, whether permanent or temporary, in proceedings under section 66. This point is dealt with in detail under the heading " Injunctions ".

As has been pointed out previously, by subsection (4) of section 66, damages for unlawful discrimination can include compensation for injury to feelings.

The point has already been made in other connections and must be re-emphasised here, that, by subsection (3) of section 60, no damages can be awarded for **covert** discrimination on the ground of sex or marital status if the body accused of such discrimination proves that the requirement or condition was not applied with the **intention** of treating the claimant unfavourably on that ground.

There is one point of difficulty in this respect, and that is that the county courts have no jurisdiction to entertain an action in tort in which the claim exceeds £1,000. In an ordinary action, if the plaintiff simply claims damages, without quantifying the amount, it is customary for the formal Statement of Claim to specify that the plaintiff abandons any amount by which his damages may be found to exceed £1,000, in order to ensure that the county court judge has jurisdiction to hear the action.

A claim in respect of an act of discrimination which is unlawful under Part III of the Act can be made the subject of civil proceedings " in like manner as any other claim in tort " by subsection (1) of section 65. Despite the provisions of section 66 the Act contains no specific provision to enable county courts to entertain claims for more than £1,000. It may be that the words at the end of subsection (2) " but all such remedies shall be obtainable in such proceedings as, apart from this subsection, would be obtainable in the High Court " can be construed as not only extending the county court jurisdiction in respect of the **kind** of remedies, but also in respect of the financial limits on them. However, until the point has been decided by the courts, it cannot be regarded as free from doubt.

By the curiously phrased subsection (5) of section 66, so far as the bodies listed in subsection (5) of section 25 are concerned (briefly, these are the local education authorities, managers or governors of local education authority schools, and the proprietors of special schools not maintained by the local education authority) the individual who suffers the discrimination prescribed by sections 22 and 23 must give notice of the claim to the Secretary of State, and wait until **either** the Minister has informed him or her that he does not want further time to consider the matter, **or** two months have elapsed, before commencing proceedings. It will be seen that, if the Minister requires time for consideration, only two months is allowed—there is no provision for extending this period.

Time limits for proceedings in County Court

The proceedings in the County Court must be commenced **within six months** of the act or omission to which they relate, under the limitation imposed by subsection (2) of section 76, but if the Minister does **not** give notice that he (or she!) requires no further time, the limit by which proceedings must be brought is extended to eight months from the date of the act or omission of the body concerned, for cases within section 66 (5).

The requirement of prior notice to the Minister, contained in subsection (5) of section 66, relates only to proceedings for a contravention of sections 22 and 23, despite the fact that the bodies involved are defined in the subsection by reference to section 25. Therefore, an individual who wishes to sue an educational body and bases the proceedings on a breach of section 29, is under no obligation whatever to give prior notice to the Minister, even if the body is within the list in section 25.

The County Court has power to hear the complaint or application by subsection (5) of section 76, even if these time limits have expired, but, obviously, this enabling power should not be relied upon unnecessarily.

As we have seen already such periods are sometimes not as short as they seem, because subsection (6) of section 76 provides that—

> (*a*) where the inclusion of any term in a contract renders the making of the contract an unlawful act that act shall be treated as extending throughout the duration of the contract, and
>
> (*b*) any act extending over a period shall be treated as done at the end of that period, and
>
> (*c*) a deliberate omission shall be treated as done when the person in question decided upon it,

and continues:

> and in the absence of evidence establishing the contrary a person shall be taken for the purposes of this section to decide upon an omission when he does an act inconsistent with doing the omitted act or, if he has done no such inconsistent act, when the period expires within which he might **reasonably have been expected to do** the omitted act if it was to be done.

The somewhat limited territorial jurisdiction of the County Courts is extended very widely indeed by subsection (8) of section 66 to include " an act done on a ship, aircraft or hovercraft outside its district, including such an act done outside Great Britain ".

Whatever the legislators intended, this extension of the territorial jurisdiction of the County Court is not limited to British ships, nor to United Kingdom territorial waters, and must be by far the widest territorial jurisdiction the United Kingdom has ever claimed for county courts.

A comment which may be useful to a person wishing to sue a Government department or body for discrimination (for, as has been noticed, section 85 applies the Act to the Crown) is that the Treasury publishes a list of Government Departments which can be sued in their own name, or in the name of another Department. If a Department or body is not on this list, proceedings should be commenced against the Attorney-General and served upon the Treasury Solicitor.

QUESTIONNAIRES FOR USE PRIOR TO PROCEEDINGS

It should, perhaps, be mentioned at this juncture that the Act specifically authorises the Secretary of State by order to prescribe:

(*a*) forms by which the person aggrieved may question the respondent on his reasons for doing any relevant act, or on any other matter which is or may be relevant;

(*b*) forms by which the respondent may if he so wishes reply to any questions,

by subsection (1) of section 74. The purpose of such forms is described by the same subsection as being:

> With a view to helping a person (" the person aggrieved ") who considers he may have been discriminated against in contravention of this Act to decide whether to institute proceedings and, if he does so, to formulate and present his case in the most effective manner.

What is far more important is subsection (2), which provides:

> (2) Where the person aggrieved questions the respondent (whether in accordance with an order under subsection (1) or not)—
>
> (*a*) the question and any reply by the respondent subject to the following provisions of this section shall be admissible as evidence in the proceedings;
>
> (*b*) if it appears to the court or tribunal that the respondent deliberately and without reasonable excuse omitted to reply within a reasonable period or that his reply is evasive or equivocal, the court or tribunal may draw any inference from that fact that it considers it just and equitable to draw, including an inference that he committed an unlawful act.

Paragraph (*a*) does not enlarge the law at all, as the county courts have always had ample provision for communications between the parties to be admissible in evidence, but paragraph (*b*) certainly does extend the existing law. Prior to the passing of the Act, it would have been impossible for any reasonable and rational court or industrial tribunal to draw, merely from the respondent's failure to reply to questions or his equivocal or evasive reply, the inference that he had committed an unlawful act.

Subsection (3) of section 74 adds:

> (3) The Secretary of State may by order—
>
> (*a*) prescribe the period within which questions must be duly served in order to be admissible under subsection (2) (*a*), and
>
> (*b*) prescribe the manner in which a question, and any reply by the respondent, may be duly served.

and subsection (4) continues:

> (4) Rules may enable the court entertaining a claim under section 66 to determine, before the date fixed for the hearing of the claim, whether a question or reply is admissible under this section or not.

NON-DISCRIMINATION NOTICES

The position with regard to non-discrimination notices, etc., against bodies in the education field is identical with the position with regard to such measures against employers, but what was said upon those matters in Chapter 4 is reproduced here for the convenience of those who are primarily interested in this Chapter.

At this point, it becomes necessary to explain the procedure for a non-discrimination notice, especially since the issue of such notices (which, in practice, establish, without a judicial inquiry, that a breach of the Act has taken place) by any body other than a local authority or government department, is somewhat of an innovation in English law.

Power of Commission to serve Notices

By subsection (2) of section 67 the Commission can only serve a non-discrimination notice in the course of a formal investigation. The procedure for a formal investigation is set out at greater length in Chapter 14, but it would seem that it is not primarily intended to be a mere routine process to be invoked whenever a complaint of unlawful discrimination is received which appears to merit investigation, but a far more substantial inquiry for the purpose of investigating, for example, specific areas of discrimination, certain parts of the country, or even, say, a specific university or local education authority.

As has been said before, this appears from the fact that a formal investigation may be initiated by the Secretary of State (section 57); that if it is initiated by the Commission they must first lay down terms of reference and either give general notice of it or notice to the persons named in the terms of reference (section 58); that a Commissioner may be nominated to conduct the formal investigation and the Commission's functions delegated to him (section 57 (3)); and that the Commission may appoint **one or more** additional Commissioners for the purposes of a formal investigation.

As already observed, it is true that subsection (2) (*b*) of section 59 contemplates a formal investigation for the purpose of establishing whether a person specified in the terms of reference has been or is discriminating unlawfully, but, in view of the formalities attendant upon a formal investigation, it would seem unlikely that such investigations are to be an everyday occurrence.

It follows from this that non-discrimination notices are normally by-products of a substantial inquiry of a general nature, and not a common-or-garden method of enforcing the provisions of the Act. Moreover, the requirements for a non-discrimination notice in subsection (5) of section 67 include prior notice to the person who is to be the object of it specifying the grounds on which the Commission contemplate serving it, an opportunity for such person to make written or oral representations, and the consideration of such representations.

A non-discrimination notice requires the person served with it not to commit (or omit) certain acts which contravene sections 22, 23 and 29, or one or other of them, to inform the Commission of changes in his arrangements to give effect to that requirement, and to inform other persons concerned of such changes. All these provisions are contained in subsection (2) of section 67, which is worded thus:

> (2) If in the course of a formal investigation the Commission becomes satisfied that a person is committing, or has committed, any such acts, the Commission may in the prescribed manner serve on him a notice in the prescribed form (" a non-discrimination notice ") requiring him—
>
> (*a*) not to commit any such acts, and
>
> (*b*) where compliance with paragraph (*a*) involves changes in any of his practices or other arrangements,
>
> (i) to inform the Commission that he has effected those changes and what the changes are, and
>
> (ii) to take such steps as may be reasonably required by the notice for the purpose of affording that information to other persons concerned.

Subsections (3) and (4) continue:

> (3) A non-discrimination notice may also require the person on whom it is served to furnish the Commission with such other information as may be reasonably required by the notice in order to verify that the notice has been complied with.
>
> (4) The notice may specify the time at which, and the manner and form in which, any information is to be furnished to the Commission, but the time at which any information is to be furnished in compliance with the notice shall not be later than five years after the notice has become final.

In addition to being one of the two grounds on which the Commission can apply to the County Court for an injunction, by the combined effect of subsection (7) of section 67 and subsection (4) of section 59, failure to comply with a requirement in a non-discrimination notice regarding making known changes in practices or other arrangements, once the notice has become final, entitles the Commission to apply to the County Court for an order to enforce compliance with that requirement. Even if the Commission has " reasonable cause to believe " that the party served with the notice intends not to comply with part of it, they may apply for such an order.

Failure " without reasonable excuse " to comply with the county court order renders the party served with the non-discrimination notice liable to a fine in a sum not exceeding

£10. What is far more important is that it gives the Commission the right to apply to Court for an injunction, as explained in the next few pages.

Appeals against non-discrimination notices

In view of the contents of the last paragraph, it may be some comfort to know that what section 22 terms " a responsible body " can appeal to a County Court against **any** requirement of a non-discrimination notice which it has received, under subsection (1) of section 68, providing it does so within six weeks of being served with the notice.

If, on hearing such an appeal, the court considers the requirement appealed against to be unreasonable, whether because it is based on an incorrect finding of fact, or for any other reason, it must quash the requirement. In most legal processes to " quash " means to annul or extinguish, but the word is given a new dimension by the Act, which permits the court, under subsection (3) of section 68, to insert some **other** requirement in the notice in place of the requirement quashed. In effect, therefore, the court can **amend** the requirement in any way it pleases.

Indeed, the County Court is completely unfettered. The words in subsection (2) of section 68 " because it is based on an incorrect finding of fact or for **any** other reason " mean that the Court can approach the matter afresh and reject the requirement for any reason, even a reason unconnected with the issue of the non-discrimination notice and the circumstances preceding the issue; whilst there is equally no restriction upon the nature of the requirement which the Court may impose in place of one quashed, and it is quite possible for it to have nothing whatever to do with the original requirement and still be within the authority given to the Court by subsection (3) of section 68.

Clearly, in view of the very serious potential situation which a non-discrimination notice produces, any " responsible body " should appeal against the requirements of such a notice, if at all possible. By subsection (4) of section 68, a requirement inserted in a non-discrimination notice by a

County Court in place of one quashed cannot, in turn, be the subject of an appeal to the Court, although it could, of course, be the subject of an appeal to the Court of Appeal.

INJUNCTIONS

Clearly, the Equal Opportunities Commission, which is established by the Act, is specifically empowered, under section 71, to apply to the County Court for an injunction in certain circumstances (or, in those circumstances, to take the equivalent action in Scotland).

The point has already been made that the Act leaves the question of whether the Court can grant an injunction to an individual in proceedings under section 66 in some doubt. The difficulty arises in the following manner:

A **temporary** injunction will normally be granted by the High Court or a county court whenever necessary in proceedings in tort, to prevent any irremediable damage occurring pending the trial of the action. A **permanent** injunction is a remedy which is available instead of damages, and only in cases in which damages, of whatever amount, will not adequately compensate the person who has suffered from the wrong. It is certainly possible to imagine instances of discrimination in education when an award of a cash sum by way of damages would not compensate the pupil who had suffered the discrimination.

The difficulty arises because subsection (1) of section 62 decrees that contraventions of the Act " shall incur as such **no sanction . . . except to the extent . . . expressly provided by this Act ".** Section 62 (2) states that " sanction " includes the granting of an injunction or declaration, so that an injunction will not be a remedy **unless** there is express provision. The question which then arises is whether the words of section 66 (1), that acts of discrimination " may be made the subject of civil proceedings in like manner as any other claim in tort " is a sufficient specific provision, as described above, to add injunctions to the armoury of sanctions provided by the Act.

In this connection, it is noteworthy that subsection (2) of section 66 reads as follows:

> (2) Proceedings under subsection (1)—
>
> (*a*) shall be brought in England and Wales only in a county court, and
>
> (*b*) shall be brought in Scotland only in a sheriff court,
>
> but all such remedies shall be obtainable in such proceedings as, apart from this subsection, would be obtainable in the High Court or the Court of Session, as the case may be.

It is certainly arguable that an injunction *is* a remedy which " apart from this subsection would be obtainable in the High Court " but this is another aspect of the Act which will be shrouded in doubt until dispelled by a Court decision.

Any individual who is suffering unlawful discrimination in the field of education and is minded to apply to Court for an injunction, moreover, should be warned that injunctions are not granted lightly, since they are considered to interfere with the freedom of the citizen (using the word here to encompass all " responsible bodies "). The injustice suffered by the individual will have to be substantial, not trivial, it must be incapable of being adequately compensated by such a sum of money as the Court would award, and the ' balance of convenience ' (*i.e.* inconvenience) must lie with making the injunction, as opposed to leaving things as they are.

Any individual proposing to apply to the County Court for an injunction must also remember that the Court would probably apply, by analogy, the time limit within which an application must be made to an industrial tribunal or county court by virtue of subsection (2) of section 76, namely, six months and that, under the equitable doctrine known as " laches " (the Court will not aid an injured party who sleeps on his rights) the time limit could be even shorter.

The fact that section 85 provides that the Act applies to the Crown (that is to say, to all Government departments and bodies) has already been noticed. The enforcement provisions are, however, subject to the Crown Proceedings Act 1947, and therefore, since the latter Act specifically does not extend the remedy of an injunction to the Crown, no injunction can be obtained against the Crown under the Sex Discrimination Act.

Injunction Applications by the Commission

As indicated above, the Equal Opportunities Commission is empowered, by section 71, to apply to the County Court in two cases, namely, first, where they have served the " responsible body " with a non-discrimination notice, or secondly, where a court or tribunal has made a finding that the " responsible body " has committed an act of unlawful discrimination or has contravened the Equal Pay Act.

It is particularly important to notice the last few words, of the last paragraph, since the " persistent discrimination " (as it is termed by the Act) to which section 71 relates need not take place in only one area covered by the Act, and a finding that, say, the governing body of a university had contravened the Equal Pay Act in respect of an **employee,** coupled with a non-discrimination notice relating to a practice *vis-a-vis* its undergraduates, would be quite sufficient to found an application for an injunction.

In each case, the Commission **may** apply for an injunction (the wording is permissive and places no obligation on the Commission to do so) if they believe that, unless restrained, the " responsible body " is likely to commit another unlawful discriminatory act or a breach of the Equal Pay Act.

The application by the Commission must be made within five years of the finding against the " responsible body " by the Court, or if it is based upon service of a non-discrimination notice, of the notice becoming " final ". Subsection (4) of section 82 defines " final ", in this context, as being when the time for appeal against the finding of the Court, or against the non-discrimination notice, has expired without an appeal being lodged, or, if an appeal is lodged, when that appeal is dismissed, withdrawn or abandoned.

It is worth noting that subsection (2) of section 71 prohibits the Commission from **alleging,** when applying to the County Court for an injunction, that the " responsible body " against whom the injunction is sought has, to quote the subsection, " done an act which is within the jurisdiction of an industrial tribunal ", unless a finding by an industrial tribunal that they have done that act has become final. This may inhibit the

Commission in attempting to prove that the " responsible body " is **likely** to contravene one or other of these Acts unless restrained, as is required by section 71 (1); in other words, it may be necessary to have two or more adverse findings by industrial tribunals or County Courts against a " responsible body ", which have become final, before an injunction can be obtained under section 71.

The somewhat inelegant phrase " done an act which is within the jurisdiction of an industrial tribunal " is explained by subsection (4) of section 73. If the references to other parts of the Act, and to section 2 of the Equal Pay Act, are followed through, the act is seen to be:

either—

(*a*) an act of discrimination which is unlawful by virtue of Part II of the Sex Discrimination Act (*i.e.* the unlawful acts described in Chapters 1, 2, 5 and 6) or

(*b*) an act of discrimination which is unlawful by virtue of sections 38, 39 or 40 (*i.e.* a discriminatory advertisement, an instruction to another person to discriminate, or an inducement to or pressure upon another person to discriminate) or

(*c*) an act contravening a term which is deemed to be included in an employee's contract, or a term in such a contract which is deemed to be modified, by an " equality clause " under the Equal Pay Act.

CERTIORARI, MANDAMUS AND PROHIBITION

A short explanation of these exotically-named High Court orders is necessary since they are, in fact, forms of appeal from inferior courts, tribunals and public bodies.

The ramifications and limitations of these procedures are far too extensive and complex to be dealt with in a book such as this, and the present exposition is inadequate to the point of being misleading in many respects, but it will, it is hoped, be sufficient to indicate where such appeal procedures may be relevant to the matters covered by the Act, and where they are inappropriate.

Certiorari is a High Court order which quashes (and here the word **really** means annuls) the proceedings of an inferior court or body having the legal right to determine questions affecting the right of subjects. It is therefore suitable as a method of appeal from some of the bodies to whom sections 22, 23, 25 and 29 apply, if it is desired to completely extinguish any decisions made by them. The order will not be made by the High Court, however, in order to quash proceedings in an area of jurisdiction which it does not itself possess, and therefore certiorari would not be a suitable method of appeal from decisions of the County Courts and industrial tribunals made under the powers conferred solely upon them by this Act.

Mandamus is an order made by the High Court, directing an inferior court, tribunal or public body to do something which is in the nature of a public duty and appertains to their office. In general, it is used to enforce statutory rights and duties, to require public officials and public bodies to carry out their duties, and to command inferior tribunals to exercise their jurisdiction. It cannot be used if the official or body has a discretion in the matter, as opposed to a strict obligation or duty. Hence, it could be used both against some of the bodies to whom sections 22, 23, 25 and 29 apply and against County Courts and industrial tribunals in the event of the latter refusing to exercise a non-discretionary power conferred upon them by this Act.

An order of prohibition by the High Court is the opposite of an order of mandamus and, as the name suggests, forbids an inferior court or tribunal to continue proceedings if it is attempting to exceed its jurisdiction. In view of the complexity of this Act, that is a situation which could well arise.

CHAPTER 10

DISCRIMINATION IN THE PROVISION OF GOODS, FACILITIES AND SERVICES

The reader who has read this far will have some idea of the nature and instances of discrimination which are made unlawful in each field of activity to which the Act relates and will, it is hoped, find it more helpful in this Chapter to learn, first, to whom and in what respects the anti-discrimination provisions relate, leaving a definition of the nature of the discrimination here dealt with until later in the Chapter.

It is immediately apparent that subsection (2) of section 29 contains a list of the facilities and services to which the section applies. The facilities and services set out in the list are, as the subsection makes clear, only **examples** of those covered by the section and, indeed, only scratch the surface of the areas of the life and activity of our nation to which the provisions of this very important section relate. Nevertheless, it is worth reproducing the list here, as some indication of the breadth of the section's provisions:

(*a*) access to and use of any place which members of the public or a section of the public are permitted to enter;

(*b*) accommodation in a hotel, boarding house or other similar establishment;

(*c*) facilities by way of banking or insurance or for grants, loans, credit or finance;

(*d*) facilities for education;

(*e*) facilities for entertainment, recreation or refreshment;

(*f*) facilities for transport or travel;

(*g*) the services of any profession or trade, or any local or other public authority.

In addition to the examples given in subsection (2), it must be realised that " goods " brings within the orbit of the section the entire manufacturing, wholesale and retail sections of trade and industry. Whilst it is mainly the retailers who are concerned with " a woman (or man) who seeks to obtain or use those goods " (the words used at the beginning of section 29), it must be remembered that many manufacturers attach conditions to the sale of their goods, accompany the retail sales with guarantees, or themselves provide credit and hire purchase facilities. Manufacturers must, therefore, ensure that those conditions, guarantees and facilities are free from the forms of discrimination proscribed by this section. " Facilities and services " extends the section to every form of advice and to all forms of brokerage and agency.

Accommodation in hotels, boarding houses and similar establishments will be dealt with in conjunction with the management and disposal of premises in the next Chapter.

The first half of subsection (1) of section 29 reads:

> It is unlawful for any person concerned with the provision (for payment or not) of goods, facilities or services to the public or a section of the public to discriminate against a woman who seeks to obtain or use those goods, facilities or services,

and continues with the instances in which discrimination is unlawful, to which reference has already been made in Chapter 8.

Reference was made in Chapter 8 to the fact that section 29 extended to the facilities and services provided by the educational bodies to which sections 22, 23 and 25 applied. It must now be appreciated that there are some bodies and firms engaged in forms of education which only come within the terms of section 29, for example, driving schools, the bodies commonly called " crammers ", and the purveyors of postal tuition courses. Likewise, a number of organisations teaching foreign languages, for example, the " modern language laboratory " operated by the Institute of Directors, will only come within section 29.

EXCEPTIONS

As with the provisions of the Act relating to employment, there is an extensive list of exceptions to section 29, and perhaps the widest is contained in subsection (3) of section 35, which provides that section 29 does not apply to any discrimination which is rendered unlawful by sections 22 and 23, nor to discrimination which would be unlawful but for the fact that it falls within the exceptions set out in sections 26, 27 and 28, and paragraph 3 of Schedule 4. Without this provision, section 29 would certainly have duplicated, as well as extended, sections 22 and 23, and would also have duplicated sections 12 to 16.

The exclusion for provisions contained in charitable instruments, discussed in detail in Chapter 1, applies to the whole Act, and, subject to the limitations discussed in that Chapter, is particularly apposite to section 29.

There is also a specific exception in subsection (3) of section 29, which declares that, where a particular **skill** is commonly exercised in a different way for men and for women, it will not be a contravention of the section for " a person who does not normally exercise it for women to insist on exercising it for a woman **only in accordance with his normal practice** ", or, if he " reasonably considers it impracticable ", to refuse or deliberately omit to exercise it. Clearly, this means that a barber could not be compelled to give a woman a permanent wave, and she might have to settle for a short back and sides; but it has a wider effect and, for example, a tailor or cutter who has spent a lifetime making men's suits might feel unable to make any reasonable fist of a suit for a woman, and *vice versa.*

Clubs and Private Associations

The wording of subsections (1) and (2) of section 29 are almost identical to section 2 of the Race Relations Act 1968.

In early 1973, the House of Lords decided, in proceedings between the Race Relations Board and Edward Charter and two other committee members of the East Ham South Conservative Club, that the words limited the operation of the section concerned to groups or sections of people in their public capacities, and therefore excluded groups of people associated together in a **private** manner, or under some **private** arrangement. The judges of the House of Lords decided that a club or association which has a procedure for the selection of would-be members, to ensure that they will be acceptable to existing members, was a private group and therefore excluded by the words " the public or a section of the public ".

This rule regarding private groups, as opposed to public groups, can be applied to groups other than clubs. For example, a few friends, or neighbours, or workmates, may combine to hire transport or buy in bulk because it is cheaper, and with such a small group there may be selection by common assent, rather than any formal procedure; for instance, members may ask one another " Shall we bring in old so-and-so ? ", or " Stan wants to join in, shall we let him ? " Such a group would be exempt from the restrictions imposed by section 29 but, obviously, the numbers would have to be small for the selection to operate in such an informal way.

Non-profit making Bodies

The Act goes much further than the Race Relations Act, because, in section 34, it excludes from the terms of sections 29 and 30 all **non-profit making** bodies unless they were set up by a statute.

This exception covers most member clubs and private associations, but it also extends to many bodies of which **membership is open to the public.** The range of such bodies is not only extensive but extremely important, since non-profit making bodies, from Housing Associations, through charities, to learned societies, are a very common and vital feature of our society.

The text of section 34 is as follows:

(1) This section applies to a body—

(*a*) the activities of which are carried on otherwise than for profit, and

(*b*) which was not set up by any enactment.

(2) Sections 29 (1) and 30 shall not be construed as rendering unlawful—

(*a*) the restriction of membership of any such body to persons of one sex (disregarding any minor exceptions), or

(*b*) the provision of benefits, facilities or services to members of any such body where the membership is so restricted,

even though membership of the body is open to the public, or to a section of the public.

(3) Nothing in section 29 or 30 shall—

(*a*) be construed as affecting a provision to which this subsection applies, or

(*b*) render unlawful an act which is done in order to give effect to such a provision.

(4) Subsection (3) applies to a provision for conferring benefits on persons of one sex only (disregarding any benefits to persons of the opposite sex which are exceptional or are relatively insignificant), being a provision which constitutes the main object of a body within subsection (1).

Before considering the section as a whole, it should be observed, in passing, that, under subsection (1) (*b*), only bodies which were " **not set up by** any enactment " are excluded. This leaves firmly within the exemption bodies such as Housing Associations which, whilst they exist under statutory provisions, are not actually brought into being by a statute, in the manner that, for example, the Equal Opportunities Commission is brought into being by the Act.

Upon close examination, the section falls into three distinct parts: subsection (1) defines the bodies to which the exemption applies, and has already been discussed. Subsection (2) specifies two forms of conduct which are exempt from the general rules in sections 29 and 30, namely: restricting **membership** of the body to one sex and the **provision of goods, facilities and services** where membership of the body **is** restricted to one sex.

Pausing there, it will be seen that membership of the non-profit making body need not be entirely single-sex in order to obtain exemption for **either** form of conduct, since paragraph (*b*) of subsection (2) interjects the words " disregarding any minor exceptions ". It will also be noticed that the closing words of subsection (2) specifically refer to membership of the body being open to the public, to put it beyond doubt that the decision in *Race Relations Board v. Charter* does not apply.

The third part of the section is contained in sub-paragraphs (3) and (4) and, in effect, gives an exemption from **all** the provisions of sections 29 and 30 to bodies which are not only non-profit making, but have **as their main object** the provision

F

of such benefits to one sex only. The **bodies** to which subsections (3) and (4) relate are therefore only a small proportion of those encompassed by subsection (2), but the forms of conduct which the former subsections render lawful are more extensive than those to which subsection (2) relates, particularly in the field of housing and accommodation.

Notwithstanding the last paragraph, it must be admitted that the wording of subsection (4) is somewhat circumspect, and whilst it includes bodies whose **activities** are not carried on for profit, whatever the **objects** may be, it would also seem to include bodies whose activities, or some of whose activities, make an incidental profit, provided the activities were not " carried on " for the purpose of so doing, by its reference to " a body within subsection (1) ".

It must then be stressed that the provision for conferring benefits on one sex only, which is the essence of the exemption, must constitute " **the** main object " of the body, which deprives non-profit making bodies with two or more main objects of equal importance, not all of which are to confer benefits upon one sex, of the exemption from section 29 provided by this subsection.

Political Parties

An exception of some interest to most people is contained in section 33, which deals with political parties. Subsection (1) of section 33 applies the exception to a political party if:

(*a*) it has as its main object, or one of its main objects, the promotion of parliamentary candidatures for the Parliament of the United Kingdom, or

(*b*) it is an affiliate of, or has as an affiliate, or has similar formal links with, a political party within paragraph (*a*).

Subsections (2) and (3) of section 33 provide that:

> Nothing in section 29 (1) shall be construed as affecting any special provision for persons of one sex only in the constitution, organisation or administration of the political party, or render unlawful an act done in order to give effect to such a special provision.

Paragraph (*b*) above was intended to cover the constituency parties of the national political parties and paragraph (*a*) the national party organisation. Whilst paragraph (*b*) may fulfil its intended function, the words " an affiliate of, or has an affiliate, or has similar formal links with ", almost certainly bring in other organisations, particularly those affiliated or connected to the smaller minority parties.

It will be seen that the exception is limited to single-sex provisions in the constitution, organisation and administration of the party. This is not, as might be suspected, a specific exception for the benefit of certain prominent women members of the Labour and Conservative parties disguised in general terms, but is to enable political parties to continue to have women's sections and committees, to confine certain offices and seats on committees to women or to men, and to hold conferences confined to women. Apparently, the Labour Party and the Conservative Party, at least, feel that it would be very undesirable for them to be prevented from organising on the basis of such separate facilities for women. This in no way affects the position of **employees** of political parties, since they come under the separate provisions of Part II of the Act.

Whilst the political parties thus enjoy the benefit of a section dedicated to certain of their activities, they are also clearly within subsections (1) and (2) of section 34 (and it is conceivable that a political party might be formed which would be within subsections (3) and (4) of section 34). Indeed, had the Government of the day thought of section 34 a little earlier than it did, section 33 might never have seen the light of day. The situation under the Act is, therefore, that, in addition to the exemptions which political parties enjoy under section 33, they can limit their membership to one sex only and, if they do so, provide benefits, facilities and services to that membership without contravening sections 29 and 30.

Miscellaneous exceptions in section 35

Subsections (1) and (2) of section 35 provide for a series of exceptions similar to some of the exceptions contained in section 7 in respect of employment, but worded rather differently. Some of these exceptions were referred to briefly in

Chapter 8, but it is now necessary to set them out in full and look at them a little more carefully. Subsection (1) reads:

> A person who provides at any place facilities or services restricted to men does not for that reason contravene section 29 (1) if—
>
> (*a*) the place is, or is part of, a hospital, reception centre provided by the Supplementary Benefits Commission or other establishment for persons requiring special care, supervision or attention, or
>
> (*b*) the place is (permanently or for the time being) occupied or used for the purposes of an organised religion, and the facilities or services are restricted to men so as to comply with the doctrines of that religion or avoid offending the religious susceptibilities of a significant number of its followers, or
>
> (*c*) the facilities or services are provided for, or are likely to be used by, two or more persons at the same time, and
>
> (i) the facilities or services are such, or those persons are such, that male users are likely to suffer serious embarrassment at the presence of a woman, or
>
> (ii) the facilities or services are such that a user is likely to be in a state of undress and a male user might reasonably object to the presence of a female user.

Here, again, the " looking-glass " provision must be stressed. At each point one must read these provisions, reversing the position of the sexes, so that paragraph (*b*), for example, refers just as much to a convent as to a monastery.

It should also be observed of paragraph (*b*), as has been said of a similar provision in section 7, that the susceptibilities must be **religious,** and not blind prejudice.

Paragraph (*c*) has hidden depths. Sub-paragraph (ii) of paragraph (*c*) obviously applies to such facilities as cubicles and dressing-rooms for changing clothes in shops, sports grounds, swimming pools, hospitals and clinics, and those whose immediate reaction is that, human nature being what it is, many male users would not object to the presence of a female user in a state of undress, are reminded of the " looking-glass " provisions, and the fact that there would be every reason to object on the female side. What is noticeable is that neither here nor in section 7 is there any exception relating to the sale of ladies' underwear, or of sanitary appliances to either sex, to be carried out by a member of the same sex as the buyer. One would have expected to have found some such provision out of respect for the feelings of those members of our society who are a little less " liberated " than others.

Similarly, having read sub-paragraph (i) of paragraph (*c*), one can readily envisage male users suffering serious embarrassment at the presence of a woman in, for example, a toilet, but the phrase " or those persons are such ", as an alternative to " the facilities or services are such ", is not so readily explicable. The phrase, presumably, relates to members of religious sects, particularly some Roman Catholic orders, whose views are such that they must shut themselves off from members of the opposite sex.

Subsection (2) omits the reference to " at any place ", found in subsection (1), and provides simply that any facilities or services restricted to one sex are exempt from the prohibitions in section 29, if they are such that physical contact between the user and another person is likely **and** the other person might **reasonably** object if of the opposite sex. This, obviously, covers the position of masseurs, but would apply equally to tailoring for both sexes.

TERRITORIAL LIMITS

Just as section 10 defined when employment was to be considered as taking place " at an establishment in Great Britain ", so section 36 exempts from the operation of section 29 goods, facilities or services outside Great Britain, except as provided in subsections (2) and (3) of section 36. The precise wording of subsection (1) of section 36 is:

(*a*) does not apply to goods, facilities or services outside Great Britain except as provided in subsections (2) and (3), and

(*b*) does not apply to facilities by way of banking or insurance or for grants, loans, credit or finance where the facilities are for a purpose to be carried out, or in connection with risks wholly or mainly arising, outside Great Britain.

It must be admitted at this point that this subsection is likely to be called into question more often, and to cause greater difficulties of interpretation, than section 10. Section 29, it will be recalled, made it unlawful for any person " concerned with the provision . . . of goods, facilities or services to the public ", and it would appear from subsection (1) of section 36 that, for example, an importer of goods can discriminate amongst would-be buyers on the ground of sex if the goods had not, at that time, entered the country.

There may also be difficulties for the provider of facilities or services. It will be seen that, whilst the exemption for " risks " (presumably insurance risks) is where they are " wholly or mainly arising " outside Great Britain, the other facilities are only exempt if they are " for a purpose to be carried out " outside Great Britain, and this must be presumed to mean " wholly carried out outside Great Britain ".

There will be many occasions when the facilities are " for a purpose " to be carried out partly in Great Britain and partly outside and it will be impossible to decide whether or not section 29 applies.

There can be no doubt that the subsection creates considerable difficulties of interpretation in certain circumstances, especially in areas of commerce so complicated and sophisticated as banking and insurance.

Subsection (2) of section 36 specifically re-applies the prohibitions in section 29 to the provision of facilities for travel outside Great Britain if the refusal or omission occurs in Great Britain, or on a ship, aircraft or hovercraft within the next subsection. In general terms, therefore, a travel agent will **not** be able to insist on dealing with men only in booking holidays abroad, or to organise package holidays restricted to single people.

Subsection (3) really needs no comment here, and is as follows:

> (3) Section 29 (1) applies on and in relation to—
>
> (*a*) any ship registered at a port of registry in Great Britain, and

(*b*) any aircraft or hovercraft registered in the United Kingdom and operated by a person who has his principal place of business or is ordinarily resident, in Great Britain,

(*c*) any ship, aircraft or hovercraft belonging to or possessed by Her Majesty in right of the Government of the United Kingdom,

even if the ship, aircraft or hovercraft is outside Great Britain.

In order not to create a conflict with the laws of any other country, this necessitates subsection (4), which provides that:

(4) This section shall not render unlawful an act done in or over a country outside the United Kingdom, or in or over that country's territorial waters, for the purpose of complying with the laws of that country.

DISCRIMINATION IN GOODS, FACILITIES AND SERVICES DEFINED

The various forms of discrimination which are forbidden by section 29 have already been quoted in Chapter 8, but it would be unreasonable not to quote the relevant words again, as this is the Chapter principally concerned with them. The discrimination is, of course, specified to be " against a woman " who seeks to obtain or use the goods, facilities or services provided by the classes of persons, firms or companies already referred to in this Chapter:

(*a*) by refusing or deliberately omitting to provide her with any of them or

(*b*) by refusing or deliberately omitting to provide her with goods, facilities or services of the like quality, in the like manner and on the like terms as are normal in his case in relation to male members of the public or (where she belongs to a section of the public) to male members of that section.

The wording of paragraph (*b*) departs from previous clauses defining unlawful discrimination, and, in particular, the reference to " goods, facilities and services **of the like quality** ", is something quite new. In all the earlier references to facilities and services, there is no mention of quality, and to that extent it would appear that the general public, in their capacity of customers or clients are to be treated better than employees, partners and the members of trade unions and other bodies.

The subsequent words " in the like manner and on the like terms ", when applied to a specific situation, are really no different in their effect to " in the way he affords her access to ", used in subsection (2) (*a*) of section 6 and other operative sections, and are certainly narrower than " subjecting her to any other detriment " in subsection (2) (*b*) of section 6 and later operative sections. What **is** different, however, is the use of the words " as are normal in his case ". This is another instance of the recognition, by the Act, of a measure of discrimination, and it means that any person, firm or company accused of discrimination in the supply of goods, facilities and services to members of the public has an excuse if they can show that any comparisons with other instances of their treatment of the opposite sex adduced against them were not " normal " in their case, but were exceptional for one reason or another.

The full definitions, or check list, for unlawful discrimination in this field is therefore as follows:

Discrimination:

(*a*) by a person or firm concerned with the provision (for payment or not)

(*b*) of goods, facilities **or** services

(*c*) to the public or a **section** of the public

(*d*) **against** an individual who

(*e*) seeks to obtain, or use, those goods, facilities or services

either by

(*f*) refusing, or deliberately omitting, to provide them
or

(*g*) refusing, or deliberately omitting, to provide that individual with goods, facilities or services of

(i) the like quality

(ii) in the like manner **and**

(iii) on the like terms

as are " normal " in **that** person's or firm's case in relation to (*h*) members of the public of the opposite sex to the individual concerned

or

(*i*) if the individual belongs to a section of the public, to members of **that section** of the public of the opposite sex to the individual concerned

in every case either—

(*j*) on the ground of the sex, or married status of that individual

or

(*k*) by applying to the individual an unfavourable requirement which that person applies, or would apply, equally to both sexes, or to the married and unmarried alike

but which

(i) is such that the proportion of married persons of the same sex, or persons of the individual's sex (as the case may be) who can comply with the requirement is **considerably** smaller than the proportion of unmarried persons " of the same sex, or persons of the opposite sex to the individual (as the case may be), who can comply with it

and

(ii) which the person providing the goods, facilities or services cannot show to be justifiable irrespective of the marital status, or the sex (as the case may be), of that individual

(*l*) always provided that the comparison of the cases of persons of different marital status, or different sex, for this purpose, is such that the relevant circumstances in the one case are the same, or not materially different, in the other.

DISCRIMINATORY CONTRACTS

Before leaving this subject, it is most important to consider the provisions of section 77, which render the term of a contract void or unenforceable if:

(*a*) its inclusion renders the making of the contract unlawful by virtue of this Act, or (*b*) it is included in furtherance of an act rendered unlawful by this Act, or

(*c*) it provides for the doing of an act which would be rendered unlawful by this Act.

Similarly, by subsection (2) of section 77, if the inclusion of a term in a contract constitutes unlawful discrimination, or is in furtherance of, or provides for, such discrimination against a party to the contract, it is **unenforceable against that party.** This is very different to the term being void because, of course, it could be enforced by **that** party against other parties to the contract—a particularly useful advantage if the term in question contains both obligations upon **and** benefits to the party discriminated against.

Subsection (4) of section 77 authorises an application to the County Court to remove or modify a contractual term to which subsection (2) applies.

Further, a term in a contract which would exclude or limit any provision of the Act is, by subsection (3) of section 77 **unenforceable by any person in whose favour the term would operate,** although the subsection does not apply to an agreement settling a complaint to an industrial tribunal with the assistance of a conciliation officer. This subsection is less favourable to the person who suffers the discrimination than subsection (2), since, if the term were sufficiently extensive to confer a benefit on that person, the benefit would be lost.

It will be seen that the effect of this section on, for example, contracts for the sale of goods, or for hire-purchase or other credit facilities may be catastrophic, particularly if the provision for payment or repayment is not clearly separated from the discriminatory term in the contract.

VICARIOUS LIABILITY

This seems a suitable point at which to mention that, by section 41, the individuals and organisations to which this Chapter relates are not only liable for unlawful discrimination by their employees 'in the course of their employment' (which seems reasonable) whether or not it was with their knowledge or approval (which does not), but also for unlawful discrimination by any agent, whether the agent's authority is express or to be implied from the circumstances, and even if the discrimination was ratified by the individual or organisation after it had occurred.

The individual or organisation has a defence, by subsection (3) of section 41, if they took " such steps as were reasonably practical to prevent the employee from doing that act, or from doing in the course of his employment acts of that description " but they have no such defence in respect of any unlawful discrimination by their agents. So far as agents are concerned, therefore, it matters only that the act or omission was within their authority.

The other side of the coin is that, in the circumstances described above, both the employee and the agent may also be liable for " knowingly aiding another person " to unlawfully discriminate under section 42, and the employee is liable even if his employer is excused because he took the steps described in subsection (3) of section 41.

Both the employee and the agent are exempted from liability by subsection (3) of section 42 if they acted in reliance on a statement made to them by the individual or organisation that, because of a provision of the Act, the discrimination would not be unlawful, and it was reasonable for them to rely upon it. This introduces a further liability on the party who makes the statement, for if he does so knowingly or recklessly he may, by subsection (4) of section 42, be fined up to £400. This is one of the several instances of criminal liability under the Act.

Similar responsibilities for such individuals and organisations are provided by sections 39 and 40. Section 39 reads as follows:

> It is unlawful for a person—
>
> (*a*) who has authority over another person, or

(*b*) in accordance with whose wishes that other person is accustomed to act,

to instruct him to do any act which is unlawful by virtue of Part II or III, or procure or attempt to procure the doing by him of any such act.

Whilst Part II of the Act relates principally to employment and training for employment, Part III includes the sale of goods and the supply of facilities and services. In fact, an individual or organisation will be liable if they instruct an employee or any other person over whom he has influence to discriminate in any manner prohibited by the Act, except by publishing a discriminatory advertisement.

It will be noticed that it is not only straightforward instructions which are contrary to the section, as it refers also to " procure or attempt to procure the doing . . . of any such act ". These words can cover a very wide variety of actions and subtle pressures, and to put the matter quite beyond doubt, section 40 provides—

(1) It is unlawful to induce, or attempt to induce, a person to do any act which contravenes Part II or III by—

(*a*) providing or offering to provide him with any benefit, or

(*b*) subjecting or threatening to subject him to any detriment.

(2) An offer or threat is not prevented from falling within subsection (1) because it is not made directly to the person in question, if it is made in such a way that he is likely to hear of it.

Neither nods nor winks to blind horses will avoid these two sections, and the only safe course is to eschew any attempt to discriminate in a manner which is contrary to the Act.

Although sections 39 and 40 do not apply to advertisements, an individual or organisation which advertises in a discriminatory manner, and informs the publisher of the advertisement that the advertisement is not unlawful because they are entitled to discriminate, whether because the discrimination is not of a kind which comes within the general prohibitions of the Act, or because it falls within an exemption to it, may be fined up to £400 if that statement is untrue. This liability is dealt with at greater length in Chapter 13.

CHAPTER 11

DISCRIMINATION IN THE PROVISION OF HOUSING AND ACCOMMODATION

In addition to the terms of section 29 covering the supply of facilities and services, which, as subsection (2) (*b*) makes clear, extends to the provision of accommodation in a hotel, boarding house or similar establishment, section 30 deals with discrimination in the disposal of premises in Great Britain, and in the management of premises. Having just dealt with the general provisions of section 29 at some length, it is proposed now to deal first with section 30, and return to section 29 later.

First, it is vital to emphasise one matter which applies to the housing and accommodation provisions of both sections 29 and 30. This is that the prohibition against discrimination on the ground that a person is married, as opposed to being single, applies just as much to these two sections as to Part II of the Act, as was explained in Chapter 1. This is likely to have very far-reaching consequences, since housing and accommodation are fields in which there is a strong tradition of discrimination on the ground of marital status (both in favour of and against those who are married) and landlords, local authorities and property management firms will have to reconsider their procedures in this respect.

SALES AND LETTINGS

Subsection (1) of section 30, which deals with disposals, begins:

> It is unlawful for a person, in relation to premises in Great Britain of which he has power to dispose, to discriminate against a woman.

The " person " here mentioned could be the owner, trustee, manager of or agent for the premises, provided he has " power to dispose ". It could even be a relation or friend of the owner who has been entrusted with the task of " disposing " of the premises in the owner's absence. It includes, of course, local authorities in respect of property which they own.

Equally, " dispose " is defined by subsection (1) of section 72 as including granting a right to occupy the premises, and would therefore also cover the sale of a freehold, the sale of a long lease, the sale of a short lease, the creation of a new lease, the creation or transfer of a tenancy, and even the creation or transfer (if the latter be possible) of a tenancy at will or licence to occupy, premises of any description.

Moreover, there is nothing in the section, or elsewhere, which restricts it to premises used for residential purposes and it applies equally to business premises. Nor is subsection (1) of section 30 limited to premises to be occupied by the individual seeking to acquire them, and it is just as applicable to premises which such an individual wishes to acquire as an investment.

The prohibited discrimination is:

(*a*) in the terms on which he offers her those premises, or

(*b*) by refusing her application for those premises, or

(*c*) in his treatment of her in relation to any list of persons in need of premises of that description.

So far as the acquisition of premises is concerned, this seems pretty comprehensive, but it omits to provide for one very general point, and that is the necessity for the owner of the property, or the leaseholder, if what is being acquired is an underlease, to give his " licence " or consent to the acquisition of the lease or underlease by the individual. Most leases of property prohibit the transfer of the lease by the lessee or tenant to another person unless the landlord has given his formal consent to the transfer to that person. The landlord would not be 'a person who has power to dispose of the premises' so far as the lease to the lessee or tenant was concerned, and therefore would not be within subsection (1) of section 30.

The landlord, and the necessity for his consent to a new lessee or tenant, is dealt with by section 31, subsection (1) of which provides:

> (1) Where the licence or consent of the landlord or of any other person is required for the disposal to any person of premises in Great Britain comprised in a tenancy, it is unlawful for the landlord or other person to discriminate against a woman by withholding the licence or consent for disposal of the premises to her.

Therefore, if a landlord or lessor withholds his consent to the transfer of a lease to a new tenant or lessee **on the ground of the new tenant's sex or married status,** it is unlawful discrimination, and the landlord or lessor will be subject to all the sanctions referred to in Chapter 12.

The words " tenancy " and " disposal " are, for the purposes of this section, separately and very broadly defined by subsection (3) thus:

> (3) In this section " tenancy " means a tenancy created by a lease or sublease, by an agreement for a lease or sub-lease, or by a tenancy agreement or in pursuance of any enactment; and " disposal ", in relation to premises comprised in a tenancy, includes assignment or assignation of the tenancy and sub-letting or parting with possession of the premises or any part of the premises.

Moreover, subsection (4) puts it beyond doubt that the section applies just as much to leases and tenancies created before the Act was passed as to those created after it became law.

There is an exception to section 31, however, to bring it into line with the exception for small dwellings contained in section 32 (which is dealt with later in this Chapter). This is contained in subsection (2) in these terms:

> (2) Subsection (1) does not apply if—
>
> (*a*) the person withholding a licence or consent, or a near relative of his (" the relevant occupier ") resides, and intends to continue to reside, on the premises, and
>
> (*b*) there is on the premises, in addition to the accommodation occupied by the relevant occupier, accommodation (not being storage accommodation or means of access)

shared by the relevant occupier with other persons residing on the premises who are not members of his household, and

(*c*) the premises are small premises as defined in section 32 (2).

This subsection should be considered in the light of the comments made upon the identical wording to be found in section 32.

Exception for Sales and Lettings

There is, however, an exception to subsection (1) of section 30 in respect of owner-occupiers: this is to be found in subsection (3) of section 30, which reads as follows:

> (3) Subsection (1) does not apply to a person who owns an estate or interest in the premises and wholly occupies them unless he uses the services of an estate agent for the purposes of the disposal of the premises, or publishes or causes to be published an advertisement in connection with the disposal.

It is understandable, perhaps, that a person who occupies, say, a large house, and wishes to sell or let a part of it should be allowed to discriminate in this way, especially when it is remembered that, under the " looking-glass " provision, the discrimination may be by a woman owner against a man lodger or tenant. It is not so clear why the exception should apply to any owner-occupier disposing of a freehold or leasehold house or flat with vacant possession on the completion of the sale, as it undoubtedly does, nor why the exception should only be available if an estate agent is not used and the premises are not advertised.

The reference to estate agents and advertisements is presumably an attempt to eliminate owner-occupiers selling with full vacant possession, since the vast majority of such vendors in England and Wales find their purchasers through estate agents or press advertisements. The tiny minority who do not do so sell to relations, friends, or purchasers who are personally introduced to them, and therefore the transaction is wholly discriminatory, in the sense that the property is never put on the open market.

Really, subsection (3) is an attempt to permit discrimination by owner-occupiers of boarding houses and private hotels, since they are the principal people who can be said to " wholly occupy " premises if they have let part of them in the past. A boarder or lodger is, in law, a mere licensee, and the landlady (or landlord) does not part with possession of their room, or, technically, cease to occupy it, but has the right to enter it at will. The wording of the subsection does, however, cover an owner-occupier letting a flat or bedsitter in their house for the first time.

It seems at first surprising that the exemption in subsection (3) does not extend to the many small boarding houses throughout the country if the landlady or landlord advertises the accommodation, especially as subsection (1) of section 82 defines " advertisement " as follows:

> " advertisement " includes every form of advertisement, whether to the public or not, and whether in a newspaper or other publication, by television or radio, by display of notices, signs, labels, showcards or goods, by distribution of samples, circulars, catalogues, price lists or other material, by exhibition of pictures, models or films, or in any other way, and references to the publishing of advertisements shall be construed accordingly.

This means that even a notice in the window saying " Vacancies " would be sufficient to lose the landlady the exemption. However, many such boarding houses are covered by the blanket exemption for small dwellings contained in section 32, which will be dealt with later.

TREATMENT DURING OCCUPATION

Turning to what happens once premises are occupied, subsection (2) of section 30 provides:

> It is unlawful for a person, in relation to premises managed by him, to discriminate against a woman occupying the premises—
>
> (*a*) in the way he affords her access to any benefits or facilities, or by refusing or deliberately omitting to afford her access to them, or
>
> (*b*) by evicting her, or subjecting her to any other detriment.

Here again, the words " in relation to premises managed by him " are wide enough to cover the owner of the freehold, the lessee who is sub-letting, the managing agent or estate agent who manages property for the landlord (but **not** an agent who merely collects the rent and has no power to manage), the friend or relation of the landlord who performs those functions, and even some individuals in a local authority's Housing Department and Surveyor's Department, as well as the local authority itself.

Equally, the " premises " may be a house, flat (whether self-contained or not) a " bedsitter ", or even an hotel or boarding house.

The subsection continues " against a woman occupying the premises " and the use of these words shows that the person concerned (for the " looking-glass " provisions apply here, too, and it need not be a woman) need not necessarily be a lessee or tenant, and, indeed, can be some one who has no legal interest in the premises at all—for example, a friend whom the tenant has allowed to occupy the premises in the tenant's absence, or even a squatter.

Subsection (2) does not refer specifically to the **terms** on which the premises are occupied, but such matters, together with any other conceivable method of discrimination, are covered by the phrase " or subjecting her to any other detriment ". Moreover, the ultimate sanction for not, say, redecorating if the tenant is responsible for doing so, or having children in the premises when children are forbidden, is eviction, and that is unlawful if a member of the opposite sex would not be evicted in the same circumstances.

DISCRIMINATION IN THE PROVISION OF ACCOMMODATION UNDER SECTION 29

The fact that section 29 also covers accommodation has already been mentioned. The example in subsection (2) of section 29 specifies accommodation in a hotel, boarding house " or other similar establishment ", but it seems possible to apply the words " facilities and services " to almost any accommodation, certainly to service flats, to furnished flats, houses and bungalows, and to caravans which are let or hired.

There is, therefore, a considerable overlap between the premises covered by section 29 and those covered by section 30. Fortunately, a careful comparison of paragraphs (*a*) and (*b*) of subsection (1) of section 29 with paragraphs (*a*), (*b*) and (*c*) of subsection (1) of section 30 shows that, although the wording is different, their effect is likely to be the same in any given set of circumstances. The opening words of subsection (1) of section 30 do not include " for payment or not ", but would certainly cover both situations. The real difference between the two subsections lies in the fact that subsection (1) of section 29 relates only to the provision of the facilities or services in question " to the public or a section of the public " (a phrase which was discussed earlier in connection with clubs) whereas subsection (1) of section 30 would make discrimination unlawful if it were practised in relation to premises being disposed of amongst members of a private association, or some other restricted group.

Paragraph (*a*) of subsection (2) of section 30 appears to be on all-fours with the relevant words of paragraph (*b*) of subsection (1) of section 29, but the words " by evicting her, or subjecting her to any other detriment " in paragraph (*b*) of the former subsection go beyond anything contained in paragraph (*b*) of the latter subsection, and section 30 therefore adds to and extends the provisions of section 29 in that respect.

Needless to say, section 30 also applies to an outright sale of premises, something which could not possibly be brought within section 29.

EXCEPTIONS TO PROVISION OF ACCOMMODATION UNDER SECTIONS 29 AND 30

The exceptions to section 29 have been discussed in detail in the preceding Chapter, and it will suffice to recall here, insofar as they relate to accommodation, that they cover premises occupied or used for the purpose of an organised religion if the discrimination is to comply with the doctrines of the religion, or to avoid offending the religious susceptibilities of its followers; facilities likely to be used by more than one person at the same time if they are such that users are likely to be in a state of undress or users of one sex are likely to suffer serious embarrassment at the presence of the other sex; or the facilities or services are such that physical contact between the user and another person is likely. All the foregoing can be found in section 35.

Small dwellings

Finally, there is the exception for small dwellings contained in section 32. This takes such dwellings out of the provisions of both sections 29 and 30 (and of both subsections (1) and (2) of the latter) if the person providing or disposing of the premises, or a near relative (either of whom is termed by the Act the " relevant occupier "):

(*a*) resides and intends to continue to reside on the premises, and

(*b*) there is on the premises, in addition to the accommodation occupied by the relevant occupier, accommodation (not being storage accommodation or means of access) shared by the relevant occupier with other persons residing on the premises who are not members of his household, and

(*c*) the premises are small premises.

It would seem that this exemption also covers owner-occupied boarding houses and private hotels, but, as will be seen presently, such establishments must not normally accommodate more than six boarders or guests if they are to come within this exemption. The wording also covers such establishments if only " a near relative " of the owner lives on the premises, and it covers properties which the owner has divided into one or more flats, or bedsitters **if** the owner or a near relative lives there **and** shares accommodation with a non-member of the household.

The first question that arises is " What is a near relative? " The answer which is provided by subsection (5) of section 82 is as follows:

(5) For the purposes of this Act, a person is a near relative of another if that person is the wife or husband, a parent or child, a grandparent or grandchild, or a brother or sister of the other (whether of full blood or half-blood or by affinity), and " child " includes an illegitimate child and the wife or husband of an illegitimate child.

The reason for extending the definition to the wife or husband of an illegitimate child, but not the wife or husband of a legitimate child, is not explained.

The next question is for how long must the owner or near relative intend to continue to reside—a week, a month, a year, or a lifetime? Unfortunately, that is not explained, either. Presumably, any " continuance ", however short, will suffice if it is genuinely " intended ".

The additional, and shared, accommodation specified in paragraph (*b*) must not be means of access, so that hallways, passages, staircases or landings will not count, but it can be a kitchen or bathroom or toilet.

The third question that arises is " What are small premises? " This is answered by subsection (2) of section 32, at some length, in the following manner:

> (2) Premises shall be treated for the purposes of subsection (1) as small premises if—
>
> (*a*) in the case of premises comprising residential accommodation for one or more households (under separate letting or similar agreements) in addition to the accommodation occupied by the relevant occupier, there is not normally residential accommodation for more than two such households and only the relevant occupier and any member of his household reside in the accommodation occupied by him;
>
> (*b*) in the case of premises not falling within paragraph (*a*), there is not normally residential accommodation on the premises for more than six persons in addition to the relevant occupier and any members of his household.

The exemption can be re-stated as follows:

For sections 29 and 30 **not** to apply, the owner, lessee or tenant of the whole premises, or a " near relative " (as defined above) must

(*a*) reside on the premises already, and

(*b*) intend to continue to reside there for a while, and

(*c*) share some part of the premises, other than a passage or staircase with (*d*) another person who lives there and who is not a member of his household

and either the premises

(*e*) are split-up to provide for one or two (but not more) additional households paying rent to the owner and

(*f*) the owner does not take in lodgers in his part of the premises or

(*g*) are used for lodgers, and

(*h*) do not normally accommodate more than six lodgers.

Exemption for non-profit making associations

As was explained in Chapter 10, non-profit making bodies which have not been set up by an Act of Parliament are exempt from the provisions of both sections 29 and 30, in some circumstances. Indeed, if the main object of such a body is to confer benefits on persons of one sex only, the provision of such benefits is wholly exempt from the restrictions in sections 29 and 30. Needless to say, these exemptions are particularly important in the field of housing and accommodation, where a number of such bodies operate. It must be stressed again that bodies which were set up by statute, including, of course, local authorities, are not within this exemption.

To come within the exemption under subsection (2) (*b*) of section 34, *i.e.* the provision of benefits, facilities or services to members, the body must be one which **restricts membership** to one sex only, disregarding (to quote the subsection) " any minor exceptions ". Providing it does this, such a non-profit making body may discriminate by providing benefits, facilities or services to its one-sex membership, even though this would otherwise be contrary to both sections 29 and 30.

The alternative under section 34 is for such non-profit making bodies that have **as their main object** the provision of benefits to one sex only (disregarding, for this purpose, any benefits to persons of the opposite sex which are exceptional or relatively minor) under subsections (3) and (4). These bodies need not confine their membership to one sex, and may discriminate in conferring benefits upon members and non-members providing the provision of those benefits are within their main object.

Communal accommodation

The Act contains particular provisions for communal accommodation. This is defined by subsections (1) and (2) of section 46 as follows:

> (1) In this section " communal accommodation " means residential accommodation which includes dormitories or other shared sleeping accommodation which for reasons of privacy or decency should be used by men only, or by women only (but which may include some shared sleeping accommodation for men, and some for women, or some ordinary sleeping accommodation)
>
> (2) In this section " communal accommodation " also includes residential accommodation all or part of which should be used by men only, or by women only, because of the nature of the sanitary facilities serving the accommodation,

which almost provokes the comment: " You pays your money and you takes your choice ". Certainly, as a definition, it begs more questions than it answers.

The section continues by providing an exemption for communal accommodation in the following terms:

> (3) Nothing in Part II or III shall render unlawful sex discrimination in the admission of persons to communal accommodation if the accommodation is managed in a way which, given the exigencies of the situation, comes as near as may be to fair and equitable treatment of men and women.
>
> (4) In applying subsection (3) account shall be taken of—
>
> (*a*) whether and how far it is reasonable to expect that the accommodation should be altered or extended, or that further alternative accommodation should be provided; and
>
> (*b*) the frequency of the demand or need for use of the accommodation by men as compared with women.

This is not much better. It seems that the proprietor of communal accommodation is exempt from sections 29 and 30 if he can prove that the accommodation is " managed in a way " which " comes as near as may be to fair and equitable treatment " of both sexes, " given the exigencies of the situation ". The difficulty of making any reasonable judgment on such generalised wording is tacitly acknowledged by the fact that some examples of criteria that might be used are contained in subsection (4), but they tend only to make confusion worse confused. Perhaps the entire section merely underlines the difficulty of attempting to legislate for " equality " in respect of such accommodation.

The reader will notice that the exemption is from the prohibitions in both section 29 and section 30.

However this may be, there is no doubt that, once the proprietor of such communal accommodation has brought himself within the wording of section 46, he is absolved from virtually all the provisions of the Act, because subsection (5) declares:

> (5) Nothing in Part II or III shall render unlawful sex discrimination against a woman as respects the provision of any benefit, facility or service if—
>
> (*a*) the benefit, facility or service cannot properly and effectively be provided except for those using communal accommodation, and
>
> (*b*) in the relevant circumstances the woman could lawfully be refused the use of the accommodation by virtue of subsection (3).

and subsection (8) provides that the section does not in any way restrict the effect of subsection (1) (*c*) of section 35 which, it will be recalled, enacts that the provision of facilities or services restricted to one sex does not contravene section 29 if:

> (*c*) the facilities or services are provided for, or are likely to be used by, two or more persons at the same time, and
>
> (i) the facilities or services are such, or those persons are such, that male users are likely to suffer serious embarrassment at the presence of a woman, or
>
> (ii) the facilities or services are such that a user is likely to be in a state of undress and a male user might reasonably object to the presence of a female user.

VICARIOUS LIABILITY

It is necessary here to add that, by section 41, an owner or trustee, lessee or local authority is not only liable for unlawful discrimination by their employees ' in the course of their employment ' (which seems reasonable) whether or not it was with their knowledge or approval (which does not), but also for unlawful discrimination by any agent, whether the agent's authority is express or to be implied from the circumstances, and even if the discrimination was only ratified by the owner after it had occurred.

The owner has a defence, by subsection (3) of section 41, if he took " such steps as were reasonably practical to prevent the employee from doing that act, or from doing in the course of his employment acts of that description " but he has no such defence in respect of any unlawful discrimination by his agents. So far as agents are concerned, therefore, it matters only that the act or omission was within their authority.

The other side of the coin is that, in the circumstances described above, both the employee and the agent may also be liable for " knowingly aiding another person " to unlawfully discriminate under section 42, and the employee is liable even if his employer is excused because he took the steps described in subsection (3) of section 41.

Both the employee and the agent are exempted from liability by subsection (3) of section 42 if they acted in reliance on a statement made to them by the owner or lessee that, because of a provision of the Act, the discrimination would not be unlawful, and it was reasonable for them to rely upon it. This introduces a further liability on the person who makes the statement, for if he does so knowingly or recklessly, he may, by subsection (4) of section 42, be fined up to £400. This is one of the several instances of criminal liability under the Act.

Similar responsibilities for the owners and lessees are provided by sections 39 and 40. Section 39 reads as follows:

> It is unlawful for a person—
>
> (*a*) who has authority over another person, or
>
> (*b*) in accordance with whose wishes that other person is accustomed to act,
>
> to instruct him to do any act which is unlawful by virtue of Part II or III, or procure or attempt to procure the doing by him of any such act.

Whilst Part II of the Act relates principally to employment and training for employment, Part III includes the sale of goods, the supply of facilities and services and the provision of accommodation. In fact, an owner or lessee will be liable if he instructs an employee or any other person over whom he has influence to discriminate in any manner prohibited by the Act, except by publishing a discriminatory advertisement.

It will be noticed that it is not only straightforward instructions which are contrary to the section, as it refers also to "procure or attempt to procure the doing . . . of any such act". These words can cover a very wide variety of actions and subtle pressures, and to put the matter quite beyond doubt, section 40 provides—

> (1) It is unlawful to induce, or attempt to induce, a person to do any act which contravenes Part II or III by—
>
> (*a*) providing or offering to provide him with any benefit, or
>
> (*b*) subjecting or threatening to subject him to any detriment.
>
> (2) An offer or threat is not prevented from falling within subsection (1) because it is not made directly to the person in question, if it is made in such a way that he is likely to hear of it.

Neither nods nor winks to blind horses will avoid these two sections, and the only safe course is to eschew any attempt to discriminate in a manner which is contrary to the Act.

Although sections 39 and 40 do not apply to advertisements, an owner or lessee who advertises in a discriminatory manner, and informs the publisher of the advertisement that the advertisement is not unlawful because he is entitled to discriminate, whether because the discrimination is not of a kind which comes within the general prohibitions of the Act, or because it falls within an exemption to it, may be fined up to £400 if that statement is untrue. This liability is dealt with at greater length in Chapter 13.

CHAPTER 12

SANCTIONS FOR DISCRIMINATION IN THE PROVISION OF GOODS, FACILITIES AND SERVICES AND ACCOMMODATION

COUNTY COURT PROCEEDINGS

Any sufferer from such discrimination as is made unlawful by sections 29 and 30 may sue the person or body which is guilty of that discrimination in the County Court (or the Sheriff Court in Scotland) " in like manner as any other claim in tort " (or in Scotland ' in reparation for breach of statutory duty '), by virtue of section 66. Whilst the section appears to align unlawful discrimination with torts such as negligence or defamation for the purpose of County Court procedure and jurisdiction, it may be doubted whether it actually **constitutes** such discrimination a tort for all purposes known to the law.

It is clear from the terms of subsections (3) and (4) of section 66 that damages are one remedy which can be obtained in any such proceedings in the County Court. What is far from clear is whether the County Court can grant an injunction, whether permanent or temporary, in proceedings under section 66. This point is dealt with in detail under the heading " Injunctions ".

As has been pointed out previously, by subsection (4) of section 66, damages for unlawful discrimination can include compensation for injury to feelings.

The point has already been made in other connections and must be re-emphasised here, that, by subsection (3) of section 66, no damages can be awarded for **covert** discrimination on the ground of sex or marital status if the body or person accused of such discrimination proves that the requirement or condition was **not** applied with the **intention** of treating the claimant unfavourably on the ground alleged against them.

There is one point of difficulty in this respect, and that is that the county courts have no jurisdiction to entertain an action in tort in which the claim exceeds £1,000. In an ordinary action, if the plaintiff simply claims damages, without quantifying the amount, it is customary for the formal Particulars of Claim to specify that the plaintiff abandons any amount by which his damages may be found to exceed £1,000, in order to ensure that the county court judge has jurisdiction to hear the action.

Despite the provisions of subsection (2) of section 66 the Act contains no specific provision to enable county courts to entertain claims for more than £1,000. It may be that the words at the end of subsection (2) " but all such remedies shall be obtainable in such proceedings as, apart from this subsection, would be obtainable in the High Court " can be construed as not only extending the county court jurisdiction in respect of the **kind** of remedies, but also in respect of the financial limits on them. However, until the point has been decided by the courts, it cannot be regarded as free from doubt.

Time limits for proceedings

The proceedings in the County Court must be commenced **within six months** of the act or omission to which they relate, under the limitation imposed by subsection (2) of section 70.

The County Court has power to hear the complaint or application by subsection (5) of section 70, even if this time limit has expired, but, obviously, this enabling power should not be relied upon unnecessarily.

As we have seen, however, such periods are sometimes not as short as they seem, because subsection (6) of section 76 provides that—

- (*a*) where the inclusion of any term in a contract renders the making of the contract an unlawful act that act shall be treated as extending throughout the duration of the contract, and
- (*b*) any act extending over a period shall be treated as done at the end of that period, and

(*c*) a deliberate omission shall be treated as done when the person in question decided upon it,

and continues:

> and in the absence of evidence establishing the contrary a person shall be taken for the purposes of this section to decide upon an omission when he does an act inconsistent with doing the omitted act or, if he has done no such inconsistent act, when the period expires within which he might reasonably have been expected to do the omitted act if it was to be done.

The somewhat limited territorial jurisdiction of the County Courts is extended very widely indeed by subsection (8) of section 66 to include " an act done on a ship, aircraft or hovercraft outside its district, including such an act done **outside Great Britain** ".

Whatever the legislators intended, this extension of the territorial jurisdiction of the County Court is not limited to British ships, nor to United Kingdom territorial waters, and must be by far the widest territorial jurisdiction the United Kingdom has ever claimed for any county court!

A comment which may be useful to a person wishing to sue a Government department or body for discrimination (for, as has been observed, section 85 applies the Act to the Crown) is that the Treasury publishes a list of Government Departments which can be sued in their own name, or in the name of another Department. If a Department or body is not on this list, proceedings should be commenced against the Attorney-General and served upon the Treasury Solicitor.

QUESTIONNAIRES FOR USE PRIOR TO PROCEEDINGS

It should, perhaps, be mentioned at this juncture that the Act specifically authorises the Secretary of State by order to prescribe:

(*a*) forms by which the person aggrieved may question the respondent on his reasons for doing any relevant act, or on any other matter which is or may be relevant;

(*b*) forms by which the respondent may if he so wishes reply to any questions,

by subsection (1) of section 74. The purpose of such forms is described by the same subsection as being:

With a view to helping a person (" the person aggrieved ") who considers he may have been discriminated against in contravention of this Act to decide whether to institute proceedings and, if he does so, to formulate and present his case in the most effective manner.

What is far more important is subsection (2), which provides:

(2) Where the person aggrieved questions the respondent (whether in accordance with an order under subsection (1) or not)—

(*a*) the question and any reply by the respondent subject to the following provisions of this section shall be admissible as evidence in the proceedings;

(*b*) if it appears to the court or tribunal that the respondent deliberately and without reasonable excuse omitted to reply within a reasonable period or that his reply is evasive or equivocal, the court or tribunal may draw any inference from that fact that it considers it just and equitable to draw, including an inference that he committed an unlawful act.

Paragraph (*a*) does not enlarge the law at all, as the county courts have always had ample provision for communications between the parties to be admissible in evidence, but paragraph (*b*) certainly does extend the existing law. Prior to the passing of the Act, it would have been impossible for any reasonable and rational court or industrial tribunal to draw, merely from the respondent's failure to reply to questions or his equivocal or evasive reply, the inference that he had committed an unlawful act.

Subsection (3) of section 74 adds:

(3) The Secretary of State may by order—

(*a*) prescribe the period within which questions must be duly served in order to be admissible under subsection (2) (*a*), and

(*b*) prescribe the manner in which a question, and any reply by the respondent, may be duly served.

and subsection (4) continues:

(4) Rules may enable the court entertaining a claim under section 66 to determine, before the date fixed for the hearing of the claim, whether a question or reply is admissible under this section or not.

NON-DISCRIMINATION NOTICES

The position with regard to non-discrimination notices, etc., against the persons and bodies to whom sections 29 and 30 apply is identical with the position with regard to such measures against employers, but what was said upon those matters in Chapter 4 is reproduced here for the convenience of those who are primarily interested in this Chapter.

At this point, it becomes necessary to explain the procedure for a non-discrimination notice, especially since the issue of such notices (which, in practice, establish without a judicial inquiry that a breach of the Act has taken place) by any body other than a local authority or government department, is somewhat of an innovation in English law.

Power of Commission to serve Notices

By subsection (2) of section 67, the Commission can **only** serve a non-discrimination notice in the course of a formal investigation. The procedure for a formal investigation is set out at greater length in Chapter 14, but it would seem that it is not primarily intended to be a mere routine process to be invoked whenever a complaint of unlawful discrimination is received which appears to merit investigation, but a far more substantial inquiry for the purpose of investigating, for example, specific areas of discrimination, certain parts of the country, or even, say, a specific individual or body.

The reasons for this conclusion have been set down in earlier chapters on sanctions.

Whilst it is true that subsection (2) (*b*) of section 59 contemplates a formal investigation for the purpose of establishing whether a person named in the terms of reference has been or is discriminating unlawfully, in view of the formalities attendant upon a formal investigation, it would seem unlikely that such investigations are to be an everyday occurrence.

It follows from what has been said earlier that non-discrimination notices are normally by-products of a substantial inquiry of a general nature, and not a common-or-garden method of enforcing the provisions of the Act. Moreover, the requirements for a non-discrimination notice in subsection (5) of section 67 include prior notice to the person who is to be the object of it, specifying the grounds on which the Commission contemplate serving it, an opportunity for such person to make written or oral representations, and the consideration of such representations.

A non-discrimination notice requires the person served with it not to commit (or omit) certain acts which contravene sections 29, 30 and 31, or one or other of them, to inform the Commission of changes in his arrangements to give effect to that requirement, and to inform other persons concerned of such changes. The latter provisions are contained in subsection (2) of section 67, which is worded thus:

> (2) If in the course of a formal investigation the Commission becomes satisfied that a person is committing, or has committed, any such acts, the Commission may in the prescribed manner serve on him a notice in the prescribed form ("a non-discrimination notice") requiring him—
>
> (*a*) not to commit any such acts, and
>
> (*b*) where compliance with paragraph (*a*) involves changes in any of his practices or other arrangements,
>
> (i) to inform the Commission that he has effected those changes and what the changes are, and
>
> (ii) to take such steps as may reasonably be required by the notice for the purpose of affording that information to other persons concerned.

Subsections (3) and (4) continue:

> (3) A non-discrimination notice may also require the person on whom it is served to furnish the Commission with such other information as may be reasonably required by the notice in order to verify that the notice has been complied with.
>
> (4) The notice may specify the time at which, and the manner and form in which, any information is to be furnished to the Commission, but the time at which any information is to be furnished in compliance with the notice shall not be later than five years after the notice has become final.

In addition to being one of the two grounds on which the Commission can apply to the County Court for an injunction, by the combined effect of subsection (7) of section 67 and subsection (4) of section 59, failure to comply with a requirement

G

in a non-discrimination notice regarding making known changes in practices or other arrangements, once the notice has become final, entitles the Commission to apply to the County Court for an order to enforce compliance with that requirement. Even if the Commission has " reasonable cause to believe " that the party served with the notice intends not to comply with part of it, they may apply for such an order.

Failure " without reasonable excuse " to comply with the County Court order renders the party served with the non-discrimination notice liable to a fine in a sum not exceeding £10. What is far more important is that it gives the Commission the right to apply to Court for an injunction, as explained in the next few pages.

Appeals against non-discrimination notices

In view of the contents of the last paragraph, it may be some comfort to know that any person or body can appeal to a County Court against **any** requirement of a non-discrimination notice which has been served upon them under subsection (1) of section 68, providing it does so within six weeks of being served with the notice.

If, on hearing such an appeal, the court considers the requirement appealed against to be unreasonable, whether because it is based on an incorrect finding of fact, or for any other reason, it must quash the requirement. In most legal processes to " quash " means to annul or extinguish, but the word is given a new dimension by the Act, which permits the court, under subsection (3) of section 68, to insert some **other** requirement in the notice in place of the requirement quashed. In effect, therefore, the court can **amend** the requirement in any way it pleases.

Indeed, the County Court is completely unfettered. The words in subsection (2) of section 68 " because it is based on an incorrect finding of fact or for **any** other reason " mean that the Court can approach the matter afresh and reject the requirement for any reason, even a reason unconnected with the issue of the non-discrimination notice and the circumstances preceding the issue; whilst there is equally no restriction upon the nature of the requirement which the Court may impose in place of one quashed, and it is quite possible for it to have nothing whatever to do with the original requirement and still be within the authority given to the Court by subsection (3) of section 68.

Clearly, in view of the very serious potential situation which a non-discrimination notice produces, any person or body which receives such a notice should appeal against it, if at all possible. By subsection (4) of section 68, a requirement inserted in a non-discrimination notice by a County Court in place of one quashed cannot, in turn, be the subject of an appeal to the Court, although it could, of course, be the subject of an appeal to the Court of Appeal.

INJUNCTIONS

The fact that section 85 provides that the Act applies to the Crown (that is to say, to all Government departments and bodies) has already been noticed. The **enforcement** provisions are, however, subject to the Crown Proceedings Act 1947, and therefore, since the latter Act specifically does not extend the remedy of an injunction to the Crown, no injunction can be obtained against the Crown under the Sex Discrimination Act.

Clearly, the Equal Opportunities Commission, which is established by the Act, is specifically empowered, under section 71, to apply to the County Court for an injunction in certain circumstances (or, in those circumstances, to take the equivalent action in Scotland).

The point has already been made that the Act leaves the question of whether the Court can grant an injunction to an individual in proceedings under section 66 in some doubt. The difficulty arises in the following manner:

A **temporary** injunction will normally be granted by the High Court or a county court whenever necessary in proceedings in tort, to prevent any irremediable damage occurring pending the trial of the action. A **permanent** injunction is a remedy which is available instead of damages, and only in cases in which damages, of whatever amount, will not adequately compensate the person who has suffered from the wrong. It is certainly possible to imagine instances of discrimination in some cases when an award of a cash sum by way of damages would not compensate the person who had suffered the discrimination.

The difficulty arises because subsection (1) of section 62 decrees that contraventions of the Act " shall incur as such **no sanction . . . except to the extent . . . expressly provided by this Act** ". Section 62 (2) states that " sanction " includes the granting of an injunction or declaration, so that an injunction will not be a remedy **unless** there is express provision. The question which then arises is whether the words of section 66 (1), that acts of discrimination " may be made the subject of civil proceedings in like manner as any other claim in tort " is a sufficient specific provision, as described above, to add injunctions to the armoury of sanctions provided by the Act.

In this connection, it is noteworthy that subsection (2) of section 66 reads as follows:

> (2) Proceedings under subsection (1)—
>
> (*a*) shall be brought in England and Wales only in a county court, and
>
> (*b*) shall be brought in Scotland only in a sheriff court,
>
> but all such remedies shall be obtainable in such proceedings as, apart from this subsection, would be obtainable in the High Court or the Court of Session, as the case may be.

It is certainly arguable that an injunction *is* a remedy which " apart from this subsection would be obtainable in the High Court " but this is another aspect of the Act which will be shrouded in doubt until dispelled by a Court decision.

Any individual who is suffering unlawful discrimination in the provision of goods, facilities or services, or accommodation and is minded to apply for an injunction. should be warned that injunctions are not granted lightly, since they are considered to interfere with the freedom of the citizen (using the word here to encompass all firms and other bodies). The injustice suffered by the individual will have to be substantial, not trivial, it must be incapable of being adequately compensated by such a sum of money as the Court would award, and the ' balance of convenience ' must lie with making the injunction, as opposed to leaving things as they are.

Any individual proposing to apply to the County Court for an injunction must also remember that the Court would probably apply, by analogy, the time limit within which an application must be made to an industrial tribunal or county court by virtue of subsection (2) of section 76, namely, six months and that, under the equitable doctrine known as " laches " (the Court will not aid an injured party who sleeps on his rights) the time limit could be even shorter.

Injunction Applications by the Commission

As indicated above, the Equal Opportunities Commission is empowered, by section 71, to apply to the county courts in two cases, namely, either where they have served the person or body concerned with a non-discrimination notice, or where a court or tribunal has made a finding that the person or body has committed an act of unlawful discrimination or has contravened the Equal Pay Act.

It is particularly important to notice the last few words of the last paragraph, since the " persistent discrimination " (as it is termed by the Act) to which section 71 relates need not take place in only one area covered by the Act, and a finding that, say, the proprietor of a wine bar had contravened the Equal Pay Act in respect of an **employee,** coupled with a non-discrimination notice relating to his refusal to admit women to the bar unless accompanied by a male, would be quite sufficient to found an application for an injunction.

In each case, the Commission may apply for an injunction (the wording is permissive and places no obligation on the Commission to do so) if they believe that, unless restrained, the person or body concerned is likely to commit another unlawful discriminatory act or a breach of the Equal Pay Act.

The application by the Commission must be made within five years of the finding by the Court against the person or body concerned, or if it is based upon service of a non-discrimination notice, of the notice becoming " final ". Subsection (4) of section 82 defines " final ", in this context, as being when the time for appeal against the finding of the Court, or against the non-discrimination notice, has expired without an appeal being lodged or, if an appeal is lodged, when that appeal is dismissed, withdrawn or abandoned.

It is worth noting that subsection (2) of section 71 and subsection (5) of section 72 prohibit the Commission from **alleging**, when applying to the County Court for an injunction, that the person or body against whom the injunction is sought has (to quote the subsection) " done an act which is within the jurisdiction of an industrial tribunal ", unless a finding by an industrial tribunal that they have done that act has become final. This may inhibit the Commission in attempting to prove that the person or body concerned is **likely** to contravene one or other of these Acts unless restrained, as is required by section 71; in other words, it may be necessary to have two or more adverse findings by industrial tribunals or county courts against a person which have become final, before an injunction can be obtained under section 71.

The somewhat inelegant phrase " done an act which is within the jurisdiction of an industrial tribunal " is explained by section 73. If the references to other parts of the Act, and to section 2 of the Equal Pay Act, are followed through, the act is seen to be either—

(*a*) an act of discrimination which is unlawful by virtue of Part II of the Sex Discrimination Act (*i.e.* the unlawful acts described in Chapters 1, 2, 5 and 6)

or

(*b*) an act of discrimination which is unlawful by virtue of sections 38, 39 or 40 (*i.e.* a discriminatory advertisement, an instruction to another person to discriminate, or an inducement to, or pressure upon, another person to discriminate)

or

(*c*) an act contravening a term which is deemed to be included in an employee's contract, or a term in such a contract which is deemed to be modified, by an " equality clause " under the Equal Pay Act.

CERTIORARI, MANDAMUS AND PROHIBITION

A short explanation of these exotically-named High Court orders is necessary, since they are, in fact, forms of appeal from inferior courts, tribunals and public bodies.

The ramifications and limitations of these procedures are far too extensive and complex to be dealt with in a book such as this, and the present exposition is inadequate to the point of being misleading in many respects, but it will, it is hoped, be sufficient to indicate where such appeal procedures may be relevant to the matters covered by the Act, and where they are inappropriate.

Certiorari is a High Court order which quashes (and here the word **really** means annuls) the proceedings of an inferior court or body having the legal right to determine questions affecting the right of subjects. It is therefore suitable as a method of appeal from some of the bodies to whom sections 29 and 30 apply, if it is desired to completely extinguish any decisions made by them. However, the order will not be made by the High Court for the purpose of quashing proceedings in an area of jurisdiction which it does not itself possess, and therefore certiorari would not be a suitable method of appeal from decisions of the county courts and industrial tribunals made under the powers conferred solely upon them by this Act.

Mandamus is an order made by the High Court, directing an inferior court, tribunal or public body to do something which is in the nature of a public duty and appertains to their office. In general, it is used to enforce statutory rights and duties, to require public officials and public bodies to carry out their duties, and to command inferior tribunals to exercise their jurisdiction. It cannot be used if the official or body has a discretion in the matter, as opposed to a strict obligation or duty. Hence, it could be used both against some of the bodies to whom sections 29 and 30 apply and against county courts and industrial tribunals in the event of the latter refusing to exercise a non-discretionary power conferred upon them by this Act.

An order of prohibition by the High Court is the opposite of an order of mandamus and, as the name suggests, forbids an inferior court or tribunal to continue proceedings if it is attempting to exceed its jurisdiction. In view of the complexity of this Act, that is a situation which could well arise.

CHAPTER 13

DISCRIMINATION IN ADVERTISEMENTS

The restrictions imposed by the Act on advertisements are in extraordinarily wide terms, terms of a kind which are usually only found in anti-avoidance provisions in taxing statutes. The fact that the wording used by the section is such as to make it possible for many entirely innocent people to be adjudged to have broken the law is, however, if not entirely excused, at least mitigated by two factors, both of which are to be found in section 72. First, only the Commission can take steps to enforce this extensive prohibition, and, secondly, the only sanctions imposed are a mere decision that the restrictions have been contravened or, if the contravention is repeated, an injunction.

The restrictions are to be found in section 38, and are phrased as follows:

> (1) It is unlawful to publish or cause to be published an advertisement which indicates, or might reasonably be understood as indicating, an intention by a person to do any act which is or might be unlawful by virtue of Part II or III.

It will be seen that the offence created by the section may be committed if the advertisement is such that it " **might reasonably be understood as indicating an intention** " to do an unlawful act. It is immaterial that the advertiser **had no such intention,** that, whatever, his intention, he never **committed** an unlawful act, and even that nobody can be found who **in fact understood** the advertisement as indicating such an intention.

Similarly, the act which the unfortunate advertiser is thus to be suspected of contemplating, whatever his real intention, need not even **be** one which is unlawful under the Act; it is sufficient that it " **might be** " unlawful.

Exceptions

The generality of subsection (1) of section 38 is, to some extent, brought within bounds by subsection (2), which declares roundly:

> (2) Subsection (1) does not apply to an advertisement if the intended act would not in fact be unlawful,

and if, having read these words, the thoughtful reader wonders whether the words " might be " in subsection (1) really have any meaning, she (or he) will not speculate alone.

The intention of subsection (2) is, of course, to make it lawful to advertise something which is specifically excluded from the operation of the Act, a job which can legitimately be restricted to one sex under the exceptions in section 7, for example, or the facilities of a single-sex school. Nevertheless, it applies just as much to anything which, although discriminatory of one sex in preference to the other, or of the single in preference to those locked in holy wedlock, cannot be brought within the four corners of the provisions of the Act, of which many instances will be found in the preceding pages of this book.

FORMS OF ADVERTISING

It was apparent from the debates in Parliament when the Act was passed that section 38 was seen by the Government as an instrument for dealing with advertisements for the recruitment of employees, and subsection (3) (referred to below) is additional evidence of that attitude. Nevertheless, there is nothing whatever in the section to restrict it to such advertisements, and it is equally applicable to advertisements for the sale of goods, and for the supply of services and facilities.

Therefore, an advertisement by, say, a textile shop, in a local newspaper, beginning: " Ladies, hurry along to our summer sale! " must be carefully considered by both the advertiser and the publisher, in case it " might reasonably be understood as indicating an intention " to sell at sale prices to women only. Whilst this particular instance admits, perhaps quite readily, of the conclusion that the advertisement could not **reasonably** be thus understood, other than by a visitor to these shores wholly unconversant with the customs of the country, in other instances the answer may not be nearly so simple.

As with goods, so with facilities. The common type of advertisement by insurance companies, for example, inviting men to make provision for their families lest they are overtaken by disablement, incapacity or death, often accompanied by graphic illustrations with an emphasis upon the suggestion that the man is the breadwinner and sole financial support of any family, may very well be unlawful by this standard. Nor is there an exemption in favour of insurance companies in this respect, for the exceptions contained in section 45 for insurance arrangements is restricted to any difference in the terms offered to men and women as a result of relying upon actuarial or other statistics, and certainly would not entitle an insurance company to offer a particular form of insurance, or type of policy, only to one sex, merely because that sex appeared to form the better market.

This leads naturally to the subject of pictures and illustrations. There is nothing whatsoever in subsection (1) of section 38 to limit its provisions to the **wording** of an advertisement, and if an advertisement is illustrated with a photograph or drawing, the **illustration,** taken together with the words, may convey the impression that the advertiser intends to discriminate far more forcefully than the words taken alone; it may certainly reinforce the impression conveyed by the words, or extend their apparent meaning so that a caption which, standing alone, is innocent, becomes a breach of section 38.

It must also be stressed that section 38 is not limited to advertisements in the press or in periodicals. Advertisements on hoardings and vehicles (even, as with the method used by one astute advertising agency, on the sides of cows in a field), announcements in shop windows, and pamphlets distributed by hand, are all within the orbit of its terms. So also, of course, are advertisements on the radio and television, in films, and by the public address systems used in departmental stores and supermarkets and at outdoor meetings and gatherings. Indeed, the word " advertisement " is defined by the ubiquitous subsection (1) of section 82 as follows:

> " advertisement " includes every form of advertisement, whether to the public or not, and whether in a newspaper or other publication, by television or radio, by display of notices, signs, labels, showcards or goods, by distribution of samples, circulars, catalogues, price lists or other material, by exhibition of pictures, models or films, or in any other way, and references to the publishing of advertisements shall be construed accordingly.

ADVERTISING FOR EMPLOYEES

To return to the far more limited purpose for which the section seems to have been designed, namely, advertisements for employees, subsection (3) of section 38 provides that the mere use of certain words will be unlawful **unless the advertisement contains an indication to the contrary.** The subsection goes much further than the more common statutory provision in such circumstances of raising a presumption of guilt which can be rebutted, as will be seen from the wording:

> (3) For the purposes of subsection (1), use of a job description with a sexual connotation (such as " waiter ", " salesgirl ", " postman " or " stewardess ") **shall** be taken to indicate an intention to discriminate, unless the advertisement contains an indication to the contrary.

Of course, some job-descriptive pronouns have an obvious sexual connotation, like those quoted in the subsection, but others are, in fact, general but have come to be associated in the minds of most people with a particular sex, such as " typist " and " manicurist ", whilst others again, are cunningly contrived in order to convey a single-sex meaning, such as " personal assistant " (or P.A. for short). There is, therefore, a considerable area in which advertisers and publishers will be unable to determine whether the terms of an advertisement contravene section 38, and that area will only gradually be narrowed and defined by decisions upon specific words by county courts and industrial tribunals.

Clearly, the safest course is for every advertisement in which a job-descriptive pronoun is used to include a specific disclaimer, by adding such words as " this advertisement is not restricted to persons of one sex", or " men and women can apply ", or " (either sex) ", following the pronoun.

RELIANCE UPON STATEMENTS OF OTHERS

Publishers, who labour under the disadvantage, in this respect, of being held liable for the sins of others, are afforded a defence by subsection (4) of section 38, which reads as follows:

> (4) The publisher of an advertisement made unlawful by subsection (1) shall not be subject to any liability under that

subsection in respect of the publication of the advertisement if he proves—

(*a*) that the advertisement was published in reliance on a statement made to him by the person who caused it to be published to the effect that, by reason of the operation of subsection (2), the publication would not be unlawful, and

(*b*) that it was reasonable for him to rely on the statement.

Since subsection (2) exempts from the provisions of section 38 any advertisement indicating an intention to do something which is **not** unlawful under the Act (but for the words " might be ", already adverted to, the proposition would be so obvious as not to require stating in a subsection!) the defence contained in subsection (4) only arises if the statement to the publisher is untrue. Subsection (5), therefore, provides that the advertiser who makes such a statement to the publisher " knowingly or recklessly " which is, in a material respect, false or misleading, commits a criminal offence for which he is liable to be fined up to £400 in a magistrates' court.

SANCTIONS

The point has already been made that only the Commission can enforce the provisions of section 38. This is due to the operation of section 72, subsection (1) of which reads as follows:

> (1) Proceedings in respect of a contravention of section 38, 39 or 40 shall be brought only by the Commission in accordance with the following provisions of this section.

This is intended to ensure that individuals will not institute what were described in the House of Commons by the Under-Secretary of State for Employment as " trivial and vexatious cases " which would bring the Act into disrepute. Certainly, having regard to the very wide net spread by this section of the Act, it should bring some reassurance to many advertisers and publishers that they are unlikely to be the subject of proceedings for contraventions of the section which are quite innocent and due to inadvertence or the use of a somewhat unfelicitous phraseology.

Further reassurance is to be obtained from subsection (2) of section 72, which provides—

> The proceedings shall be—
>
> (*a*) an application for a decision whether the alleged contravention occurred, or
>
> (*b*) an application under subsection (4) below,
>
> or both.

Subsection (4) reads:

> (4) If it appears to the Commission—
>
> (*a*) that a person has done an act which by virtue of section 38, 39 or 40 was unlawful, and
>
> (*b*) that unless restrained he is likely to do further acts which by virtue of that section are unlawful,
>
> the Commission may apply to a county court for an injunction, or to a sheriff court for an order, restraining him from doing such acts; and the court, if satisfied that the application is well-founded, may grant the injunction or order in the terms applied for or more limited terms.

Therefore, although an advertisement which comes within the terms of section 38 is unlawful, the worst that can happen to the transgressor is that he (or she, for even transgressors can be women!) will be ordered not to repeat the offence, upon pain of being in contempt of court. Before even that sanction is applied, the Commission will have to convince the Court that the transgressor is **likely** to repeat the offence, if not restrained.

Since subsection (5) of section 72 contains the provision met elsewhere in the Act prohibiting the Commission from alleging, in such proceedings, that the transgressor has " done . . . an act within the jurisdiction of an industrial tribunal " unless a finding to that effect by such a tribunal has become final, it is unlikely that the Commission will seek an injunction unless the party concerned has committed repeated breaches of the Act.

As has been said elsewhere, the somewhat inelegant phrase " an act which is within the jurisdiction of an industrial tribunal " is explained by subsection (4) of section 73. If the references to other parts of the Act, and to section 2 of the Equal Pay Act, are followed through, the act is seen to be:

either—

(*a*) an act of discrimination which is unlawful by virtue of Part II of the Sex Discrimination Act (*i.e.* the unlawful acts described in Chapters 1, 2, 5 and 6), or

(*b*) an act of discrimination which is unlawful by virtue of sections 38, 39 or 40 (*i.e.* a discriminatory advertisement, an instruction to another person to discriminate, or an inducement to or pressure upon another person to discriminate), or

(*c*) an act contravening a term which is deemed to be included in an employee's contract, or a term in such a contract which is deemed to be modified, by an " equality clause " under the Equal Pay Act.

Having said that, the point must again be made that a finding that the same person or body has been held by a court or industrial tribunal to be in breach of some other, quite different, provision of the Act may be used to show the likelihood that the contravention of section 38 will be repeated.

CHAPTER 14

THE EQUAL OPPORTUNITIES COMMISSION

The Equal Opportunities Commission is established by the provisions of section 53 of the Act, and the Third Schedule. It is a corporate body with perpetual succession and its own seal, like, for example, the Church Commissioners. The Commissioners may be either full-time or part-time, they must number at least eight and not more than fifteen, and paragraph 2 of the Third Schedule specifically provides that they are not civil servants.

By subsection (1) of section 53, the Commission is charged with the following tasks:

(*a*) to work towards the elimination of discrimination.

(*b*) to promote equality of opportunity between men and women generally, and

(*c*) to keep under review the working of this Act and the Equal Pay Act 1970 and, when they are so required by the Secretary of State or otherwise think it necessary, draw up and submit to the Secretary of State proposals for amending them.

In addition, by section 54, the Commission may undertake, or assist others to undertake, such research or educational activities as seem to them to be necessary for the tasks quoted above; by section 52 they must keep under review the statutory provisions which require men and women to be treated differently, and submit proposals for amending them when necessary; and, as we have seen already, they can conduct " formal investigations " and have various powers in connection with the enforcement of the Act.

FORMAL INVESTIGATIONS

The power to conduct formal investigations is contained in subsection (1) of section 57, by which " the Commission may, if they think fit, and shall, if required by the Secretary of State, conduct a formal investigation for any purpose connected with the carrying out of those duties ".

Subsection (3) of section 57 provides that " the Commission may nominate one or more Commissioners, either with or without one or more additional Commissioners, to conduct a formal investigation on their behalf, and may delegate any of their functions in relation to the investigation to the persons so nominated ", whilst subsection (2) empowers the Commissioners to appoint one or more individuals as additional Commissioners for the purposes of a formal investigation, either on a full-time or part-time basis, but only with the approval of the Secretary of State.

It appears from this that additional Commissioners, although appointed for the purposes of a formal investigation, cannot conduct such an investigation without a permanent Commissioner, whereas a permanent Commissioner does not need the assistance of additional Commissioners but can conduct such an investigation alone.

Section 58 lays down requirements for terms of reference for a formal investigation and notice of it in the following words:

> (1) The Commission shall not embark on a formal investigation unless the requirements of this section have been complied with.
>
> (2) Terms of reference for the investigation shall be drawn up by the Commission or, if the Commission were required by the Secretary of State to conduct the investigation, by the Secretary of State, after consulting the Commission.
>
> (3) It shall be the duty of the Commission to give general notice of the holding of the investigation unless the terms of reference confine it to activities of persons named in them, but in such a case the Commission shall in the prescribed manner give those persons notice of the holding of the investigation.
>
> (4) The Commission, or, if the Commission were required by the Secretary of State to conduct the investigation, the Secretary of State after consulting the Commission, may from time to time revise the terms of reference; and subsections (1) and (3) shall apply to the revised investigation and terms of reference as they applied to the original.

If, during the course of the formal investigation, or after its conclusion, it seems necessary or expedient to the Commission to do so, in the light of any of their findings, they may:

(*a*) make to any persons, with a view to promoting equality of opportunity between men and women who are affected by any of their activities, recommendations for changes in their policies or procedures, or as to any other matters, or

(*b*) make to the Secretary of State any recommendations, whether for changes in the law or otherwise,

by sub-section (1) of section 60.

By subsection (3) of the same section, whenever the Commission are required by the Secretary of State to conduct a formal investigation, they must deliver a report of their findings to him, and he must publish the report. Conversely, the Commission is forbidden to publish such a report in respect of a formal investigation initiated by the Secretary of State unless he requires them to do so. The Commission is required to publish or make available for inspection a formal report of any formal investigation which they initiate by subsection (4) of section 60.

The sum total of all these provisions is that a formal investigation **really is a formal affair,** and, as has been said before in these pages, is not to be an everyday occurrence. Indeed, it is manifest that the Commission cannot have too many formal investigations on foot at the same time if, as envisaged by subsection (3) of section 57, a Commissioner is to be in charge of each investigation, since the maximum number of Commissioners is fifteen.

OBTAINING INFORMATION IN FORMAL INVESTIGATIONS

The Act sets out a code of practice for the Commission to follow, in order to obtain information during the course of formal investigations, in section 59. Needless to say, the powers contained in section 59 are of great importance to the Commission in its triple functions of enforcing the law, initiating research and education, and proposing law reform, in respect of sex discrimination in all fields.

Subsection (1) of section 59 gives the Commission power " for the purposes of a formal investigation " to serve a notice requiring information, but subsection (2) restricts the power to certain circumstances, namely, where:

(*a*) service of the notice was authorised by an order made by or on behalf of the Secretary of State, or (*b*) the terms of reference of the investigation state that the Commission believe that a person named in them may have done or may be doing acts of all or any of the following descriptions:

(i) unlawful discriminatory acts,

(ii) contraventions of section 37,

(iii) contraventions of sections 38, 39 or 40, and

(iv) acts in breach of a term modified or included by virtue of an equality clause,

and confine the investigation to those acts.

At first sight, it might seem that the Commission would seldom be in the position of investigating an individual, firm or body whose discriminatory practices are so notorious or obvious that they can be named in advance by the Commission in the manner suggested in paragraph (*b*). Doubtless, there will be some such cases, but it will be recalled, also, that subsection (4) of section 58 gives the Commission power to revise from time to time the terms of reference which it has drawn up for a formal investigation, and therefore the Commission can, at any stage of the investigation, add to the terms of reference a statement that they believe that a specified person " may have done or may be doing " acts which contravene the Sex Discrimination Act or the Equal Pay Act, and proceed to serve on that person a notice requiring information.

Moreover, the restrictions do not apply if the Commission is engaged upon a special kind of formal investigation for the purpose of determining whether any requirement of a non-discrimination notice is being or has been carried out, and that purpose is stated in the terms of reference, together with the fact that subsection (2) (*b*) of section 59, quoted above, does not apply. This exception to the rule is contained in section 69.

In such investigations, providing, first, that notice of holding the investigation is given to the persons concerned, in accordance with subsection (3) of section 58, within five years of the non-discrimination notice " becoming final " (a phrase which is defined in the pages dealing with non-discrimination notices which follow) and, secondly, the notice requiring information is served upon the person concerned within two years of the

Commission giving notice of holding the investigation, or five years of the non-discrimination notice becoming final (whichever provides the longer period for the notice requiring information), the Commission do not need the consent of the Secretary of State before serving the notice requiring information.

The notice must be in the form and served in the manner prescribed by the Secretary of State, by subsection (1) of section 59, which continues by providing that the notice:

> (*a*) may require any person to furnish such written information as may be described in the notice, and may specify the time at which, and the manner and form in which, the information is to be furnished;
>
> (*b*) may require any person to attend at such time and place as is specified in the notice and give oral information about, and produce all documents in his possession or control relating to, any matter specified in the notice.

These are sweeping powers indeed, but they are limited to some degree by subsection (3), which directs that:

> (3) A notice under subsection (1) shall not require a person—
>
> (*a*) to give information, or produce any documents, which he could not be compelled to give in evidence, or produce in civil proceedings before the High Court or the Court of Sessions, or
>
> (*b*) to attend at any place unless the necessary expenses of his journey to and from that place are paid or tendered to him.

The section continues with strong provisions for the enforcement of such notices.

First, subsection (4) empowers the Commission to apply to the county court for an order requiring the person served with a notice to comply with it, not merely if the person concerned has failed to comply with it, but even *if they have reasonable cause to believe that he intends not to comply with it.* The subsection extends the penalty provided for neglecting to obey a witness summons contained in section 84 of the County Court Act 1959, namely, the forfeiture of a sum not exceeding £10, to failure **without reasonable excuse** to comply with any order the county court may make on such an application. There are thus two steps to be taken after non-compliance with a notice requiring information before the penalty is imposed, namely, an order by the county court and non-compliance with that order.

Secondly, subsection (6) makes it a criminal offence if a person:

(*a*) wilfully alters, suppresses, conceals or destroys a document which he has been required by a notice or order under this section to produce, or

(*b*) in complying with such a notice or order, knowingly or recklessly makes any statement which is false in a material particular,

for which the offender may be summoned before the magistrates and fined up to £400.

Each magistrates' court exercises jurisdiction over a comparatively small area of the country, and so that there may be no doubt about which court should be used, subsection (7) provides that proceedings for such an offence may be taken:

(*a*) against any person at any place at which he has an office or other place of business;

(*b*) against an individual at any place where he resides, or at which he is for the time being.

NON-DISCLOSURE OF INFORMATION OBTAINED IN FORMAL INVESTIGATIONS

Although it relates to all information obtained by the Commission in connection with a formal investigation, and not merely information obtained by use of the Commission's powers of compulsion just described, this is a suitable point at which to refer to the prohibition on disclosure of information thus obtained by the Commission. This is contained in section 61, in the following terms:

> (1) No information given to the Commission by any person (" the informant ") in connection with a formal investigation shall be disclosed by the Commission, or by any person who is or has been a Commissioner, additional Commissioner or employee, of the Commission, except—
>
> (*a*) on the order of any court, or
>
> (*b*) with the informant's consent, or

(*c*) in the form of a summary or other general statement published by the Commission which does not identify the informant or any other person to whom the information relates, or

(*d*) in a report of the investigation published by the Commission or made available for inspection under section 60 (4), or

(*e*) to Commissioners, additional Commissioners or employees of the Commission, or, so far as may be necessary for the proper performance of the functions of the Commission, to other persons, or

(*f*) for the purpose of any civil proceedings under this Act to which the Commission are a party, or any criminal proceedings.

Paragraph (*d*) would seem to be a substantial loophole in these restrictions, but that, in turn, is restricted by subsection (3) of section 61, which says:

> (3) in preparing any report for publication or for inspection the Commission shall exclude, so far as is consistent with their duties and the object of the report, any matter which relates to the private affairs of any individual or business interests of any person where the publication of that matter might, in the opinion of the Commission, prejudicially affect that individual or person.

It may be argued that this still leaves a very wide discretion with the Commission, and it is eminently possible for an individual, firm or body to suffer grave prejudice by the disclosure in a report of information which the Commission has obtained in the course of a formal investigation. Clearly, Parliament has tried to strike a balance between ensuring individual privacy and enabling the Commission to publish reports in clear and definite terms, which would provide all necessary information and enable the right conclusions to be drawn, both by the public and those in authority. In the event, much will depend upon the discretion of the Commission.

Subsection (2) renders it a criminal offence to disclose information contrary to the provisions of subsection (1), quoted above, which the magistrates may punish by a fine, with the standard limit for this Act of £400.

NON-DISCRIMINATION NOTICES

Another function, or power, of the Commission is the issue and enforcement of non-discrimination notices. The requirements of and procedure in respect of such notices has been discussed in detail in each of the Chapters upon sanctions, and can therefore be treated here in a more summary fashion.

It will be recalled that, by subsection (2) of section 67, non-discrimination notices may only issue if the Commission have become "*satisfied in the course of a formal investigation*" that a person is contravening the provisions of the Act or the Equal Pay Act, and also that the notice can require him to cease certain specified acts and, where necessary, to make changes in his practices or other arrangements and inform all those concerned, including the Commission, that he has done so.

The Act goes on to provide, in section 68, for appeal against such notices, and, in section 70, for the Commission to keep a register of all non-discrimination notices that have "become final". By subsection (4) of section 82, a non-discrimination notice "becomes final" when an appeal against the notice is dismissed, withdrawn or abandoned, or when the time for appealing (six weeks) has expired without an appeal; and for this purpose an appeal is taken to be dismissed if the court or tribunal hearing the appeal amend the notice under the provisions of subsection (3) of section 68.

The full terms of section 70 are as follows:

> (1) The Commission shall establish and maintain a register ("the register") of non-discrimination notices which have become final.
>
> (2) Any person shall be entitled, on payment of such fee (if any) as may be determined by the Commission—
>
> (*a*) to inspect the register during ordinary office hours and take copies of any entry, or
>
> (*b*) to obtain from the Commission a copy, certified by the Commission to be correct, of any entry in the register.
>
> (3) The Commission may, if they think fit, determine that the right conferred by subsection (2) (*a*) shall be exercisable in relation to a copy of the register instead of, or in addition to, the original.

> (4) The Commission shall give general notice of the place or places where, and the times when, the register or a copy of it may be inspected.

As was seen in the pages dealing with the powers of the Commission to obtain information in the course of formal investigations, section 69 envisages a formal investigation with special terms of reference as part of the armoury of enforcement provisions for non-discrimination notices. Subsection (1) of section 69 begins thus:

> (1) If—
>
> (*a*) the terms of reference of a formal investigation state that its purpose is to determine whether any requirements of a non-discrimination notice are being or have been carried out, but section 59 (2) (*b*) does not apply, and
>
> (*b*) Section 58 (3) is complied with in relation to the investigation on a date (" the commencement date ") not later than the expiration of the period of five years beginning when the non-discrimination notice became final . . .

and the section goes on to provide that, subject to certain conditions, the Commission can, for the purposes of the investigation, serve notices requiring information (with all the enforcement powers in relation to such notices contained in section 59) without the necessity for the consent of the Secretary of State required by subsection (2) (*a*) of section 59. It will be recalled that subsection (3) of section 58, referred to in paragraph (*b*), is the subsection that imposes a duty on the Commission to give notice of holding a formal investigation.

The Chapters dealing with sanctions have also described in detail the powers of the Commission to obtain an injunction against a person who has been served with a non-discrimination notice, or who has been adjudged by a court or tribunal to have contravened the Act or the Equal Pay Act. These are contained in section 71, and, as explained in those Chapters, it may be difficult for the Commission to contend that a person, firm or body is likely to contravene one or other of the Acts " if not restrained ", as required by section 71, if a non-discrimination notice or finding by an industrial tribunal which is the first in respect of that person, firm or body is under appeal.

The Commission is, as has been explained already, solely empowered to take proceedings to enforce section 38 (which deals with advertisements indicating an intention to contravene the Act) and sections 39 and 40 (which respectively deal with instructions and inducements to third parties to discriminate). This power is conferred on them by section 72, and is to obtain an order of an industrial tribunal or county court, as the case may be, that the party proceeded against has contravened one of the three sections and, when the Commission believes such a person will contravene the same section if not restrained, an injunction.

The Commission can also, by section 73, make a complaint to an industrial tribunal that a person has contravened sections 39 or 40 of the Act, or sections 6 to 21 (which, broadly, deal with discrimination in employment, against contract workers, by partners, trade unions and professional and employers' organisations against members, by qualifying bodies in awarding qualifications, and by vocational training bodies and employment agencies) sections 41 or 42 (which deal with vicarious liability for agents and employees, and aiding unlawful acts, respectively) or the Equal Pay Act, and obtain a finding against that person. In cases referring to a contravention of sections 6 to 21, such a finding can be coupled with an order declaring the rights of the parties and requiring specific action to be taken by the person concerned.

A complaint under section 73 is specifically envisaged by the section to be a prelude to an application to Court for an injunction under sections 71 (1) or 72 (4); or to an application to an industrial tribunal for a declaratory order or a recommendation that the party concerned take appropriate action under section 65; or under the Equal Pay Act. It will be recalled that an industrial tribunal cannot award compensation to a person who has suffered discrimination if the application to the tribunal is made by the Commission unless, of course, the party to whom a recommendation is made fails to comply with that recommendation without reasonable justification, when a compensation order can be made under subsection (3) (*b*) of section 65.

QUESTIONNAIRES FOR USE PRIOR TO PROCEEDINGS

Although not referring to a function of the Commission, it should, perhaps, be mentioned at this juncture that the Act specifically authorises the Secretary of State by Order to prescribe:

> (*a*) forms by which the person aggrieved may question the respondent on his reasons for doing any relevant act, or on any other matter which is or may be relevant;
>
> (*b*) forms by which the respondent may if he so wishes reply to any such questions,

by subsection (1) of section 74. The purpose of such forms is described by the same subsection as being:

> With a view to helping a person (" the person aggrieved ") who considers he may have been discriminated against in contravention of this Act to decide whether to institute proceedings and, if he does so, to formulate and present his case in the most effective manner.

What is far more important is subsection (2), which provides:

> (2) Where the person aggrieved questions the respondent (whether in accordance with an order under subsection (1) or not)—
>
> (*a*) the question and any reply by the respondent subject to the following provisions of this section shall be admissible as evidence in the proceedings;
>
> (*b*) if it appears to the court or tribunal that the respondent deliberately and without reasonable excuse omitted to reply within a reasonable period or that his reply is evasive or equivocal, the court or tribunal may draw any inference from that fact that it considers it just and equitable to draw, including an inference that he committed an unlawful act.

Paragraph (*a*) does not enlarge the law at all, as the county courts have always had ample provision for communications between the parties to be admissible in evidence, but paragraph (*b*) certainly does extend the existing law. Prior to the passing of the Act, it would have been impossible for any reasonable and rational court or industrial tribunal to draw, merely from the respondent's failure to reply to questions or his equivocal or evasive reply, the inference that he had committed an unlawful act.

Subsection (3) of section 74 adds:

> (3) The Secretary of State may by order—
>
> (*a*) prescribe the period within which questions must be duly served in order to be admissible under subsection (2) (*a*), and
>
> (*b*) prescribe the manner in which a question, and any reply by the respondent, may be duly served.

and subsection (4) continues:

> (4) Rules may enable the court entertaining a claim under section 66 to determine, before the date fixed for the hearing of the claim, whether a question or reply is admissible under this section or not.

ASSISTANCE BY COMMISSION IN RELATION TO PROCEEDINGS

By the next section, section 75, the Commission is authorised to assist an individual who " is an actual or prospective complainant or claimant " if they consider:

> (*a*) the case raises a question of principle, or
>
> (*b*) it is unreasonable, having regard to the complexity of the case or the applicant's position in relation to the respondent or another person involved or any other matter, to expect the applicant to deal with the case unaided,

or if they think fit to do so " by reason of any other special consideration ". The individual need not have actually commenced proceedings, but he must apply to the Commission for assistance—they cannot grant it of their own volition.

The assistance which the Commission may give, by subsection (2), includes:

> (*a*) giving advice;
>
> (*b*) procuring or attempting to procure the settlement of any matter in dispute;
>
> (*c*) arranging for the giving of advice or assistance by a solicitor or counsel;
>
> (*d*) arranging for representation by any person including all such assistance as is usually given by a solicitor or counsel in the steps preliminary or incidental to any

proceedings, or in arriving at or giving effect to a compromise to avoid or bring to an end any proceedings,

but paragraph (d) shall not affect the law and practice regulating the descriptions of persons who may appear in, conduct, defend and address the Court in, any proceedings.

Subsection (3) of section 75 then gives the Commission a first charge on any costs ordered to be paid to the complainant or claimant, or any " rights under any compromise or settlement " to the extent necessary to enable the Commission to recoup any expenses they incur in giving that person the assistance specified in this section, in the same way that the Law Society has a first charge for the same purpose under the Legal Aid Act 1974.

This description of the composition, functions and powers of the Equal Opportunities Commission would not be complete without some reference to the annual report upon their activities which the Commission is required to make by section 56. By subsection (2) of that section, each annual report must include a general survey of developments in respect of matters falling within the scope of the Commission's duties during the period to which it relates. By subsection (1) the report must be made to the Secretary of State as soon as possible after the end of each calendar year, and by subsection (3) he must cause it to be published. This should provide excellent evidence, not only of the manner and extent to which the Commission is carrying out its functions, but also of whether the Act is fulfilling its purpose and living up to the hopes and intentions of all those who laboured so hard and so long, in one way or another, to bring it into existence.

SEX DISCRIMINATION ACT 1975

ARRANGEMENT OF SECTIONS

Part I

Discrimination to Which Act applies

Section
1. Sex discrimination against women.
2. Sex discrimination against men.
3. Discrimination against married persons in employment field.
4. Discrimination by way of victimisation.
5. Interpretation.

Part II

Discrimination in the Employment Field

Discrimination by employers

6. Discrimination against applicants and employees.
7. Exception where sex is a genuine occupational qualification.
8. Equal Pay Act 1970.
9. Discrimination against contract workers.
10. Meaning of employment at establishment in Great Britain.

Discrimination by other bodies

11. Partnerships.
12. Trade unions etc.
13. Qualifying bodies.
14. Vocational training bodies.
15. Employment agencies.
16. Manpower Service Commission etc.

Special cases

17. Police.
18. Prison officers.
19. Ministers of religion etc.
20. Midwives.
21. Mineworkers.

PART III

DISCRIMINATION IN OTHER FIELDS

Education

Section

22. Discrimination by bodies in charge of educational establishments.
23. Other discrimination by local education authorities.
24. Designated establishments.
25. General duty in public sector of education.
26. Exception for single-sex establishments.
27. Exception for single-sex establishments turning co-educational.
28. Exception for physical training.

Goods, facilities, services and premises

29. Discrimination in provision of goods, facilities or services.
30. Discrimination in disposal or management of premises.
31. Discrimination: consent for assignment or subletting.
32. Exception for small dwellings.
33. Exception for political parties.
34. Exception for voluntary bodies.
35. Further exceptions from ss. 29(1) and 30.

Extent

36. Extent of Part III.

PART IV

OTHER UNLAWFUL ACTS

37. Discriminatory practices.
38. Discriminatory advertisements.
39. Instructions to discriminate.
40. Pressure to discriminate.
41. Liability of employers and principals.
42. Aiding unlawful acts.

PART V

GENERAL EXCEPTIONS FROM PARTS II TO IV

43. Charities.
44. Sport etc.
45. Insurance etc.
46. Communal accommodation.
47. Discriminatory training by certain bodies.
48. Other discriminatory training etc.
49. Trade unions etc.: elective bodies.

Section
50. Indirect access to benefits etc.
51. Acts done under statutory authority.
52. Acts safeguarding national security.

PART VI

EQUAL OPPORTUNITIES COMMISSION

General

53. Establishment and duties of Commission.
54. Research and education.
55. Review of discriminatory provisions in health and safety legislation.
56. Annual reports.

Investigations

57. Power to conduct formal investigations.
58. Terms of reference.
59. Power to obtain information.
60. Recommendations and reports on formal investigations.
61. Restriction on disclosure of information.

PART VII

ENFORCEMENT

General

62. No further sanctions for breach of Act.

Enforcement in employment field

63. Jurisdiction of industrial tribunals.
64. Conciliation in employment cases.
65. Remedies on complaint under section 63.

Enforcement of Part III

66. Claims under Part III.

Non-discrimination notices

67. Issue of non-discrimination notice.
68. Appeal against non-discrimination notice.
69. Investigation as to compliance with non-discrimination notice.
70. Register of non-discrimination notices.

Other enforcement by Commission

71. Persistent discrimination.
72. Enforcement of ss. 38 to 40.
73. Preliminary action in employment cases.

Help for persons suffering discrimination

Section

74. Help for aggrieved persons in obtaining information etc.
75. Assistance by Commission.

Period within which proceedings to be brought

76. Period within which proceedings to be brought.

PART VIII

SUPPLEMENTAL

77. Validity and revision of contracts.
78. Educational charities in England and Wales.
79. Educational endowments, etc. to which Part VI of the Education (Scotland) Act 1962 applies.
80. Power to amend certain provisions of Act.
81. Orders.
82. General interpretation provisions.
83. Transitional and commencement provisions, amendments and repeals.
84. Financial provisions.
85. Application to Crown.
86. Government appointments outside section 6.
87. Short title and extent.

SCHEDULES:

Schedule 1—Equal Pay Act 1970.
Schedule 2—Transitional exemption orders for educational admissions.
Schedule 3—Equal Opportunities Commission.
Schedule 4—Transitional provisions.
Schedule 5—Minor and consequential amendments.
Schedule 6—Further repeals.

SEX DISCRIMINATION ACT 1975

An Act to render unlawful certain kinds of sex discrimination and discrimination on the ground of marriage, and establish a Commission with the function of working towards the elimination of such discrimination and promoting equality of opportunity between men and women generally; and for related purposes. [12th November 1975]

BE IT ENACTED by the Queen's most Excellent Majesty, by and with the advice and consent of the Lords Spiritual and Temporal, and Commons, in this present Parliament assembled, and by the authority of the same, as follows:—

PART I

DISCRIMINATION TO WHICH ACT APPLIES

Sex discrimination against women.

1.—(1) A person discriminates against a woman in any circumstances relevant for the purposes of any provision of this Act if—

(*a*) on the ground of her sex he treats her less favourably than he treats or would treat a man, or

(*b*) he applies to her a requirement or condition which he applies or would apply equally to a man but—

(i) which is such that the proportion of women who can comply with it is considerably smaller than the proportion of men who can comply with it, and

(ii) which he cannot show to be justifiable irrespective of the sex of the person to whom it is applied, and

(iii) which is to her detriment because she cannot comply with it.

(2) If a person treats or would treat a man differently according to the man's marital status, his treatment of a woman is for the purposes of subsection (1) (*a*) to be compared to his treatment of a man having the like marital status.

Sex discrimination against men.

2.—(1) Section 1, and the provisions of Parts II and III relating to sex discrimination against women, are to be read as applying equally to the treatment of men, and for that purpose shall have effect with such modifications as are requisite.

(2) In the application of subsection (1) no account shall be taken of special treatment afforded to women in connection with pregnancy or childbirth.

Discrimination against married persons in employment field.

3.—(1) A person discriminates against a married person of either sex in any circumstances relevant for the purposes of any provision of Part II if—

(*a*) on the ground of his or her marital status he treats that person less favourably than he treats or would treat an unmarried person of the same sex, or

(*b*) he applies to that person a requirement or condition which he applies or would apply equally to an unmarried person but—

(i) which is such that the proportion of married persons who can comply with it is considerably smaller than the proportion of unmarried persons of the same sex who can comply with it, and

(ii) which he cannot show to be justifiable irrespective of the marital status of the person to whom it is applied, and

(iii) which is to that person's detriment because he cannot comply with it.

(2) For the purposes of subsection (1), a provision of Part II framed with reference to discrimination against women shall be treated as applying equally to the treatment of men, and for that purpose shall have effect with such modifications as are requisite.

Discrimination by way of victimisation.

4.—(1) A person (" the discriminator ") discriminates against another person (" the person victimised ") in any circumstances relevant for the purposes of any provision of this Act if he treats the person victimised less favourably than in those circumstances he treats or would treat other persons, and does so by reason that the person victimised has—

(*a*) brought proceedings against the discriminator or any other person under this Act or the Equal Pay Act 1970, or

(*b*) given evidence or information in connection with proceedings brought by any person against the discriminator or any other person under this Act or the Equal Pay Act 1970, or

(*c*) otherwise done anything under or by reference to this Act or the Equal Pay Act 1970 in relation to the discriminator or any other person, or

(*d*) alleged that the discriminator or any other person has committed an act which (whether or not the allegation so states) would amount to a contravention of this Act or give rise to a claim under the Equal Pay Act 1970, or by reason that the discriminator knows the person victimised intends to do any of those things, or suspects the person victimised has done, or intends to do, any of them.

(2) Subsection (1) does not apply to treatment of a person by reason of any allegation made by him if the allegation was false and not made in good faith.

(3) For the purposes of subsection (1), a provision of Part II or III framed with reference to discrimination against women shall be treated as applying equally to the treatment of men and for that purpose shall have effect with such modifications as are requisite.

Interpretation.

5.—(1) In this Act—

(*a*) references to discrimination refer to any discrimination falling within sections 1 to 4; and

(*b*) references to sex discrimination refer to any discrimination falling within section 1 or 2,

and related expressions shall be construed accordingly.

(2) In this Act—

" woman " includes a female of any age, and

" man " includes a male of any age.

(3) A comparison of the cases of persons of different sex or marital status under section 1(1) or 3(1) must be such that the relevant circumstances in the one case are the same, or not materially different, in the other.

Part II

Discrimination in the Employment Field

Discrimination by employers

Discrimination against applicants and employees.

6.—(1) It is unlawful for a person, in relation to employment by him at an establishment in Great Britain, to discriminate against a woman—

(*a*) in the arrangements he makes for the purpose of determining who should be offered that employment, or

(*b*) in the terms on which he offers her that employment, or

(*c*) by refusing or deliberately omitting to offer her that employment.

(2) It is unlawful for a person, in the case of a woman employed by him at an establishment in Great Britain, to discriminate against her—

(*a*) in the way he affords her access to opportunities for promotion, transfer or training, or to any other benefits, facilties or services, or by refusing or deliberately omitting to afford her access to them, or

(*b*) by dismissing her, or subjecting her to any other detriment.

(3) Except in relation to discrimination falling within section 4, subsections (1) and (2) do not apply to employment—

(*a*) for the purposes of a private household, or

(*b*) where the number of persons employed by the employer, added to the number employed by any associated employers of his, does not exceed five (disregarding any persons employed for the purposes of a private household).

(4) Subsections (1)(*b*) and (2) do not apply to provision in relation to death or retirement.

(5) Subject to section 8(3), subsection (1)(*b*) does not apply to any provision for the payment of money which, if the woman in question were given the employment, would be included (directly or by reference to a collective agreement or otherwise) in the contract under which she was employed.

(6) Subsection (2) does not apply to benefits consisting of the payment of money when the provision of those benefits is regulated by the woman's contract of employment.

(7) Subsection (2) does not apply to benefits, facilities or services of any description if the employer is concerned with the provision (for payment or not) of benefits, facilities or services of that description to the public, or to a section of the public comprising the woman in question, unless—

(*a*) that provision differs in a material respect from the provision of the benefits, facilities or services by the employer to his employees, or

(*b*) the provision of the benefits, facilities or services to the woman in question is regulated by her contract of employment, or

(*c*) the benefits, facilities or services relate to training.

Exception where sex is a genuine occupational qualification.

7.—(1) In relation to sex discrimination—

(*a*) section 6(1)(*a*) or (*c*) does not apply to any employment where being a man is a genuine occupational qualification for the job, and

(*b*) section 6(2)(*a*) does not apply to opportunities for promotion or transfer to, or training for, such employment.

(2) Being a man is a genuine occupational qualification for a job only where—

(*a*) the essential nature of the job calls for a man for reasons of physiology (excluding physical strength or stamina) or, in dramatic performances or other entertainment, for reasons of authenticity, so that the essential nature of the job would be materially different if carried out by a woman; or

(*b*) the job needs to be held by a man to preserve decency or privcay because—

(i) it is likely to involve physical contact with men in circumstances where they might reasonably object to its being carried out by a woman, or

(ii) the holder of the job is likely to do his work in circumstances where men might reasonably object to the presence of a woman because they are in a state of undress or are using sanitary facilities; or

(*c*) the nature or location of the establishment makes it impracticable for the holder of the job to live elsewhere than in premises provided by the employer, and—

(i) the only such premises which are available for persons holding that kind of job are lived in, or normally lived in, by men and are not equipped with separate sleeping accommodation for women and sanitary facilities which could be used by women in privacy from men, and

(ii) it is not reasonable to expect the employer either to equip those premises with such accommodation and facilities or to provide other premises for women; or

(*d*) the nature of the establishment, or of the part of it within which the work is done, requires the job to be held by a man because—

(i) it is, or is part of, a hospital, prison or other establishment for persons requiring special care, supervision or attention, and

(ii) those persons are all men (disregarding any woman whose presence is exceptional), and

(iii) it is reasonable, having regard to the essential character of the establishment or that part, that the job should not be held by a woman; or

(*e*) the holder of the job provides individuals with personal services promoting their welfare or education, or similar personal services, and those services can most effectively be provided by a man, or

(*f*) the job needs be held by a man because of restrictions imposed by the laws regulating the employment of women, or

(*g*) the job needs to be held by a man because it is likely to involve the performance of duties outside the United Kingdom in a country whose laws or customs are such that the duties could not, or could not effectively, be performed by a woman, or

(*h*) the job is one of two to be held by a married couple.

(3) Subsection (2) applies where some only of the duties of the job fall within paragraphs (*a*) to (*g*) as well as where all of them do.

(4) Paragraph (*a*), (*b*), (*c*), (*d*), (*e*), (*f*) or (*g*) of subsection (2) does not apply in relation to the filling of a vacancy at a time when the employer already has male employees—

(*a*) who are capable of carrying out the duties falling within that paragraph, and

(*b*) whom it would be reasonable to employ on those duties, and

(*c*) whose numbers are sufficient to meet the employer's likely requirements in respect of those duties without undue inconvenience.

Equal Pay Act 1970.

8.—(1) In section 1 of the Equal Pay Act 1970, the following are substituted for subsections (1) to (3)—

" (1) If the terms of a contract under which a woman is employed at an establishment in Great Britain do not include (directly or by reference to a collective agreement or otherwise) an equality clause they shall be deemed to include one.

(2) An equality clause is a provision which relates to terms (whether concerned with pay or not) of a contract under which a woman is employed (the " woman's contract "), and has the effect that—

(*a*) where the woman is employed on like work with a man in the same employment—

(i) if (apart from the equality clause) any term of the woman's contract is or becomes less favourable to the woman than a term of a similar kind in the contract under which that man is employed, that term of the woman's contract shall be treated as so modified as not to be less favourable, and

(ii) if (apart from the equality clause) at any time the woman's contract does not include a term corresponding to a term benefiting that man included in the contract under which he is employed, the woman's contract shall be treated as including such a term;

(*b*) where the woman is employed on work rated as equivalent with that of a man in the same employment—

(i) if (apart from the equality clause) any term of the woman's contract determined by the rating of the work is or becomes less favourable to the woman than a term of a similar kind in the contract under which that man is employed, that term of the woman's contract shall be treated as so modified as not to be less favourable, and

(ii) if (apart from the equality clause) at any time the woman's contract does not include a term corresponding to a term benefiting that man included in the contract under which he is employed and determined by the rating of the work, the woman's contract shall be treated as including such a term.

(3) An equality clause shall not operate in relation to a variation between the woman's contract and the man's contract if the employer proves that the variation is genuinely due to a material difference (other than the difference of sex) between her case and his."

(2) Section 1(1) of the Equal Pay Act 1970 (as set out in subsection (1) above) does not apply in determining for the purposes of section 6(1)(*b*) of this Act the terms on which employment is offered.

(3) Where a person offers a woman employment on certain terms, and if she accepted the offer then, by virtue of an equality clause, any of those terms would fall to be modified, or any additional term would fall to be included, the offer shall be taken to contravene section 6(1)(*b*).

(4) Where a person offers a woman employment on certain terms, and subsection (3) would apply but for the fact that, on her acceptance of the offer, section 1(3) of the Equal Pay Act 1970 (as set out in subsection (1) above) would prevent the equality clause from operating, the offer shall be taken not to contravene section 6(1)(*b*).

(5) An act does not contravene section 6(2) if—

(*a*) it contravenes a term modified or included by virtue of an equality clause, or

(*b*) it would contravene such a term but for the fact that the equality clause is prevented from operating by section 1(3) of the Equal Pay Act 1970.

(6) The Equal Pay Act 1970 is further amended as specified in Part I of Schedule 1, and accordingly has effect as set out in Part II of Schedule 1.

Discrimination against contract workers.

9.—(1) This section applies to any work for a person (" the principal ") which is available for doing by individuals (" contract workers ") who are employed not by the principal himself but by another person, who supplies them under a contract made with the principal.

(2) It is unlawful for the principal, in relation to work to which this section applies, to discriminate against a woman who is a contract worker—

(*a*) in the terms on which he allows her to do that work, or

(*b*) by not allowing her to do it or continue to do it, or

(*c*) in the way he affords her access to any benefits, facilities or services or by refusing or deliberately omitting to afford her access to them, or

(*d*) by subjecting her to any other detriment.

(3) The principal does not contravene subsection (2)(*b*) by doing any act in relation to a woman at a time when if the work were to be done by a person taken into his employment being a man would be a genuine occupational qualification for the job.

(4) Subsection (2) (*c*) does not apply to benefits, facilities or services of any description if the principal is concerned with the provision (for payment or not) of benefits, facilities or services of that description to the public, or to a section of the public to which the woman belongs, unless that provision differs in a material respect from the provision of the benefits, facilities or services by the principal to his contract workers.

Meaning of employment at establishment in Great Britain.

10.—(1) For the purposes of this Part and section 1 of the Equal Pay Act 1970 (" the relevant purposes "), employment is to be regarded as being at an establishment in Great Britain unless the employee does his work wholly or mainly outside Great Britain.

(2) Subsection (1) does not apply to—

(*a*) employment on board a ship registered at a port of registry in Great Britain, or

(*b*) employment on aircraft or hovercraft registered in the United Kingdom and operated by a person who has his principal place of business, or is ordinarily resident, in Great Britain;

but for the relevant purposes such employment is to be regarded as being at an establishment in Great Britain unless the employee does his work wholly outside Great Britain.

(3) In the case of employment on board a ship registered at a port of registry in Great Britain (except where the employee does his work wholly outside Great Britain, and outside any area added under subsection (5)) the ship shall for the relevant purposes be deemed to be the establishment.

(4) Where work is not done at an establishment it shall be treated for the relevant purposes as done at the establishment from which it is done or (where it is not done from any establishment) at the establishment with which it has the closest connection.

(5) In relation to employment concerned with exploration of the sea bed or subsoil or the exploitation of their natural resources, Her Majesty may by Order in Council provide that subsections (1) and (2) shall each have effect as if the last reference to Great Britain included any area for the time being designated under section 1(7) of the Continental Shelf Act 1964, except an area or part of an area in which the law of Northern Ireland applies.

(6) An Order in Council under subsection (5) may provide that, in relation to employment to which the Order applies, this Part and section 1 of the Equal Pay Act 1970 are to have effect with such modifications as are specified in the Order.

(7) An Order in Council under subsection (5) shall be of no effect unless a draft of the Order was laid before and approved by each House of Parliament.

Discrimination by other bodies

Partnerships.

11.—(1) It is unlawful for a firm consisting of six or more partners, in relation to a position as partner in the firm, to discriminate against a woman—

(*a*) in the arrangements they make for the purpose of determining who should be offered that position, or
(*b*) in the terms on which they offer her that position, or
(*c*) by refusing or deliberately omitting to offer her that position, or
(*d*) in a case where the woman already holds that position—
(i) in the way they afford her access to any benefits, facilities or services, or by refusing or deliberately omitting to afford her access to them, or
(ii) by expelling her from that position, or subjecting her to any other detriment.

(2) Subsection (1) shall apply in relation to persons proposing to form themselves into a partnership as it applies in relation to a firm.

(3) Subsection (1)(*a*) and (*c*) do not apply to a position as partner where, if it were employment, being a man would be a genuine occupational qualification for the job.

(4) Subsection (1)(*b*) and (*d*) do not apply to provision made in relation to death or retirement.

(5) In the case of a limited partnership references in subsection (1) to a partner shall be construed as references to a general partner as defined in section 3 of the Limited Partnerships Act 1907.

Trade unions etc.

12.—(1) This section applies to an organisation of workers, an organisation of employers, or any other organisation whose members carry on a particular profession or trade for the purposes of which the organisation exists.

(2) It is unlawful for an organisation to which this section applies, in the case of a woman who is not a member of the organisation, to discriminate against her—

(*a*) in the terms on which it is prepared to admit her to membership, or

(*b*) by refusing, or deliberately omitting to accept, her application for membership.

(3) It is unlawful for an orgainsation to which this section applies, in the case of a woman who is a member of the organisation, to discriminate against her—

(*a*) in the way it affords her access to any benefits, facilities or services, or by refusing or deliberately omitting to afford her access to them, or

(*b*) by depriving her of membership, or varying the terms on which she is a member, or

(*c*) by subjecting her to any other detriment.

(4) This section does not apply to provision made in relation to the death or retirement from work of a member.

Qualifying bodies.

13.—(1) It is unlawful for an authority or body which can confer an authorisation or qualification which is needed for, or facilitates, engagement in a particular profession or trade to discriminate against a woman—

(*a*) in the terms on which it is prepared to confer on her that authorisation or qualification, or

(*b*) by refusing or deliberately omitting to grant her application for it, or

(*c*) by withdrawing it from her or varying the terms on which she holds it.

(2) Where an authority or body is required by law to satisfy itself as to his good character before conferring on a person an authorisation or qualification which is needed for, or facilitates, his engagement in any profession or trade then, without prejudice to any other duty to which it is subject, that requirement shall be taken to impose on the authority or body a duty to have regard to any evidence tending to show that he, or any of his employees or agents (whether past or present), has practised unlawful discrimination in, or in connection with, the carrying on of any profession or trade.

(3) In this section—

(*a*) " authorisation or qualification " includes recognition, registration, enrolment, approval and certification,

(*b*) " confer " includes renew or extend.

(4) Subsection (1) does not apply to discrimination which is rendered unlawful by section 22 or 23.

Vocational training bodies.

14.—(1) It is unlawful for a person to whom this subsection applies, in the case of a woman seeking or undergoing training which would help to fit her for any employment, to discriminate against her—

(*a*) in the terms on which that person affords her access to any training courses or other facilities, or

(*b*) by refusing or deliberately omitting to afford her such assess, or

(*c*) by terminating her training.

(2) Subsection (1) applies to—

(*a*) industrial training boards established under section 1 of the Industrial Training Act 1964;

(*b*) the Manpower Services Commission, the Employment Service Agency, and the Training Services Agency;

(*c*) any association which comprises employers and has as its principal object, or one of its principal objects, affording their employees access to training facilities;

(*d*) any other person providing facilities for training for employment, being a person designated for the purposes of this paragraph in an order made by or on behalf of the Secretary of State.

(3) Subsection (1) does not apply to discrimination which is rendered unlawful by section 22 or 23.

Employment agencies.

15.—(1) It is unlawful for an employment agency to discriminate against a woman—

(*a*) in the terms on which the agency offers to provide any of its services, or

(*b*) by refusing or deliberately omitting to provide any of its services, or

(*c*) in the way it provides any of its services.

(2) It is unlawful for a local education authority or an education authority to do any act in the performance of its functions under section 8 of the Employment and Training Act 1973 which constitutes discrimination.

(3) References in subsection (1) to the services of an employment agency include guidance on careers and any other services related to employment.

(4) This section does not apply if the discrimination only concerns employment which the employer could lawfully refuse to offer the woman.

(5) An employment agency or local education authority or an education authority shall not be subject to any liability under this section if it proves—

(*a*) that it acted in reliance on a statement made to it by the employer to the effect that, by reason of the operation of subsection (4), its action would not be unlawful, and

(*b*) that it was reasonable for it to rely on the statement.

(6) A person who knowingly or recklessly makes a statement such as is referred to in subsection (5)(*a*) which in a material respect is false or misleading commits an offence, and shall be liable on summary conviction to a fine not exceeding £400.

Manpower Services Commission etc.

16.—(1) It is unlawful for any of the following bodies to discriminate in the provision of facilities or services under section 2 of the Employment and Training Act 1973—

(*a*) the Manpower Services Commission;

(*b*) the Employment Service Agency;

(*c*) the Training Services Agency.

(2) This section does not apply in a case where—

(*a*) section 14 applies, or

(*b*) the body is acting as an employment agency.

Special cases

Police.

17.—(1) For the purposes of this Part, the holding of the office of constable shall be treated as employment—

(*a*) by the chief officer of police as respects any act done by him in relation to a constable or that office;

(*b*) by the police authority as respects any act done by them in relation to a constable or that office.

(2) Regulations made under section 33, 34 or 35 of the Police Act 1964 shall not treat men and women differently except—

(*a*) as to requirements relating to height, uniform or equipment, or allowances in lieu of uniform or equipment, or

(*b*) so far as special treatment is accorded to women in connection with pregnancy or childbirth, or

(*c*) in relation to pensions to or in respect of special constables or police cadets.

(3) Nothing in this Part renders unlawful any discrimination

between male and female constables as to matters such as are mentioned in subsection (2)(*a*).

(4) There shall be paid out of the police fund—

(*a*) any compensation, costs or expenses awarded against a chief officer of police in any proceedings brought against him under this Act, and any costs or expenses incurred by him in any such proceedings so far as not recovered by him in the proceedings; and

(*b*) any sum required by a chief officer of police for the settlement of any claim made against him under this Act if the settelment is approved by the police authority.

(5) Any proceedings under this Act which, by virtue of subsection (1), would lie against a chief officer of police shall be brought against the chief officer of police for the time being or, in the case of a vacancy in that office, against the person for the time being performing the functions of that office; and references in subsection (4) to the chief officer of police shall be construed accordingly.

(6) Subsections (1) and (3) apply to a police cadet and appointment as a police cadet as they apply to a constable and the office of constable.

(7) In this section—

" chief officer of police "—

(*a*) in relation to a person appointed, or an appointment falling to be made, under a specified Act, has the same meaning as in the Police Act 1964,

(*b*) in relation to any other person or appointment means the officer who has the direction and control of the body of constables or cadets in question;

" police authority "—

(*a*) in relation to a person appointed, or an appointment falling to be made, under a specified Act, has the same meaning as in the Police Act 1964,

(*b*) in relation to any other person or appointment, means the authority by whom the person in question is or on appointment would be paid;

" police cadet " means any person appointed to undergo training with a view to becoming a constable;

" police fund " in relation to a chief officer of police within paragraph (*a*) of the above definition of that term has the same meaning as in the Police Act 1964, and in any other case means money provided by the police authority;

"specified Act" means the Metropolitan Police Act 1829, the City of London Police Act 1839 or the Police Act 1964.

(8) In the application of this section to Scotland, in subsection (7) for any reference to the Police Act 1964 there shall be substituted a reference to the Police (Scotland) Act 1967, and for the reference to sections 33, 34 and 35 of the former Act in subsection (2) there shall be substituted a reference to sections 26 and 27 of the latter Act.

Prison officers.

18.—(1) Nothing in this Part renders unlawful any discrimination between male and female prison officers as to requirements relating to height.

(2) In section 7(2) of the Prison Act 1952 the words "and if women only are received in a prison the Governor shall be a woman" are repealed.

Ministers of religion etc.

19.—(1) Nothing in this Part applies to employment for purposes of an organised religion where the employment is limited to one sex so as to comply with the doctrines of the religion or avoid offending the religious susceptibilities of a significant number of its followers.

(2) Nothing in section 13 applies to an authorisation or qualification (as defined in that section) for purposes of an organised religion where the authorisation or qualification is limited to one sex so as to comply with the doctrines of the religion or avoid offending the religious susceptibilities of a significant number of its followers.

Midwives.

20.—(1) Section 6(1) does not apply to employment as a midwife.

(2) Section 6(2)(*a*) does not apply to promotion, transfer or training as a midwife.

(3) Section 14 does not apply to training as a midwife.

(4) In the Midwives Act 1951 the following section is inserted after section 35—

"**Extension of Act to men.** 35A. From 1st January 1976 references in this Act to women (except to a woman in childbirth) apply equally to men."

(5) In the Midwives (Scotland) Act 1951 the said section 35A is inserted after section 37 of that Act as section 37A.

Mineworkers.

21.—(1) The following shall be substituted for section 124(1) of the Mines and Quarries Act 1954 (which provides that no female shall be employed below ground at a mine)—

"(1) No female shall be employed in a job the duties of which ordinarily require the employee to spend a significant proportion of his time below ground at mine which is being worked ".

(2) Throughout the Coal Mines Regulation Act 1908, for " workman " or " man " there is substituted " worker ", and for " workmen " or " men " there is substituted " workers ".

Part III

Discrimination in Other Fields

Education

Discrimination by bodies in charge of educational establishments.

22. It is unlawful, in relation to an educational establishment falling within column 1 of the following table, for a person indicated in relation to the establishment in column 2 (the " responsible body ") to discriminate againat a woman—

(*a*) in the terms on which it offers to admit her to the establishment as a pupil, or

(*b*) by refusing or deliberately omitting to accept an application for her admission to the establishment as a pupil, or

(*c*) where she is a pupil of the establishment—

(i) in the way it affords her access to any benefits, facilities or services, or by refusing or deliberately omitting to afford her access to them, or

(ii) by excluding her from the establishment or subjecting her to any other detriment.

TABLE

Establishment	*Responsible body*
ENGLAND AND WALES	
1. Educational establishment maintained by a local education authority.	Local education authority or managers or governors, according to which of them has the function in question.
2. Independent school not being a special school.	Proprietor.
3. Special school not maintained by a local education authority.	Proprietor.
4. University.	Governing body.
5. Establishment (not falling within paragraphs 1 to 4) providing full-time or part-time education, being an establishment designated under section 24(1).	Governing body.
SCOTLAND	
6. Educational establishment managed by an education authority.	Education authority.
7. Educational establishment in respect of which the managers are for the time being receiving grants under section 75(*c*) or (*d*) of the Education (Scotland) Act 1962.	Managers of the educational establishment.
8. University.	Governing body.
9. Independent school.	Proprietor.
10. Any other educational establishment (not falling within paragraphs 6, 7 and 9) providing full or part-time school education or further education.	Managers of the educational establishment.

Other discrimination by local education authorities.

23.—(1) It is unlawful for a local education authority, in carrying out such of its functions under the Education Acts 1944 to 1975 as do not fall under section 22, to do any act which constitutes sex discrimination.

(2) It is unlawful for an education authority, in carrying out such of its functions under the Education (Scotland) Acts 1939 to 1974

as do not fall under section 22, to do any act which constitutes sex discrimination.

Designated establishments.

24.—(1) The Secretary of State may by order designate for the purposes of paragraph 5 of the table in section 22 such establishments of the description mentioned in that paragraph as he thinks fit.

(2) An establishment shall not be designated under subsection (1) unless—

(*a*) it is recognised by the Secretary of State as a polytechnic, or

(*b*) it is an establishment in respect of which grants are payable out of money provided by Parliament, or

(*c*) it is assisted by a local education authority in accordance with a scheme approved under section 42 of the Education Act 1944, or

(*d*) it provides full-time education for persons who have attained the upper limit of compulsory school age but not the age of nineteen.

(3) A designation under subsection (1) shall remain in force until revoked notwithstanding that the establishment ceases to be within subsection (2).

General duty in public sector of education.

25.—(1) Without prejudice to its obligation to comply with any other provision of this Act, a body to which this subsection applies shall be under a general duty to secure that facilities for education provided by it, and any ancillary benefits or services, are provided without sex discrimination.

(2) The following provisions of the Education Act 1944, namely—

(*a*) section 68 (power of Secretary of State to require duties under that Act to be exercised reasonably), and

(*b*) section 99 (powers of Secretary of State where local education authorities etc. are in default),

shall apply to the performance by a body to which subsection (1) applies of the duties imposed by sections 22 and 23 and shall also apply to the performance of the general duty imposed by subsection (1) as they apply to the performance by a local education authority of a duty imposed by that Act.

(3) Section 71 of the Education (Scotland) Act 1962 (power of the Secretary of State to require duties in that Act to be exercised) shall apply to the performance by a body to which subsection (1) applies of the duties imposed by sections 22 and 23 and shall also

apply to the performance of the general duty imposed by subsection (1) as the said section 71 applies to the performance by an education authority of a duty imposed by that Act.

(4) The sanctions in subsections (2) and (3) shall be the only sanctions for breach of the general duty in subsection (1), but without prejudice to the enforcement of sections 22 and 23 under section 66 or otherwise (where the breach is also a contravention of either of those sections).

(5) The Secretary of State shall have the power to cause a local inquiry to be held into any matter arising from subsection (3) under section 68 of the Education (Scotland) Act 1962.

(6) Subsection (1) applies to—

(*a*) local education authorities in England and Wales;

(*b*) education authorities in Scotland;

(*c*) any other body which is a responsible body in relation to—

(i) an establishment falling within paragraph 1, 3 or 7 of the table in section 22;

(ii) an establishment designated under section 24(1) as falling within paragraph (*a*) or (*c*) of section 24(2);

(iii) an establishment designated under section 24(1) as falling within paragraph (*b*) of section 24(2) where the grants in question are payable under section 100 of the Education Act 1944.

Exception for single-sex establishments.

26.—(1) Sections 22(*a*) and (*b*) and 25 do not apply to the admission of pupils to any establishment (a " single-sex establishment ") which admits pupils of one sex only, or which would be taken to admit pupils of one sex only if there were disregarded pupils of the opposite sex—

(*a*) whose admission is exceptional, or

(*b*) whose numbers are comparatively small and whose admission is confined to particular courses of instruction or teaching classes.

(2) Where a school which is not a single-sex establishment has some pupils as boarders and others as non-boarders, and admits as boarders pupils of one sex only (or would be taken to admit as boarders pupils of one sex only if there were disregarded boarders of the opposite sex whose numbers are comparatively small), sections 22(*a*) and (*b*) and 25 do not apply to the admission of boarders and sections 22(*c*)(i) and 25 do not apply to boarding facilities.

(3) Where an establishment is a single-sex establishment by reason of its inclusion in subsection (1)(*b*), the fact that pupils of

one sex are confined to particular couses of instruction or teaching classes shall not be taken to contravene section 22(*c*)(i) or the duty in section 25.

Exception for single-sex establishments turning co-educational.

27.—(1) Where at any time—

(*a*) the responsible body for a single-sex establishment falling within column 1 of the table in section 22 determines to alter its admissions arrangements so that the establishment will cease to be a single-sex establishment, or

(*b*) section 26(2) applies to the admission of boarders to a school falling within column 1 of that table but the responsible body determines to alter its admissions arrangements so that section 26(2) will cease so to apply,

the responsible body may apply in accordance with Schedule 2 for an order (a " transitional exemption order ") authorising discriminatory admissions during the transitional period specified in the order.

(2) Where during the transitional period specified in a transitional exemption order applying to an establishment the responsible body refuses or deliberately omits to accept an application for the admission of a person to the establishment as a pupil the refusal or omission shall not be taken to contravene any provision of this Act.

(3) Subsection (2) does not apply if the refusal or mission contravenes any condition of the transitional exemption order.

(4) Except as mentioned in subsection (2), a transitional exemption order shall not afford any exemption from liability under this Act.

(5) Where, during the period between the making of an application for a transitional exemption order in relation to an establishment and the determination of the application, the responsible body refuses or deliberately omits to accept an application for the admission of a person to the establishment as a pupil the refusal or omission shall not be taken to contravene any provision of this Act.

Exception for physical training.

28. Sections 22, 23 and 25 do not apply to any further education course being—

(*a*) a course in physical training, or

(*b*) a course designed for teachers of physical training.

Goods, facilities, services and premises

Discrimination in provision of goods, facilities or services.

29.—(1) It is unlawful for any person concerned with the provision (for payment or not) of goods, facilities or services to the public or a section of the public to discriminate against a woman who seeks to obtain or use those goods, facilities or services—

(*a*) by refusing or deliberately omitting to provide her with any of them, or

(*b*) by refusing or deliberately omitting to provide her with goods, facilities or services of the like quality, in the like manner and on the like terms as are normal in his case in relation to male members of the public or (where she belongs to a section of the public) to male members of that section.

(2) The following are examples of the facilities and services mentioned in subsection (1)—

(*a*) access to and use of any place which members of the public or a section of the public are permitted to enter;

(*b*) accommodation in a hotel, boarding house or other similar establishment;

(*c*) facilities by way of banking or insurance or for grants, loans, credit or finance;

(*d*) facilities for education;

(*e*) facilities for entertainment, recreation or refreshment;

(*f*) facilities for transport or travel;

(*g*) the services of any profession or trade, or any local or other public authority.

(3) For the avoidance of doubt it is hereby declared that where a particular skill is commonly exercised in a different way for men and for women it does not contravene subsection (1) for a person who does not normally exercise it for women to insist on exercising it for a woman only in accordance with his normal practice or, if he reasonably considers it impracticable to do that in her case, to refuse or deliberately omit to exercise it.

Discrimination in disposal or management of premises.

30.—(1) It is unlawful for a person, in relation to premises in Great Britain of which he has power to dispose, to discriminate against a woman—

(*a*) in the terms on which he offers her those premises, or

(*b*) by refusing her application for those premises, or

(*c*) in his treatment of her in relation to any list of persons in need of premises of that description.

(2) It is unlawful for a person, in relation to premises managed by him, to discriminate against a woman occupying the premises—

(*a*) in the way he affords her access to any benefits or facilities, or by refusing or deliberately omitting to afford her access to them, or

(*b*) by evicting her, or subjecting her to any other detriment.

(3) Subsection (1) does not apply to a person who owns an estate or interest in the premises and wholly occupies them unless he

uses the services of an estate agent for the purposes of the disposal of the premises, or publishes or causes to be published an advertisement in connection with the disposal.

Discrimination: consent for assignment or sub-letting.

31.—(1) Where the licence or consent of the landlord or of any other person is required for the disposal to any person of premises in Great Britain comprised in a tenancy, it is unlawful for the landlord or other person to discriminate against a woman by withholding the licence or consent for disposal of the premises to her.

(2) Subsection (1) does not apply if—

(*a*) the person withholding a licence or consent, or a near relative of his ("the relevant occupier") resides, and intends to continue to reside, on the presmises, and

(*b*) there is on the premises, in addition to the accommodation occupied by the relevant occupier, accommodation (not being storage accommodation or means of access) shared by the relevant occupier with other persons residing on the premises who are not members of his household, and

(*c*) the premises are small premises as defined in section 32(2).

(3) In this section "tenancy" means a tenancy created by a lease or sub-lease, by an agreement for a lease or sub-lease or by a tenancy agreement or in pursuance of any enactment; and "disposal", in relation to premises comprised in a tenancy, includes assignment or assignation of the tenancy and sub-letting or parting with possession of the premises or any part of the premises.

(4) This section applies to tenancies created before the passing of this Act, as well as to others.

Exception for small dwellings.

32.—(1) Sections 29(1) and 30 do not apply to the provision by a person of accommodation in any premises, or the disposal of premises by him, if—

(*a*) that person or a near relative of his ("the relevant occupier") resides, and intends to continue to reside, on the premises, and

(*b*) there is on the premises, in addition to the accommodation occupied by the relevant occupier, accommodation (not being storage accommodation or means of access) shared by the relevant occupier with other persons residing on the premises who are not members of his household, and

(*c*) the premises are small premises.

(2) Premises shall be treated for the purposes of subsection (1) as small premises if—

(*a*) in the case of premises comprising residential accommodation for one or more households (under separate letting or similar agreements) in addition to the accommodation occupied by the relevant occupier, there is not normally residential accommodation for more than two such households and only the relevant occupier and any member of his household reside in the accommodation occupied by him;

(*b*) in the case of premises not falling within paragraph (*a*), there is not normally residential accommodation on the premises for more than six persons in addition to the relevant occupier and any members of his household.

Exception for political parties.

33.—(1) This section applies to a political party if—

(*a*) it has as its main object, or one of its main objects, the promotion of parliamentary candidatures for the Parliament of the United Kingdom, or

(*b*) it is an affiliate of, or has as an affiliate, or has similar formal links with, a political party within paragraph (*a*).

(2) Nothing in section 29(1) shall be construed as affecting any special provision for persons of one sex only in the constitution, organisation or administration of the political party.

(3) Nothing in section 29(1) shall render unlawful an act done in order to give effect to such a special provision.

Exception for voluntary bodies.

34.—(1) This section applies to a body—

(*a*) the activities of which are carried on otherwise than for profit, and

(*b*) which was not set up by any enactment.

(2) Sections 29(1) and 30 shall not be construed as rendering unlawful—

(*a*) the restriction of membership of any such body to persons of one sex (disregarding any minor exceptions), or

(*b*) the provision of benefits, facilities or services to members of any such body where the membership is so restricted,

even though membership of the body is open to the public, or to a section of the public.

(3) Nothing in section 29 or 30 shall—

(*a*) be construed as affecting a provision to which this subsection applies, or

(*b*) render unlawful an act which is done in order to give effect to such a provision.

(4) Subsection (3) applies to a provision for conferring benefits on persons of one sex only (disregarding any benefits to persons of the opposite sex which are exceptional or are relatively insignifi-

cant), being a provision which constitutes the main object of a body within subsection (1).

Further exceptions from ss. 29(1) and 30.

35.—(1) A person who provides at any place facilities or services restricted to men does not for that reason contravene section 29(1) if—

(*a*) the place is, or is part of, a hospital, reception centre provided by the Supplementary Benefits Commission or other establishment for persons requiring special care, supervision or attention, or

(*b*) the place is (permanently or for the time being) occupied or used for the purposes of an organised religion, and the facilities or services are restricted to men so as to comply with the doctrines of that religion or avoid offending the religious susceptibilities of a significant number of its followers, or

(*c*) the facilities or services are provided for, or are likely to be used by, two or more persons at the same time, and

(i) the facilities or services are such, or those persons are such, that male users are likely to suffer serious embarrassment at the presence of a woman, or

(ii) the facilities or services are such that a user is likely to be in a state of undress and a male user might reasonably object to the presence of a female user.

(2) A person who provides facilities or services restricted to men does not for that reason contravene section 29(1) if the services or facilities are such that physical contact between the user and any other person is likely, and that other person might reasonably object if the user were a woman.

(3) Sections 29(1) and 30 do not apply—

(*a*) to discrimination which is rendered unlawful by any provision in column 1 of the table below, or

(*b*) to discrimination which would be so unlawful but for any provision in column 2 of that table, or

(*c*) to discrimination which contravenes a term modified or included by virtue of an equality clause.

TABLE

Provision creating illegality	*Exception*
Part II	Sections 6(3), 7(1)(*b*), 15(4), 19 and 20. Schedule 4 paragraphs 1 and 2.
Section 22 or 23	Sections 26, 27 and 28. Schedule 4 paragraph 4.

Extent

Extent of Part III.

36.—(1) Section 29(1)—

(*a*) does not apply to goods, facilities or services outside Great Britain except as provided in subsections (2) and (3), and

(*b*) does not apply to facilities by way of banking or insurance or for grants, loans, credit or finance, where the facilities are for a purpose to be carried out, or in connection with risks wholly or mainly arising, outside Great Britain.

(2) Section 29(1) applies to the provision of facilities for travel outside Great Britain where the refusal or omission occurs in Great Britain or on a ship, aircraft or hovercraft within subsection (3).

(3) Section 29(1) applies on and in relation to—

(*a*) any ship registered at a port of registry in Great Britain, and

(*b*) any aircraft or hovercraft registered in the United Kingdom and operated by a person who has his principal place of business, or is ordinarily resident, in Great Britain,

(*c*) any ship, aircraft or hovercraft belonging to or possessed by Her Majesty in right of the Government of the United Kingdom,

even if the ship, aircraft or hovercraft is outside Great Britain.

(4) This section shall not render unlawful an act done in or over a country outside the United Kingdom, or in or over that country's territorial waters, for the purpose of complying with the laws of that country.

(5) Sections 22, 23 and 25 do not apply to benefits, facilities or services outside Great Britain except—

(*a*) travel on a ship registered at a port of registry in Great Britain, and

(*b*) benefits, facilities or services provided on a ship so registered.

PART IV

OTHER UNLAWFUL ACTS

Discriminatory practices.

37.—(1) In this section " discriminatory practice " means the application of a requirement or condition which results in an act of discrimination which is unlawful by virtue of any provision of Part II or III taken with section 1(1)(*b*) or 3(1)(*b*) or which would be likely to result in such an act of discrimination if the persons to whom it is applied were not all of one sex.

(2) A person acts in contravention of this section if and so long as—

(*a*) he applies a discriminatory practice, or

(*b*) he operates practices or other arrangements which in any circumstances would call for the application by him of a discriminatory practice.

(3) Proceedings in respect of a contravention of this section shall be brought only by the Commission in accordance with sections 67 to 71.

Discriminatory advertisements.

38.—(1) It is unlawful to publish or cause to be published an advertisement which indicates, or might reasonably be understood as indicating, an intention by a person to do any act which is or might be unlawful by virtue of Part II or III.

(2) Subsection (1) does not apply to an advertisement if the intended act would not in fact be unlawful.

(3) For the purposes of subsection (1), use of a job description with a sexual connotation (such as " waiter ", " salesgirl ", " postman " or " stewardess ") shall be taken to indicate an intention to discriminate, unless the advertisement contains an indication to the contrary.

(4) The publisher of an advertisement made unlawful by subsection (1) shall not be subject to any liability under that subsection in respect of the publication of the advertisement if he proves—

(*a*) that the advertisement was published in reliance on a statement made to him by the person who caused it to be published to the effect that, by reason of the operation of subsection (2), the publication would not be unlawful, and

(*b*) that it was reasonable for him to rely on the statement.

(5) A person who knowingly or recklessly makes a statement such as is referred to in subsection (4) which in a material respect is false or misleading commits an offence, and shall be liable on summary conviction to a fine not exceeding £400.

Instructions to discriminate.

39.—It is unlawful for a person—

(*a*) who has authority over another person, or

(*b*) in accordance with whose wishes that other person is accustomed to act,

to instruct him to do any act which is unlawful by virtue of Part II or III, or procure or attempt to procure the doing by him of any such act.

Pressure to discriminate.

40.—(1) It is unlawful to induce, or attempt to induce, a person to do any act which contravenes Part II or III by—

(*a*) providing or offering to provide him with any benefit, or

(*b*) subjecting or threatening to subject him to any detriment.

(2) An offer or threat is not prevented from falling within subsection (1) because it is not made directly to the person in question, if it is made in such a way that he is likely to hear of it.

Liability of employers and principals.

41.—(1) Anything done by a person in the course of his employment shall be treated for the purposes of this Act as done by his employer as well as by him, whether or not it was done with the employer's knowledge or approval.

(2) Anything done by a person as agent for another person with the authority (whether express or implied, and whether precedent or subsequent) of that other person shall be treated for the purposes of this Act as done by that other person as well as by him.

(3) In proceedings brought under this Act against any person in respect of an act alleged to have been done by an employee of his it shall be a defence for that person to prove that he took such steps as were reasonably practicable to prevent the employee from doing that act, or from doing in the course of his employment acts of that description.

Aiding unlawful acts.

42.—(1) A person who knowingly aids another person to do an act made unlawful by this Act shall be treated for the purposes of this Act as himself doing an unlawful act of the like description.

(2) For the purposes of subsection (1) an employee or agent for whose act the employer or principal is liable under section 41 (or would be so liable but for section 41(3)) shall be deemed to aid the doing of the act by the employer or principal.

(3) A person does not under this section knowingly aid another to do an unlawful act if—

(*a*) he acts in reliance on a statement made to him by that other person that, by reasons of any provision of this Act, the act which he aids would not be unlawful, and

(*b*) it is reasonable for him to rely on the statement.

(4) A person who knowingly or recklessly makes a statement such as is referred to in subsection (3)(*a*) which in a material respect is false or misleading commits an offence, and shall be liable on summary conviction to a fine not exceeding £400.

PART V

GENERAL EXCEPTIONS FROM PARTS II TO IV

Charities.

43.—(1) Nothing in Parts II to IV shall—

(*a*) be construed as affecting a provision to which this subsection applies, or (*b*) render unlawful an act which is done in order to give effect to such a provision.

(2) Subsection (1) applies to a provision for conferring benefits on persons of one sex only (disregarding any benefits to persons of the opposite sex which are exceptional or are relatively insignificant), being a provision which is contained in a charitable instrument.

(3) In the application of this section to England and Wales—

(*a*) " charitable instrument " means an enactment or other instrument passed or made for charitable purposes, or an enactment or other instrument so far as it relates to charitable purposes;

(*b*) " charitable purposes " means purposes which are exclusively charitable according to the law of England and Wales.

(4) In this application of this section to Scotland " charitable instrument " means an enactment or instrument passed or made by or on behalf of a body of persons or trust established for charitable purposes only.

Sport etc.

44. Nothing in Parts II to IV shall, in relation to any sport, game or other activity of a competitive nature where the physical strength, stamina or physique of the average woman puts her at a disadvantage to the average man, render unlawful any act related to the participation of a person as a competitor in events involving that activity which are confined to competitors of one sex.

Insurance etc.

45. Nothing in Parts II to IV shall render unlawful the treatment of a person in relation to an annuity, life assurance policy, accident insurance policy, or similar matter involving the assessment of risk, where the treatment—

(*a*) was effected by reference to actuarial or other data from a source on which it was reasonable to rely, and

(*b*) was reasonable having regard to the data and any other relevant factors.

Communal accommodation.

46.—(1) In this section " communal accommodation " means residential accommodation which includes dormitories or other shared sleeping accommodation which for reasons of privacy or decency should be used by men only, or by women only (but which may include some shared sleeping accommodation for men, and some for women, or some ordinary sleeping accommodation).

(2) In this section " communal accommodation " also includes residential accommodation all or part of which should be used by

men only, or by women only, because of the nature of the sanitary facilities serving the accommodation.

(3) Nothing in Part II or III shall render unlawful sex discrimination in the admission of persons to communal accommodation if the accommodation is managed in a way which, given the exigencies of the situation, comes as near as may be to fair and equitable treatment of men and women.

(4) In applying subsection (3) account shall be taken of—

(*a*) whether and how far it is reasonable to expect that the accommodation should be altered or extended, or that further alternative accommodation should be provided; and

(*b*) the frequency of the demand or need for use of the accommodation by men as compared with women.

(5) Nothing in Part II or III shall render unlawful sex discrimination against a woman, or against a man, as respects the provision of any benefit, facility or service if—

(*a*) the benefit, facility or service cannot properly and effectively be provided except for those using communal accommodation, and

(*b*) in the relevant circumstances the woman or, as the case may be, the man could lawfully be refused the use of the accommodation by virtue of subsection (3).

(6) Neither subsection (3) nor subsection (5) is a defence to an act of sex discrimination under Part II unless such arrangements as are reasonably practicable are made to compensate for the detriment caused by the discrimination; but in considering under subsection (5)(*b*) whether the use of communal accommodation could lawfully be refused (in a case based on Part II), it shall be assumed that the requirements of this subsection have been complied with as respects subsection (3).

(7) Section 25 shall not apply to sex discrimination within subsection (3) or (5).

(8) This section is without prejudice to the generality of section 35(1)(*c*).

Discriminatory training by certain bodies.

47.—(1) Nothing in Parts II to IV shall render unlawful any act done in relation to particular work by a training body in, or in connection with—

(*a*) affording women only, or men only, access to facilities for training which would help to fit them for that work, or

(*b*) encouraging women only, or men only, to take advantage of opportunities for doing that work,

where it appears to the training body that at any time within the 12 months immediately preceding the doing of the act there were no persons of the sex in question doing that work in Great Britain, or the number of persons of that sex doing the work in Great Britain was comparatively small.

(2) Where in relation to particular work it appears to a training body that although the condition for the operation of subsection (1) is not met for the whole of Great Britain it is met for an area within Great Britain, nothing in Parts II to IV shall render unlawful any act done by the training body in, or in connection with—

(*a*) affording persons who are of the sex in question, and who appear likely to take up that work in that area, access to facilities for training which would help to fit them for that work, or

(*b*) encouraging persons of that sex to take advantage of opportunities in the area for doing that work.

(3) Nothing in Parts II to IV shall render unlawful any act done by a training body in, or in connection with, affording persons access to facilities for training which would help to fit them for employment, where it appears to the training body that those persons are in special need of training by reason of the period for which they have been discharging domestic or family responsibilities to the exclusion of regular full time employment.

The discrimination in relation to which this subsection applies may result from confining the training to persons who have been discharging domestic or family responsibilities, or from the way persons are selected for training, or both.

(4) In this section " training body " means—

(*a*) a person mentioned in section 14(2)(*a*) or (*b*), or

(*b*) any other person being a person designated for the purposes of this section in an order made by or on behalf of the Secretary of State,

and a person may be designated under paragraph (*b*) for the purposes of subsections (1) and (2) only, or of subsection (3) only, or for all those subsections.

Other discriminatory training etc.

48.—(1) Nothing in Parts II to IV shall render unlawful any act done by an employer in relation to particular work in his employment, being an act done in, or in connection with,—

(*a*) affording his female employees only, or his male employees only, acces to facilities for training which would help to fit them for that work, or

(*b*) encouraging women only, or men only, to take advantage of opportunities for doing that work,

where at any time within the twelve months immediately preceding the doing of the act there were no persons of the sex in question among those doing that work or the number of persons of that sex doing the work was comparatively small.

(2) Nothing in section 12 shall render unlawful any act done by an organisation to which that section applies in, or in connection with,—

(*a*) affording female members of the organisation only, or male members of the organisation only, access to facilities for training which would help to fit them for holding a post of any kind in the organisation, or

(*b*) encouraging female members only, or male members only, to take advantage of opportunities for holding such posts in the organisation,

where at any time within the twelve months immediately preceding the doing of the act there were no persons of the sex in question among persons holding such posts in the organisation or the number of persons of that sex holding such posts was comparatively small.

(3) Nothing in Parts II to IV shall render unlawful any act done by an organisation to which section 12 applies in, or in connection with, encouraging women only, or men only, to become members of the organisation where at any time within the twelve months immediately preceding the doing of the act there were no persons of the sex in question among those members or the number of persons of that sex among the members was comparatively small.

Trade unions etc.: elective bodies.

49.—(1) If an organisation to which section 12 applies comprises a body the membership of which is wholly or mainly elected, nothing in section 12 shall render unlawful provision which ensures that a minimum number of persons of one sex are members of the body—

(*a*) by reserving seats on the body for persons of that sex, or

(*b*) by making extra seats on the body available (by election or co-option or otherwise) for persons of that sex on occasions when the number of persons of that sex in the other seats is below the minimum,

where in the opinion of the organisation the provision is in the circumstances needed to secure a reasonable lower limit to the number of members of that sex serving on the body, and nothing in Parts II to IV shall render unlawful any act done in order to give effect to such a provision.

(2) This section shall not be taken as making lawful—

(*a*) discrimination in the arrangements for determining the persons entitled to vote in an election of members of the body, or otherwise to choose the persons to serve on the body, or

(*b*) discrimination in any arrangements concerning membership of the organisation itself.

Indirect access to benefits etc.

50.—(1) References in this Act to the affording by any person of access to benefits, facilities or services are not limited to benefits, facilities or services provided by that person himself, but include any means by which it is in that person's power to facilitate access to benefits, facilities or services provided by any other person (the " actual provider ").

(2) Where by any provision of this Act the affording by any person of access to benefits, facilities or services in a discriminatory way is in certain circumstances prevented from being unlawful, the effect of the provision shall extend also to the liability under this Act of any actual provider.

Acts done under statutory authority.

51.—(1) Nothing in Parts II to IV shall render unlawful any act done by a person if it was necessary for him to do it in order to comply with a requirement—

(*a*) of an Act passed before this Act; or

(*b*) of an instrument made or approved (whether before or after the passing of this Act) by or under an Act passed before this Act.

(2) Where an Act passed after this Act re-enacts (with or without modification) a provision of an Act passed before this Act, subsection (1) shall apply to that provision as re-enacted as if it continued to be contained in an Act passed before this Act.

Acts safeguarding national security.

52.—(1) Nothing in Parts II to IV shall render unlawful an act done for the purpose of safeguarding national security.

(2) A certificate purporting to be signed by or on behalf of a Minister of the Crown and certifying that an act specified in the certificate was done for the purpose of safeguarding national security shall be conclusive evidence that it was done for that purpose.

(3) A document purporting to be a certificate such as is mentioned in subsection (2) shall be received in evidence and, unless the contrary is proved, shall be deemed to be such a certificate.

PART VI
EQUAL OPPORTUNITIES COMMISSION

Establishment and duties of Commission.

53.—(1) There shall be a body of Commissioners named the Equal Opportunities Commission, consisting of at least eight but not more than fifteen individuals each appointed by the Secretary of State on a full-time or part-time basis, which shall have the following duties—

(*a*) to work towards the elimination of discrimination,

(*b*) to promote equality of opportunity between men and women generally, and

(*c*) to keep under review the working of this Act and the Equal Pay Act 1970 and, when they are so required by the Secretary of State or otherwise think it necessary, draw up and submit to the Secretary of State proposals for amending them.

(2) The Secretary of State shall appoint—

(*a*) one of the Commissioners to be chairman of the Commission, and

(*b*) either one or two of the Commissioners (as the Secretary of State thinks fit) to be deputy chairman or deputy chairmen of the Commission.

(3) The Secretary of State may by order amend subsection (1) so far as it regulates the number of Commissioners.

(4) Schedule 3 shall have effect with respect to the Commission.

Research and education.

54.—(1) The Commission may undertake or assist (financially or otherwise) the undertaking by other persons of any research, and any educational activities, which appear to the Commission necessary or expedient for the purposes of section 53(1).

(2) The Commission may make charges for educational or other facilities or services made available by them.

Review of discriminatory provisions in health and safety legislation.

55.—(1) Without prejudice to the generality of section 53(1), the Commission, in pursuance of the duties imposed by paragraphs (*a*) and (*b*) of that subsection—

(*a*) shall keep under review the relevant statutory provisions in so far as they require men and women to be treated differently, and

(*b*) if so required by the Secretary of State, make to him a report on any matter specified by him which is connected with those duties and concerns the relevant statutory provisions.

Any such report shall be made within the time specified by the Secretary of State, and the Secretary of State shall cause the report to be published.

(2) Whenever the Commission think it necessary, they shall draw up and submit to the Secretary of State proposals for amending the relevant statutory provisions.

(3) The Commission shall carry out their duties in relation to the relevant statutory provisions in consultation with the Health and Safety Commission.

(4) In this section " the relevant statutory provisions " has the meaning given by section 53 of the Health and Safety at Work etc. Act 1974.

Annual reports.

56.—(1) As soon as practicable after the end of each calendar year the Commission shall make to the Secretary of State a report on their activities during the year (an " annual report ").

(2) Each annual report shall include a general survey of developments, during the period to which it relates, in respect of matters falling within the scope of the Commission's duties.

(3) The Secretary of State shall lay a copy of every annual report before each House of Parliament, and shall cause the report to be published.

Investigations

Power to conduct formal investigations.

57.—(1) Without prejudice to their general power to do anything requisite for the performance of their duties under section 53(1), the Commission may if they think fit, and shall if required by the Secretary of State, conduct a formal investigation for any purpose connected with the carrying out of those duties.

(2) The Commission may, with the approval of the Secretary of State, appoint, on a full-time or part-time basis, one or more individuals as additional Commissioners for the purposes of a formal investigation.

(3) The Commission may nominate one or more Commissioners, with or without one or more additional Commissioners, to conduct a formal investigation on their behalf, and may delegate any of their functions in relation to the investigation to the persons so nominated.

Terms of reference.

58.—(1) The Commission shall not embark on a formal investigation unless the requirements of this section have been complied with.

(2) Terms of reference for the investigation shall be drawn up by the Commission or, if the Commission were required by the

Secretary of State to conduct the investigation, by the Secretary of State after consulting the Commission.

(3) It shall be the duty of the Commission to give general notice of the holding of the investigation unless the terms of reference confine it to activities of persons named in them, but in such a case the Commission shall in the prescribed manner give those persons notice of the holding of the investigation.

(4) The Commission or, if the Commission were required by the Secretary of State to conduct the investigation, the Secretary of State after consulting the Commission may from time to time revise the terms of reference; and subsections (1) and (3) shall apply to the revised investigation and terms of reference as they applied to the original.

Power to obtain information.

59.—(1) For the purposes of a formal investigation the Commission, by a notice in the prescribed form served on him in the prescribed manner,—

(*a*) may require any person to furnish such written information as may be described in the notice, and may specify the time at which, and the manner and form in which, the information is to be furnished;

(*b*) may require any person to attend at such time and place as is specified in the notice and give oral information about, and produce all documents in his possession or control relating to, any matter specified in the notice.

(2) Except as provided by section 69, a notice shall be served under subsection (1) only where—

(*a*) service of the notice was authorised by an order made by or on behalf of the Secretary of State, or

(*b*) the terms of reference of the investigation state that the Commission believe that a person named in them may have done or may be doing acts of all or any of the following descriptions—

(i) unlawful discriminatory acts,

(ii) contraventions of section 37,

(iii) contraventions of sections 38, 39 or 40, and

(iv) acts in breach of a term modified or included by virtue of an equality clause,

and confine the investigation to those acts.

(3) A notice under subsection (1) shall not require a person—

(*a*) to give information, or produce any documents, which he could not be compelled to give in evidence, or produce, in civil proceedings before the High Court or the Court of Session, or (*b*) to attend at any place unless the necessary expenses of his journey to and from that place are paid or tendered to him.

(4) If a person fails to comply with a notice served on him under subsection (1) or the Commission has reasonable cause to believe that he intends not to comply with it, the Commission may apply to a county court for an order requiring him to comply with it or wich such directions for the like purpose as may be contained in the order; and section 84 (penalty for neglecting witness summons) of the County Courts Act 1959 shall apply to failure without reasonable excuse to comply with any such order as it applies in the cases there provided.

(5) In the application of subsection (4) to Scotland—

(*a*) for the reference to a county court there shall be substituted a reference to a sheriff court, and

(*b*) for the words after " order; and " to the end of the subsection there shall be substituted the words " paragraph 73 of the First Schedule to the Sheriff Courts (Scotland) Act 1907 (power of sheriff to grant second diligence for compelling the attendances of witnesses or havers) shall apply to any such order as it applies in proceedings in the sheriff court ".

(6) A person commits an offence if he—

(*a*) wilfully alters, suppresses, conceals or destroys a document which he has been required by a notice or order under this section to produce, or

(*b*) in complying with such a notice or order, knowingly or recklessly makes any statement which is false in a material particular,

and shall be liable on summary conviction to a fine not exceeding £400.

(7) Proceedings for an offence under subsection (6) may (without prejudice to any jurisdiction exercisable apart from this subsection) be instituted—

(*a*) against any person at any place at which he has an office or other place of business;

(*b*) against an individual at any place where he resides, or at which he is for the time being.

Recommendations and reports on formal investigations.

60.—(1) If in the light of any of their findings in a formal investigation it appears to the Commission necessary or expedient, whether during the course of the investigation or after its conclusion,—

(*a*) to make to any persons, with a view to promoting equality of opportunity between men and women who are affected by any of their activities, recommendations for changes in their policies or procedures, or as to any other matters, or

(*b*) to make to the Secretary of State any recommendations, whether for changes in the law or otherwise,

the Commission shall make those recommendations accordingly.

(2) The Commission shall prepare a report of their findings in any formal investigation conducted by them.

(3) If the formal investigation is one required by the Secretary of State—

(*a*) the Commission shall deliver the report to the Secretary of State, and

(*b*) the Secretary of State shall cause the report to be published,

and unless required by the Secretary of State the Commission shall not publish the report.

(4) If the formal investigation is not one required by the Secretary of State, the Commission shall either publish the report, or make it available for inspection in accordance with subsection (5).

(5) Where under subsection (4) a report is to be made available for inspection, any person shall be entitled, on payment of such fee (if any) as may be determined by the Commission—

(*a*) to inspect the report during ordinary office hours and take copies of all or any part of the report, or

(*b*) to obtain from the Commission a copy, certified by the Commission to be correct, of the report.

(6) The Commission may if they think fit determine that the right conferred by subsection (5)(*a*) shall be exercisable in relation to a copy of the report instead of, or in addition to, the original.

(7) The Commission shall give general notice of the place or places where, and the times when, reports may be inspected under subsection (5).

Restriction on disclosure of information.

61.—(1) No information given to the Commission by any person (" the informant ") in connection with a formal investigation shall be disclosed by the Commission, or by any person who is or has been a Commissioner, additional Commissioner or employee of the Commission, except—

(*a*) on the order of any court, or
(*b*) with the informant's consent, or
(*c*) in the form of a summary or other general statement published by the Commission which does not identify the informant or any other person to whom the information relates, or
(*d*) in a report of the investigation published by the Commission or made available for inspection under section 60(5), or
(*e*) to the Commissioners, additional Commissioners or employees of the Commission, or, so far as may be necessary for the proper performance of the functions of the Commission, to other persons, or
(*f*) for the purpose of any civil proceedings under this Act to which the Commission are a party, or any criminal proceedings.

(2) Any person who discloses information in contravention of subsection (1) commits an offence and shall be liable on summary conviction to a fine not exceeding £400.

(3) In preparing any report for publication or for inspection the Commission shall exclude, so far as is consistent with their duties and the object of the report, any matter which relates to the private affairs of any individual or business interests of any person where the publication of that matter might, in the opinion of the Commission, prejudicially affect that individual or person.

Part VII

Enforcement

General

No further sanctions for breach of Act.

62.—(1) A contravention of this Act shall incur as such no sanction, whether civil or criminal, except to the extent (if any) expressly provided by this Act.

(2) In subsection (1) " sanction " includes the granting of an injunction or declaration, but does not include the making of an order of certiorari, mandamus or prohibition.

(3) Subsection (2) does not affect the remedies available under section 66(2), notwithstanding that subsection (2) would prevent those remedies being obtainable in the High Court.

(4) In relation to Scotland in subsection (1) " sanction " includes the granting of an interdict or of a declarator or a decree ad factum praestandum, but otherwise nothing in this Act shall affect any right to bring any proceedings, whether civil or criminal, which might have been brought if this Act had not been passed.

Enforcement in employment field

Jurisdiction of industrial tribunals.

63.—(1) A complaint by any person (" the complainant ") that another person (" the respondent ")—

(*a*) has committed an act of discrimination against the complainant which is unlawful by virtue of Part II, or

(*b*) is by virtue of section 41 or 42 to be treated as having committed such an act of discrimination against the complainant,

may be presented to an industrial tribunal.

(2) Subsection (1) does not apply to a complaint under section 13(1) of an act in respect of which an appeal, or proceedings in the nature of an appeal, may be brought under any enactment.

Conciliation in employment cases.

64.—(1) Where a complaint has been presented to an industrial tribunal under section 63, or under section 2(1) of the Equal Pay Act 1970, and a copy of the complaint has been sent to a conciliation officer, it shall be the duty of the conciliation officer—

(*a*) if he is requested to do so both by the complainant and the respondent, or

(*b*) if, in the absence of requests by the complainant and the respondent, he considers that he could act under this subsection with a reasonable prospect of success,

to endeavour to promote a settlement of the complaint without its being determined by an industrial tribunal.

(2) Where, before a complaint such as is mentioned in subsection (1) has been presented to an industrial tribunal, a request is made to a conciliation officer to make his services available in the matter by a person who, if the complaint were so presented, would be the complainant or respondent, subsection (1) shall apply as if the complaint had been so presented and a copy of it had been sent to the conciliation officer.

(3) In proceeding under subsection (1) or (2), a conciliation officer shall where appropriate have regard to the desirability of encouraging the use of other procedures available for the settlement of grievances.

(4) Anything communicated to a conciliation officer in connection with the performance of his functions under this section shall not be admissible in evidence in any proceedings before an industrial tribunal except with the consent of the person who communicated it to that officer.

Remedies on complaint under section 63.

65.—(1) Where an industrial tribunal finds that a complaint presented to it under section 63 is well-founded the tribunal shall make such of the following as it considers just and equitable—

(*a*) an order declaring the rights of the complainant and the respondent in relation to the act to which the complaint relates;

(*b*) an order requiring the respondent to pay to the complainant compensation of an amount corresponding to any damages he could have been ordered by a county court or by a sheriff court to pay to the complainant if the complaint had fallen to be dealt with under section 66;

(*c*) a recommendation that the respondent take within a specified period action appearing to the tribunal to be practicable for the purpose of obviating or reducing the adverse effect on the complainant of any act of discrimination to which the complaint relates.

(2) The amount of compensation awarded to a person under subsection (1)(*b*) shall not exceed the amount for the time being specified in paragraph 20(1)(*b*) of Schedule I to the Trade Union and Labour Relations Act 1974.

(3) If without reasonable justification the respondent to a complaint fails to comply with a recommendation made by an industrial tribunal under subsection (1)(*c*), then, if they think it just and equitable to do so—

(*a*) the tribunal may increase the amount of compensation required to be paid to the complainant in respect of the complaint by an order made under subsection (1)(*b*), or

(*b*) if an order under subsection (1)(*b*) could have been made but was not, the tribunal may make such an order.

Enforcement of Part III

Claims under Part III.

66.—(1) A claim by any person (" the claimant ") that another person (" the respondent ")—

(*a*) has committed an act of discrimination against the claimant which is unlawful by virtue of Part III, or

(*d*) is by virtue of section 41 or 42 to be treated as having committed such an act of discrimination against the claimant,

may be made the subject of civil proceedings in like manner as any other claim in tort or (in Scotland) in reparation for breach of statutory duty.

(2) Proceedings under subsection (1)—

(*a*) shall be brought in England and Wales only in a county court, and

(*b*) shall be brought in Scotland only in a sheriff court,

but all such remedies shall be obtainable in such proceedings as, apart from this subsection, would be obtainable in the High Court or the Court of Session, as the case may be.

(3) As respects an unlawful act of discrimination falling within section 1(1)(*b*) (or, where this section is applied by section 65(1)(*b*) section 3(1)(*b*)) no award of damages shall be made if the respondent proves that the requirement or condition in question was not applied with the intention of treating the claimant unfavourably on the ground of his sex or marital status as the case may be.

(4) For the avoidance of doubt it is hereby declared that damages in respect of an unlawful act of discrimination may include compensation for injury to feelings whether or not they include compensation under any other head.

(5) Civil proceedings in respect of a claim by any person that he has been discriminated against in contravention of section 22 or 23 by a body to which section 25(1) applies shall not be instituted unless the claimant has given notice of the claim to the Secretary of State and either the Secretary of State has by notice informed the claimant that the Secretary ot State does not require further time to consider the matter, or the period of two months has elapsed since the claimant gave notice to the Secretary of State; but nothing in this subsection applies to a counterclaim.

(6) For the purposes of proceedings under subsection (1)—

(*a*) section 91(1) (power of judge to appoint assessors) of the County Courts Act 1959 shall apply with the omission of the words " on the application of any party ", and

(*b*) the remuneration of assessors appointed under the said section 91(1) shall be at such rate as may be determined by the Lord Chancellor with the approval of the Minister for the Civil Service.

(7) For the purpose of proceedings before the sheriff, provision may be made by act of sederunt for the appointment of assessors by him, and the remuneration of any assessors so appointed shall be at such rate as the Lord President of the Court of Session with the approval of the Minister foı the Civil Service may determine.

(8) A county court or sheriff court shall have jurisdiction to entertain proceedings under subsection (1) with respect to an act done on a ship, airfraft or hovercraft outside its district, including such an act done outside Great Britain.

Non-discrimination notices

Issue of non-discrimination notice.

67.—(1) This section applies to—

(*a*) an unlawful discriminatory act, and
(*b*) a contravention of section 37, and
(*c*) a contravention of section 38, 39 or 40, and
(*d*) an act in breach of a term modified or included by virtue of an equality clause,

and so applies whether or not proceedings have been brought in respect of the act.

(2) If in the course of a formal investigation the Commission become satisfied that a person is committing, or has committed, any such acts, the Commission may in the prescribed manner serve on him a notice in the prescribed form (" a non-discrimination notice ") requiring him—

(*a*) not to commit any such acts, and
(*b*) where compliance with paragraph (*a*) involves changes in any of his practices or other arrangements—

(i) to inform the Commission that he has effected those changes and what those changes are, and

(ii) to take such steps as may be reasonably required by the notice for the purpose of affording that information to other persons concerned.

(3) A non-discrimination notice may also require the person on whom it is served to furnish the Commission with such other information as may be reasonably required by the notice in order to verify that the notice has been complied with.

(4) The notice may specify the time at which, and the manner and form in which, any information is to be furnished to the Commission, but the time at which any information is to be furnished in compliance with the notice shall not be later than five years after the notice has become final.

(5) The Commission shall not serve a non-discrimination notice in respect of any person unless they have first—

(*a*) given him notice that they are minded to issue a non-discrimination notice in his case, specifying the grounds on which they contemplate doing so, and
(*b*) offered him an opportunity of making oral or written representations in the matter (or both oral and written representations if he thinks fit) within a period of not less than 28 days specified in the notice, and
(*c*) taken account of any representations so made by him.

(6) Subsection (2) does not apply to any acts in respect of which the Secretary of State could exercise the powers conferred on him

by section 25(2) and (3); but if the Commission become aware of any such acts they shall give notice of them to the Secretary of State.

(7) Section 59(4) shall apply to requirements under subsection (2)(*b*), (3) and (4) contained in a non-discrimination notice which has become final as it applies to requirements in a notice served under section 59(1).

Appeal against non-discrimination notice.

68.—(1) Not later than six weeks after a non-discrimination notice is served on any person he may appeal against any requirement of the notice—

(*a*) to an industrial tribunal, so far as the requirement relates to acts which are within the jurisdiction of the tribunal;

(*b*) to a county court or to a sheriff court so far as the requirement relates to acts which are within the jurisdiction of the court and are not within the jurisdiction of an industrial tribunal.

(2) Where the court or tribunal considers a requirement in respect of which an appeal is brought under subsection (1) to be unreasonable because it is based on an incorrect finding of fact or for any other reason, the court or tribunal shall quash the requirement.

(3) On quashing a requirement under subsection (2) the court or tribunal may direct that the non-discrimination notice shall be treated as if, in place of the requirement quashed, it had contained a requirement in terms specified in the direction.

(4) Subsection (1) does not apply to a requirement treated as included in a non-discrimination notice by virtue of a direction under subsection (3).

Investigation as to compliance with non-discrimination notice.

69.—(1) If—

(*a*) the terms of reference of a formal investigation state that its purpose is to determine whether any requirements of a non-discrimination notice are being or have been carried out, but section 59(2)(*b*) does not apply, and

(*b*) section 58(3) is complied with in relation to the investigation on a date (" the commencement date ") not later than the expiration of the period of five years beginning when the non-discrimination notice became final,

the Commission may within the period referred to in subsection (2) serve notices under section 59(1) for the purposes of the investigation without needing to obtain the consent of the Secretary of State.

(2) The said period begins on the commencement date and ends on the later of the following dates—

(*a*) the date on which the period of five years mentioned in subsection (1)(*b*) expires;

(*b*) the date two years after the commencement date.

Register of non-discrimination notices.

70.—(1) The Commission shall establish and maintain a register (" the register ") of non-discrimination notices which have become final.

(2) Any person shall be entitled, on payment of such fee (if any) as may be determined by the Commission,—

(*a*) to inspect the register during ordinary office hours and take copies of any entry, or

(*b*) to obtain from the Commission a copy, certified by the Commission to be correct, of any entry in the register.

(3) The Commission may, if they think fit, determine that the right conferred by subsection (2)(*a*) shall be exercisable in relation to a copy of the register instead of, or in addition to, the original.

(4) The Commission shall give general notice of the place or places where, and the times when, the register or a copy of it may be inspected.

Other enforcement by Commission

Persistent discrimination.

71.—(1) If, during the period of five years beginning on the date on which either of the following became final in the case of any person, namely,—

(*a*) a non-discrimination notice served on him,

(*b*) a finding by a court or tribunal under section 63 or 66, or section 2 of the Equal Pay Act 1970, that he has done an unlawful discriminatory act or an act in breach of a term modified or included by virtue of an equality clause,

it appears to the Commission that unless restrained he is likely to do one or more acts falling within paragraph (*b*), or contravening section 37, the Commission may apply to a county court for an injunction, or to the sheriff court for an order, restraining him from doing so; and the court, if satisfied that the application is well-founded, may grant the injunction or order in the terms applied for or in more limited terms.

(2) In proceedings under this section the Commission shall not allege that the person to whom the proceedings relate has done an act which is within the jurisdiction of an industrial tribunal unless a finding by an industrial tribunal that he did that act has become final.

Enforcement of ss. 38 to 40.

72.—(1) Proceedings in respect of a contravention of section 38, 39 or 40 shall be brought only by the Commission in accordance with the following provisions of this section.

(2) The proceedings shall be—

(*a*) an application for a decision whether the alleged contravention occurred, or

(*b*) an application under subsection (4) below,

or both.

(3) An application under subsection (2)(*a*) shall be made—

(*a*) in a case based on any provision of Part II, to an industrial tribunal, and

(*b*) in any other case to a county court or sheriff court.

(4) If it appears to the Commission—

(*a*) that a person has done an act which by virtue of section 38, 39 or 40 was unlawful, and

(*b*) that unless restrained he is likely to do further acts which by virtue of that section are unlawful,

the Commission may apply to a county court for an injunction, or to a sheriff court for an order, restraining him from doing such acts; and the court, if satisfied that the application is well-founded, may grant the injunction or an order in the terms applied for or more limited terms.

(5) In proceedings under subsection (4) the Commission shall not allege that the person to whom the proceedings relate has done an act which is unlawful under this Act and within the jurisdiction of an industrial tribunal unless a finding by an industrial tribunal that he did that act has become final.

Preliminary action in employment cases.

73.—(1) With a view to making an application under section 71(1) or 72(4) in relation to a person the Commission may present to an industrial tribunal a complaint that he has done an act within the jurisdiction of an industrial tribunal, and if the tribunal considers that the complaint is well-founded they shall make a finding to that effect and, if they think it just and equitable to do so in the case of an act contravening any provision of Part II may also (as if the complaint had been presented by the person discriminated against) make an order such as is referred to in section 65(1)(*a*), or a recommendation such as is referred to in section 65(1)(*c*), or both.

(2) Subsection (1) is without prejudice to the jurisdiction conferred by section 72(2).

(3) Any finding of an industrial tribunal under—

(*a*) this Act, or

(*b*) the Equal Pay Act 1970,

in respect of any act shall, if it has become final, be treated as conclusive—

(i) by the county court or sheriff court on an application under section 71(1) or 72(4) or in proceedings on an equality clause,

(ii) by an industrial tribunal on a complaint made by the person affected by the act under section 63 or in relation to an equality clause.

(4) In sections 71 and 72 and this section, the acts " within the jurisdiction of an industrial tribunal " are those in respect of which such jurisdiction is conferred by sections 63 and 72 and by section 2 of the Equal Pay Act 1970.

Help for persons suffering discrimination

Help for aggrieved persons in obtaining information etc.

74.—(1) With a view to helping a person (" the person aggrieved ") who considers he may have been discriminated against in contravention of this Act to decide whether to institute proceedings and, if he does so, to formulate and present his case in the most effective manner, the Secretary of State shall by order prescribe—

(*a*) forms by which the person aggrieved may question the respondent on his reasons for doing any relevant act, or on any other matter which is or may be relevant;

(*b*) forms by which the respondent may if he so wishes reply to any questions.

(2) Where the person aggrieved questions the respondent (whether in accordance with an order under subsection (1) or not)—

(*a*) the question, and any reply by the respondent (whether in accordance with such an order or not) shall, subject to the following provisions of this section, be admissible as evidence in the proceedings;

(*b*) if it appears to the court or tribunal that the respondent deliberately, and without reasonable excuse omitted to reply within a reasonable period or that his reply is evasive or equivocal, the court or tribunal may draw any inference from that fact that it considers it just and equitable to draw, including an inference that he committed an unlawful act.

(3) The Secretary of State may by order—

(*a*) prescribe the period within which questions must be duly served in order to be admissible under subsection (2)(*a*), and

(*b*) prescribe the manner in which a question, and any reply by the respondent, may be duly served.

(4) Rules may enable the court entertaining a claim under section 66 to determine, before the date fixed for the hearing of the claim, whether a question or reply is admissible under this section or not.

(5) This section is without prejudice to any other enactment or rule of law regulating interlocutory and preliminary matters in proceedings before a county court, sheriff court or industrial tribunal, and has effect subject to any enactment or rule of law regulating the admissibility of evidence in such proceedings.

(6) In this section " respondent " includes a prospective respondent and " rules "—

(*a*) in relation to county court proceedings, means county court rules;

(*b*) in relation to sheriff court proceedings, means sheriff court rules.

Assistance by Commission.

75.—(1) Where, in relation to proceedings or prospective proceedings either under this Act or in respect of an equality clause, an individual who is an actual or prospective complainant or claimant applies to the Commission for assistance under this section, the Commission shall consider the application and may grant it if they think fit to do so on the ground that—

(*a*) the case raises a question of principle, or

(*b*) it is unreasonable, having regard to the complexity of the case or the applicant's position in relation to the respondent or another person involved or any other matter, to expect the applicant to deal with the case unaided,

or by reason of any other special consideration.

(2) Assistance by the Commission under this section may include—

(*a*) giving advice;

(*b*) procuring or attempting to procure the settlement of any matter in dispute;

(*c*) arranging for the giving of advice or assistance by a solicitor or counsel;

(*d*) arranging for representation by any person including all such assistance as is usually given by a solicitor or counsel in the steps preliminary or incidental to any proceedings, or in arriving at or giving effect to a compromise to avoid or bring to an end any proceedings, but paragraph (*d*) shall not affect the law and practice regulating the descriptions of persons who may appear in, conduct, defend and address the court in, any proceedings.

(3) In so far as expenses are incurred by the Commission in providing the applicant with assistance under this section the recovery of those expenses (as taxed or assessed in such manner as may be prescribed by rules or regulations) shall constitute a first charge for the benefit of the Commission—

(*a*) on any costs or expenses which (whether by virtue of a judgment or order of a court or tribunal or an agreement or otherwise) are payable to the applicant by any other person in respect of the matter in connection with which the assistance is given, and

(*b*) so far as relates to any costs or expenses, on his rights under any compromise or settlement arrived at in connection with that matter to avoid or bring to an end any proceedings.

(4) The charge conferred by subsection (3) is subject to any charge under the Legal Aid Act 1974, or any charge or obligation for payment in priority to other debts under the Legal Aid and Advice (Scotland) Acts 1967 and 1972, and is subject to any provision in any of those Acts for payment of any sum into the legal aid fund.

(5) In this section " respondent " includes a prospective respondent and " rules or regulations "—

(*a*) in relation to county court proceedings, means county court rules;

(*b*) in relation to sheriff court proceedings, means sheriff court rules;

(*c*) in relation to industrial tribunal proceedings, means regulations made under paragraph 21 of Schedule 1 to the Trade Union and Labour Relations Act 1974.

Period within which proceedings to be brought

Period within which proceedings to be brought.

76.—(1) An industrial tribunal shall not consider a complaint under section 63 unless it is presented to the tribunal before the end of the period of three months beginning when the act complained of was done.

(2) A county court or a sheriff court shall not consider a claim under section 66 unless proceedings in respect of the claim are instituted before the end of the period of six months beginning—

(*a*) when the act complained of was done, or

(*b*) in a case to which section 66(5) applies, when the restriction on the institution of proceedings imposed by that provision ceased to operate.

(3) A county court or sheriff court shall not consider an application under section 72 unless it is made before the end of the period of six months beginning when the act to which it relates was done.

(4) An industrial tribunal shall not consider a complaint under section 73(1) unless it is presented to the tribunal before the end of the period of six months beginning when the act complained of was done.

(5) A court or tribunal may nevertheless consider any such complaint, claim or application which is out of time if, in all the circumstances of the case, it considers that it is just and equitable to do so.

(6) For the purposes of this section—

(*a*) where the inclusion of any term in a contract renders the making of the contract an unlawful act that act shall be treated as extending throughout the duration of the contract, and

(*b*) any act extending over a period shall be treated as done at the end of that period, and

(*c*) a deliberate omission shall be treated as done when the person in question decided upon it,

and in the absence of evidence establishing the contrary a person shall be taken for the purposes of this section to decide upon an omission when he does an act inconsistent with doing the omitted act or, if he has done no such inconsistent act, when the period expires within which he might reasonably have been expected to do the omitted act if it was to be done.

Part VIII

Supplemental

Validity and revision of contracts.

77.—(1) A term of a contract is void where—

(*a*) its inclusion renders the making of the contract unlawful by virtue of this Act, or

(*b*) it is included in furtherance of an act rendered unlawful by this Act, or

(*c*) it provides for the doing of an act which would be rendered unlawful by this Act.

(2) Subsection (1) does not apply to a term the inclusion of which constitutes, or is in furtherance of, or provides for, unlawful discrimination against a party to the contract, but the term shall be unenforceable against that party.

(3) A term in a contract which purports to exclude or limit any provision of this Act or the Equal Pay Act 1970 is unenforceable by any person in whose favour the term would operate apart from this subsection.

(4) Subsection (3) does not apply—

(*a*) to a contract settling a complaint to which section 63(1) of this Act or section 2 of the Equal Pay Act 1970 applies where the contract is made with the assistance of a conciliation officer;

(*b*) to a contract settling a claim to which section 66 applies.

(5) On the application of any person interested in a contract to which subsection (2) applies, a county court or sheriff court may make such order as it thinks just for removing or modifying any term made unenforceable by that subsection; but such an order shall not be made unless all persons affected have been given notice of the application (except where under rules of court notice may be dispensed with) and have been afforded an opportunity to make representations to the court.

(6) An order under subsection (5) may include provision as respects any period before the making of the order.

Educational charities in England and Wales.

78.—(1) This section applies to any trust deed or other instrument—

(*a*) which concerns property applicable for or in connection with the provision of education in any establishment in paragraphs 1 to 5 of the Table in section 22, and

(*b*) which in any way restricts the benefits available under the instrument to persons of one sex.

(2) If on the application of the trustees, or of the responsible body (as defined in section 22), the Secretary of State is satisfied that the removal or modification of the restriction would conduce to the advancement of education without sex discrimination, he may by order make such modifications of the instrument as appear to him expedient for removing or modifying the restriction, and for any supplemental or incidental purposes.

(3) If the trust was created by gift or bequest, no order shall be made until 25 years after the date on which the gift or bequest took effect, unless the donor or his personal representatives, or the personal representatives of the testator, have consented in writing to the making of the application for the order.

(4) The Secretary of State shall require the applicant to publish notice—

(*a*) containing particulars of the proposed order, and

(*b*) stating that representations may be made to the Secretary of State within a period specified in the notice.

(5) The period specified in the notice shall not be less than one month from the date of the notice.

(6) The applicants shall publish the notice in such manner as may be specified by the Secretary of State, and the cost of any publication of the notice may be defrayed out of the property of the trust.

(7) Before making the order the Secretary of State shall take into account any representations duly made in accordance with the notice.

(8) This section does not apply in Scotland.

Educational endowments etc. to which Part VI of the Education (Scotland) Act 1962 applies.

79.—(1) This section applies to any educational endowment to which Part VI of the Education (Scotland) Act 1962 applies and which in any way restricts the benefit of the endowment to persons of one sex and any reference to an educational endowment in this section includes a reference to

(*a*) a scheme made or approved for that endowment under that Part of the Education (Scotland) Act 1962;

(*b*) any endowment which is, by virtue of section 121(1) of that Act, dealt with as if it were an educational endowment; and

(*c*) a university endowment, the Carnegie Trust, a theological endowment and a new endowment.

(2) If, on the application of the governing body of an educational endowment, the Secretary of State is satisfied that the removal or modification of the provision which restricts the benefit of the endowment to persons of one sex would conduce to the advancement of education without sex discrimination, he may, by order, make such modifications to the endowment as appear to him expedient for removing or modifying the restriction and for any supplemental or incidental purposes.

(3) Where the Secretary of State proposes to make an order under this section, he shall publish a notice, in such manner as he thinks sufficient for giving information to persons whom he considers may be interested in the endowment

(*a*) containing particulars of the proposed order; and

(*b*) stating that representations may be made with respect thereto within such period as may be specified in the notice, not being less than one month from the date of publication of the notice,

and the cost of publication of any such notice shall be paid out of the funds of the endowment to which the notice relates.

(4) Before making any order under this section, the Secretary of

State shall consider any representations duly made in accordance with the said notice and he may cause a local inquiry to be held into such representations under section 68 of the Education (Scotland) Act 1962.

(5) Without prejudice to section 81(5) of this Act, any order made under this section may be varied or revoked in a scheme made or approved under Part VI of the Education (Scotland) Act 1962.

(6) For paragraph (*b*) of section 123(1) of the Education (Scotland) Act 1962, there shall be substituted the following paragraph—

" (*b*) where he considers it expedient to do so, provide for extending to both sexes the benefit of the endowment".

(7) This section shall be construed as one with Part VI of the Education (Scotland) Act 1962.

Power to amend certain provisions of Act.

80.—(1) The Secretary of State may by an order the draft of which has been approved by each House of Parliament—

(*a*) amend any of the following provisions, namely, sections 6(3), 7, 19, 20(1), (2) and (3), 31(2), 32, 34, 35 and 43 to 48 (including any such provision as amended by a previous order under this subsection);

(*b*) amend or repeal any of the following provisions, namely, sections 11(4), 12(4), 33 and 49 (including any such provision as amended by a previous order under this subsection);

(*c*) amend Part II, III or IV so as to render lawful an act which, apart from the amendment, would be unlawful by reason of section 6(1) or (2), 29(1), 30 or 31;

(*d*) amend section 11(1) so as to alter the number of partners specified in that provision.

(2) The Secretary of State shall not lay before Parliament the draft of an order under subsection (1) unless he has consulted the Commission about the contents of the draft.

(3) An order under subsection (1)(*c*) may make such amendments to the list of provisions given in subsection (1)(*a*) as in the opinion of the Secretary of State are expedient having regard to the contents of the order.

Orders.

81.—(1) Any power of the Secretary of State to make orders under the provisions of this Act (except sections 14(2)(*d*), 27, 47(4)(*b*) and 59(2)) shall be exercisable by statutory instrument.

(2) An order made by the Secretary of State under the preceding provisions of this Act (except sections 14(2)(*d*), 27, 47(4)(*b*), 59(2)

and 80(1)) shall be subject to annulment in pursuance of a resolution of either House of Parliament.

(3) Subsections (1) and (2) do not apply to an order under section 78 or 79, but—

(*a*) an order under section 78 which modifies an enactment, and

(*b*) any order under section 79 other than one which relates to an endowment to which section 128 of the Education (Scotland) Act 1962 (small endowments) applies,

shall be made by statutory instrument subject to annulment in pursuance of a resolution of either House of Parliament.

(4) An order under this Act may make different provision in relation to different cases or classes of case, may exclude certain cases or classes of case, and may contain transitional provisions and savings.

(5) Any power conferred by this Act to make orders includes power (exercisable in the like manner and subject to the like conditions) to vary or revoke any order so made.

General interpretation provisions.

82.—(1) In this Act, unless the context otherwise requires—

" access " shall be construed in accordance with section 50;

" act " includes a deliberate omission;

" advertisement " includes every form of advertisement, whether to the public or not, and whether in a newspaper or other publication, by television or radio, by display of notices, signs, labels, showcards or goods, by distribution of samples, circulars, catalogues, price lists or other material, by exhibition of pictures, models or films, or in any other way, and references to the publishing of advertisements shall be construed accordingly;

" associated employer " shall be construed in accordance with subsection (2);

" the Commission " means the Equal Opportunities Commission;

" Commissioner " means a member of the Commission;

" conciliation officer " means a person appointed under paragraph 26(1) of Schedule 1 to the Trade Union and Labour Relations Act 1974;

" designate " shall be construed in accordance with subsection (3);

" discrimination " and related terms shall be construed in accordance with section 5(1);

" dispose ", in relation to premises, includes granting a right to occupy the premises, and any reference to acquiring premises shall be construed accordingly;

" education " includes any form of training or instruction;

" education authority " and " educational establishment " in relation to Scotland have the same meaning as they have respectively in section 145(16) and (17) of the Education (Scotland) Act 1962;

" employment " means employment under a contract of service or of apprenticeship or a contract personally to execute any work or labour, and related expressions shall be construed accordingly;

" employment agency " means a person who, for profit or not, provides services for the purpose of finding employment for wokers or supplying employers with workers;

" equality clause " has the meaning given in section 1(2) of the Equal Pay Act 1970 (as set out in section 8(1) of this Act);

" estate agent " means a person who, by way of profession or trade, provides services for the purpose of finding premises for persons seeking to acquire them or assisting in the disposal of premises;

" final " shall be construed in accordance with subsection (4);

" firm " has the meaning given by section 4 of the Partnership Act 1890;

" formal investigation " means an investigation under section 57;

" further education " has the meaning given by section 41(*a*) of the Education Act 1944 and in Scotland has the meaning given by section 145(21) of the Education (Scotland) Act 1962;

" general notice ", in relation to any person, means a notice published by him at a time and in a manner appearing to him suitable for securing that the notice is seen within a reasonable time by persons likely to be affected by it;

" genuine occupational qualification " shall be construed in accordance with section 7(2);

" Great Britain " includes such of the territorial waters of the United Kingdom as are adjacent to Great Britain;

" independent school " has the meaning given by section 114(1) of the Education Act 1944 and in Scotland has the meaning given by section 145(23) of the Education (Scotland) Act 1962;

" industrial tribunal " means a tribunal established under section 12 of the Industrial Training Act 1964;

" man " includes a male of any age;

" managers " has the same meaning for Scotland as in section 145(26) of the Education (Scotland) Act 1962;

" near relative " shall be construed in accordance with subsection (5);

" non-discrimination notice " means a notice under section 67;

" notice " means a notice in writing;

" prescribed " means prescribed by regulations made by the Secretary of State by statutory instrument;

" profession " includes any vocation or occupation;

" proprietor ", in relation to any school, has the meaning given by section 114(1) of the Education Act 1944 and in Scotland has the meaning given by section 145(37) of the Education (Scotland) Act 1962;

" pupil " in Scotland includes a student of any age;

" retirement " includes retirement (whether voluntary or not) on grounds of age, length of serivce or incapacity;

" school " has the meaning given by section 114(1) of the Education Act 1944, and in Scotland has the meaning given by section 145(42) of the Education (Scotland) Act 1962;

" school education " has the meaning given by section 145(43A) of the Education (Scotland) Act 1962;

" trade " includes any business;

" training " includes any form of education or instruction;

" university " includes a university college and the college, school or hall of a university;

" upper limit of compulsory school age " means, subject to section 9 of the Education Act 1962, the age that is that limit by virtue of section 35 of the Education Act 1944 and the Order in Council made under that section;

" woman " includes a female of any age.

(2) For the purposes of this Act two employers are to be treated as associated if one is a company of which the other (directly or indirectly) has control or if both are companies of which a third person (directly or indirectly) has control.

(3) Any power conferred by this Act to designate establishments or persons may be exercised either by naming them or by identifying them by reference to a class or other description.

(4) For the purposes of this Act a non-discrimination notice or a finding by a court or tribunal becomes final when an appeal against the notice or finding is dismissed, withdrawn or abandoned or when the time for appealing expires without an appeal having been brought; and for this purpose an appeal against a non-discrimination notice shall be taken to be dismissed if, notwithstanding that a requirement of the notice is quashed on appeal, a direction is given in respect of it under section 68(3).

(5) For the purposes of this Act a person is a near relative of another if that person is the wife or husband, a parent or child, a grandparent or grandchild, or a brother or sister of the other (whether of full blood or half-blood or by affinity), and " child " includes an illegitimate child and the wife or husband of an illegitimate child.

(6) Except so far as the context otherwise requires, any reference in this Act to an enactment shall be construed as a reference to that enactment as amended by or under any other enactment, including this Act.

(7) In this Act, except where otherwise indicated—

(*a*) a reference to a numbered Part, section or Schedule is a reference to the Part or section of, or the Schedule to, this Act so numbered, and

(*b*) a reference in a section to a numbered subsection is a reference to the subsection of that section so numbered, and

(*c*) a reference in a section, subsection or Schedule to a numbered paragraph is a reference to the paragraph of that section, subsection or Schedule so numbered, and

(*d*) a reference to any provision of an Act (including this Act) includes a Schedule incorporated in the Act by that provision.

Transitional and commencement provisions, amendments and repeals.

83.—(1) The provisions of Schedule 4 shall have effect for making transitional provision for the purposes of this Act.

(2) Parts II to VII shall come into operation on such day as the Secretary of State may by order appoint, and different days may be so appointed for different provisions and for different purposes.

(3) Subject to subsection (4)—

(*a*) the enactments specified in Schedule 5 shall have effect subject to the amendments specified in that Schedule (being minor amendments or amendments consequential on the preceding provisions of this Act), and

(*b*) the enactments specified in Schedule 6 are hereby repealed to the extent shown in column 3 of that Schedule.

(4) The Secretary of State shall by order provide for the coming into operation of the amendments contained in Schedule 5 and the repeals contained in Schedule 6, and those amendments and repeals shall have effect only as provided by an order so made.

(5) An order under this section may make such transitional provision as appears to the Secretary of State to be necessary or expedient in connection with the provisions thereby brought into operation, including such adaptations of those provisions, or of any provisions of this Act then in operation, as appear to the Secretary of State necessary or expedient in consequence of the partial operation of this Act.

Financial provisions.

84. There shall be defrayed out of money provided by Parliament—

(*a*) sums required by the Secretary of State for making payments under paragraph 5 or 14 of Schedule 3, and for defraying any other expenditure falling to be made by him under or by virtue of this Act;

(*b*) payments falling to be made under section 66(6)(*b*) or (7) in respect of the remuneration of assessors; and

(*c*) any increase attributable to the provisions of this Act in the sums payable out of money provided by Parliament under any other Act.

Application to Crown.

85.—(1) This Act applies—

(*a*) to an act done by or for purposes of a Minister of the Crown or government department, or

(*b*) to an act done on behalf of the Crown by a statutory body, or a person holding a statutory office,

as it applies to an act done by a private person.

(2) Parts II and IV apply to—

(*a*) service for purposes of a Minister of the Crown or government department, other than service of a person holding a statutory office, or

(*b*) service on behalf of the Crown for purposes of a person holding a statutory office or purposes of a statutory body,

as they apply to employment by a private person, and shall so apply as if references to a contract of employment included references to the terms of service.

(3) Subsections (1) and (2) have effect subject to section 17.

(4) Subsections (1) and (2) do not apply in relation to service in—

(*a*) the naval, military or air forces of the Crown, or

(*b*) any women's service administered by the Defence Council.

(5) Nothing in this Act shall render unlawful discrimination in admission to the Army Cadet Force, Air Training Corps, Sea Cadet Corps or Combined Cadet Force, or any other cadet training corps for the time being administered by the Ministry of Defence.

(6) This Act (except section 8(1) and (6)) does not apply to employment in the case of which the employee may be required to serve in support of a force or service mentioned in subsection 4(*a*) or (*b*).

(7) Subsection (2) of section 10 shall have effect in relation to any ship, aircraft or hovercraft belonging to or possessed by Her

Majesty in right of the Government of the United Kingdom as it has effect in relation to a ship, aircraft or hovercraft mentioned in paragraph (*a*) or (*b*) of that subsection, and section 10(5) shall apply accordingly.

(8) The provisions of Parts II to IV of the Crown Proceedings Act 1947 shall apply to proceedings against the Crown under this Act as they apply to proceedings in England and Wales which by virtue of section 23 of that Act are treated for the purposes of Part II of that Act as civil proceedings by or against the Crown, except that in their application to proceedings under this Act section 20 of that Act (removal of proceedings from county court to High Court) shall not apply.

(9) The provisions of Part V of the Crown Proceedings Act 1947 shall apply to proceedings against the Crown under this Act as they apply to proceedings in Scotland which by virtue of the said Part are treated as civil proceedings by or against the Crown, except that in their application to proceedings under this Act the proviso to section 44 of that Act (removal of proceedings from the sheriff court to the Court of Session) shall not apply.

(10) In this section " statutory body " means a body set up by or in pursuance of an enactment, and " statutory office " means an office so set up; and service " for purposes of " a Minister of the Crown or government department does not include service in any office in Schedule 2 (Ministerial offices) to the House of Commons Disqualification Act 1975 as for the time being in force.

Government appointments outside section 6.

86.—(1) This section applies to any appointment by a Minister of the Crown or government department to an office or post where section 6 does not apply in relation to the appointment.

(2) In making the appointment, and in making the arrangements for determining who should be offered the office or post, the Minister of the Crown or government department shall not do an act which would be unlawful under section 6 if the Crown were the employer for the purposes of this Act.

Short title and extent.

87.—(1) This Act may be cited as the Sex Discrimination Act 1975.

(2) This Act (except paragraph 16 of Schedule 3) does not extend to Northern Ireland.

SCHEDULES

SCHEDULE 1

Section 8.

EQUAL PAY ACT 1970

PART I

AMENDMENTS OF ACT

1.—(1) In section 1(6), paragraph (*b*) is repealed and the following is inserted after paragraph (*c*): " and men shall be treated as in the same employment with a woman if they are men employed by her employer or any associated employer at the same establishment or at establishments in Great Britain which include that one and at which common terms and conditions of employment are observed either generally or for employees of the relevant classes ".

(2) Section 1(7) is repealed.

(3) The following is substituted for section 1(8)—

" (8) This section shall apply to

(*a*) service for purposes of a Minister of the Crown or government department, other than service of a person holding a statutory office, or

(*b*) service on behalf of the Crown for purposes of a person holding a statutory office or purposes of a statutory body,"

as it applies to employment by a private person, and shall so apply as if references to a contract of employment included references to the terms of service.

(9) Subsection (8) does not apply in relation to service in—

(*a*) the naval, military or air forces of the Crown, or

(*b*) any women's service administered by the Defence Council.

(10) In this section " statutory body " means a body set up by or in pursuance of an enactment, and " statutory office " means an office so set up; and service " for purposes of " a Minister of the Crown or government department does not include service in any office in Schedule 2 (Ministerial offices) to the House of Commons Disqualification Act 1975 as for the time being in force."

(4) The following subsections are inserted at the end of section 1—

" (11) For the purposes of this Act it is immaterial whether the law which (apart from this subsection) is the proper law of a contract is the law of any part of the United Kingdom or not.

(12) In this Act " Great Britain " includes such of the territorial waters of the United Kingdom as are adjacent to Great Britain.

(13) Provisions of this section and section 2 below framed with reference to women and their treatment relative to men are to be read as applying equally in a converse case to men and their treatment relative to women ".

2.—(1) The following is substituted for section 2(1)—

" (1) Any claim in respect of the contravention of a term modified or included by virtue of an equality clause, including a claim for arrears of remuneration or damages in respect of the contravention, may be presented by way of a complaint to an industrial tribunal."

(2) After section 2(1) there is inserted—

" (1A) Where a dispute arises in relation to the effect of an equality clause the employer may apply to an industrial tribunal for an order declaring the rights of the employer and the employee in relation to the matter in question."

(3) In section 2(2)—

(*a*) for " failing to comply with their equal pay clauses " there is substituted " contravening a term modified or included by virtue of their equality clauses ", and

(*b*) after " the question may be referred by him " there is inserted " as respects all or any of them ", and

(*c*) after " claim by the women " there is inserted " or woman ".

(4) Section 2(6) is repealed.

(5) In section 2(7), the words " and there shall be paid " onwards are repealed.

3. In section 6 the following is substituted for subsection (1)—

" (1) Neither an equality clause nor the provisions of section 3(4) above shall operate in relation to terms—

(*a*) affected by compliance with the laws regulating the employment of women, or

(*b*) affording special treatment to women in connection with pregnancy or childbirth.

(1A) An equality clause and those provisions—

(*a*) shall operate in relation to terms relating to membership of an occupational pension scheme (within the meaning of the Social Security Penions Act 1975) so far as those terms relate to any matter in respect of which the scheme has to conform with the equal access requirements of Part IV of that Act; but

(*b*) subject to this, shall not operate in relation to terms related to death or retirement, or to any provision made in connection with death or retirement."

4. Section 8 is repealed.

5. In section 9(1), the words " Except as provided by subsection (2) below ", and sections 9(2) to (5) and 10(4) are repealed.

6.—(1) For references to an equal pay clause in each place where they occur there are substituted references to an equality clause.

(2) For the words " the Industrial Court ", in each place where they occur, there are substituted the words " the Industrial Arbitration Board "; in sections 4 and 10 for the words " Court " and " Court's " in each place where they occur there are substituted respectively " Board " and " Board's ", and in section 5 for the word " Board " in each place where it occurs there is substituted " Agricultural Wages Board " and for the word " Court " in each place where it occurs there is substituted " Industrial Arbitration Board ".

PART II

ACT AS AMENDED

[*In the provisions set out in this Schedule words inserted by the Act are printed in* **bold type** *and omissions are denoted by dots.*]

1970 CHAPTER 41

An Act to prevent discrimination, as regards terms and conditions of employment, between men and women. [29th May 1970]

BE IT ENACTED by the Queen's Most Excellent Majesty, by and with the advice and consent of the Lords Spiritual and Temporal, and Commons, in this present Parliament assembled, and by the authority of the same, as follows:—

1.—(1) If the terms of a contract under which a woman is employed at an establishment in Great Britain do not include (directly or by reference to a collective agreement or otherwise) an equality clause they shall be deemed to include one.

(2) An equality clause is a provision which relates to terms (whether concerned with pay or not) of a contract under which a woman is employed (the " woman's contract "), and has the effect that—

(a) where the woman is employed on like work with a man in the same employment—

(i) if (apart from the equality clause) any term of the women's contract is or becomes less favourable to the woman than a term of a similar kind in the contract under which that man is employed, that term of the woman's contract shall be treated as so modified as not to be less favourable, and

(ii) if (apart from the equality clause) at any time the woman's contract does not include a term corresponding to a term benefiting that man included in the contract under which he is employed, the woman's contract shall be treated as including such a term;

(b) where the woman is employed on work rated as equivalent with that of a man in the same employment—

(i) if (part from the equality clause) any term of the woman's contract determined by the rating of the work is or becomes less favourable to the woman than a term of a similar kind in the contract under which that man is employed, that term of the woman's contract shall be treated as so modified as not to be less favourable, and

(ii) if (part from the equality clause) at any time the woman's contract does not include a term corresponding to a term benefiting that man included in the contract under which he is employed and determined by the rating of the work, the woman's contract shall be treated as including such a term.

(3) An equality clause shall not operate in relation to a variation between the woman's contract and the man's contract if the employer proves that the variation is genuinely due to a material difference (other than the difference of sex) between her case and his.

(4) A woman is to be regarded as employed on like work with men if, but only if, her work and theirs is of the same or a broadly similar nature, and the differences (if any) between the things she does and the things they do are not of practical importance in relation to terms and conditions of employment; and accordingly in comparing her work with theirs regard shall be had to the frequency or otherwise with which any such differences occur in practice as well as to the nature and extent of the differences.

(5) A woman is to be regarded as employed on work rated as equivalent with that of any man if, but only if, her job and their job have been given an equal value, in terms of the demand made on a worker under various headings (for instance effort, skill, decision), on a study undertaken with a view to evaluating in those terms the jobs to be done by all or any of the employees in an undertaking or group of undertakings, or would have been given an equal value but for the evaluation being made on a system setting different values for men and women on the same demand under any heading.

(6) Subject to the following subsections, for purposes of this section—

(*a*) " employed " means employed under a contract of service or of apprenticeship or a contract personally to execute

K

any work or labour, and related expressions shall be construed accordingly;

. . . .

(*c*) two employers are to be treated as associated if one is a company of which the other (directly or indirectly) has control or if both are companies of which a third person (directly or indirectly) has control,

and men shall be treated as in the same employment with a woman if they are men employed by her employer or any associated employer at the same establishment or at establishments in Great Britain which include that one and at which common terms and conditions of employment are observed either generally or for employees of the relevant classes.

. . . .

(8) This section shall apply to

(a) service for purposes of a Minister of the Crown or government department, other than service of a person holding a statutory office, or

(b) service on behalf of the Crown for purposes of a person holding a statutory office or purposes of a statutory body,

as it applies to employment by a private person, and shall so apply as if references to a contract of employment included references to the terms of service.

(9) Subsection (8) does not apply in relation to service in—

(a) the naval, military or air forces of the Crown, or

(b) any women's service administered by the Defence Council.

(10) In this section " statutory body " means a body set up by or in pursuance of an enactment, and " statutory office " means an office so set up; and service " for purposes of " a Minister of the Crown or government department does not include service in any office in Schedule 2 (Ministerial offices) to the House of Commons Disqualification Act 1975 as for the time being in force.

(11) For the purposes of this Act it is immaterial whether the law which (apart from this subsection) is the proper law of a contract is the law of any part of the United Kingdom or not.

(12) In this Act " Great Britain " includes such of the territorial waters of the United Kingdom as are adjacent to Great Britain.

(13) Provisions of this section and section 2 below framed with reference to women and their treatment relative to men are to be read as applying equally in a converse case to men and their treatment relative to women.

Disputes as to, and enforcement of, requirement of equal treatment.

2.—(1) Any claim in respect of the contravention of a term modified or included by virtue of an equality clause, including a claim for

arrears of remuneration or damages in respect of the contravention, may be presented by way of a complaint to an industrial tribunal.

(1A) Where a dispute arises in relation to the effect of an equality clause the employer may apply to an industrial tribunal for an order declaring the rights of the employer and the employee in relation to the matter in question.

(2) Where it appears to the Secretary of State that there may be a question whether the employer of any women is or has been **contravening a term modified or included by virtue of their equality clauses,** but that it is not reasonable to expect them to take steps to have the question determined, the question may be referred by him **as respects all or any of them** to an industrial tribunal and shall be dealt with as if the reference were of a claim by the women **or woman** against the employer.

(3) Where it appears to the court in which any proceedings are pending that a claim or counterclaim in respect of the operation of an **equality** clause could more conveniently be disposed of separately by an industrial tribunal, the court may direct that the claim or counterclaim shall be struck out; and (without prejudice to the foregoing) where in proceedings before any court a question arises as to the operation of an **equality** clause, the court may on the application of any party to the proceedings or otherwise refer that question, or direct it to be referred by a party to the proceedings, to an industrial tribunal for determination by the tribunal, and may stay or sist the proceedings in the meantime.

(4) No claim in respect of the operation of an **equality** clause relating to a woman's employment shall be referred to an industrial tribunal otherwise than by virtue of subsection (3) above, if she has not been employed in the employment within the six months preceding the date of the reference.

(5) A woman shall not be entitled, in proceedings brought in respect of a failure to comply with an **equality** clause (including proceedings before an industrial tribunal), to be awarded any payment by way of arrears of remuneration or damages in respect of a time earlier than two years before the date on which the proceedings were instituted.

. . . .

(7) in this section " industrial tribunal " means a tribunal established under section 12 of the Industrial Training Act 1964 . . .

Collective agreements and pay structures.

3.—(1) Where a collective agreement made before or after the commencement of this Act contains any provision applying specifically to men only or to women only, the agreement may be referred, by any party to it or by the Secretary of State, to the Industrial **Arbitration Board** constituted under Part I of the Industrial Courts

Act 1919 to declare what amendments need to be made in the agreement, in accordance with subsection (4) below, so as to remove that discrimination between men and women.

(2) Where on a reference under subsection (1) above the Industrial **Arbitration Board** have declared the amendments needing to be made in a collective agreement in accordance with that subsection, then—

(*a*) in so far as the terms and conditions of a person's employment are dependent on that agreement, they shall be ascertained by reference to the agreement as so amended, and any contract regulating those terms and conditions shall have effect accordingly; and

(*b*) if the Industrial **Arbitration Board** make or have made, under section 8 of the Terms and Conditions of Employment Act 1959 or any other enactment, an award or determination requiring an employer to observe the collective agreement, the award or determination shall have effect by reference to the agreement as so amended.

(3) On a reference under subsection (1) above the Industrial **Arbitration Board** may direct that all or any of the amendments needing to be made in the collective agreement shall be treated as not becoming effective until a date after their decision, or as having been effective from a date before their decision but not before the reference to them, and may specify different dates for different purposes; and subsection (2) above and any such contract, award or determination as is there mentioned shall have or be deemed to have had effect accordingly.

(4) Subject to section 6 below, the amendments to be made in a collective agreement under this section shall be such as are needed—

(*a*) to extend to both men and women any provision applying specifically to men only or to women only; and

(*b*) to eliminate any resulting duplication in the provisions of the agreement in such a way as not to make the terms and conditions agreed for men, or those agreed for women, less favourable in any respect than they would have been without the amendments;

but the amendments shall not extend the operation of the collective agreement to men or to women not previosly falling within it, and where accordingly a provision applying specifically to men only or to women only continues to be required for a category of men or of women (there being no provision in the agreement for women or, as the case may be, for men of that category), then the provision shall be limited to men or women of that category but there shall be made to it such amendments, if any, as are needed to secure that the terms and conditions of the men or women of that category are not in any respect less favourable than those of all persons of the other sex to whom the agreement applies.

(5) For purposes of this section " collective agreement " means any agreement as to terms and conditions of employment, being an agreement between—

(*a*) parties who are or represent employers or organisations of employers or associations of such organisations; and

(*b*) parties who are or represent organisations of employees or associations of such organisations;

but includes also any award modifying or supplementing such an agreement.

(6) Subsections (1) to (4) above (except subsection (2)(*b*) and subsection (3) in so far as it relates to subsection (2)(*b*)) shall have effect in relation to an employer's pay structure as they have effect in relation to a collective agreement, with the adaptation that a reference to the Industrial **Arbitration Board** may be made by the employer or by the Secretary of State; and for this purpose " pay structure " means any arrangements adopted by an employer (with or without any associated employer) which fix common terms and conditions of employment for his employees or any class of his employees, and of which the provisions are generally known or open to be known by the employees concerned.

(7) In this section the expression " employment " and related expressions, and the reference to an associated employer, shall be construed in the same way as in section 1 above, and section 1(8) shall have effect in relation to this section as well as in relation to that section.

Wages regulation orders.

4.—(1) Where a wages regulation order made before or after the commencement of this Act contains any provision applying specifically to men only or to women only, the order may be referred by the Secretary of State to the Industrial **Arbitration Board** to declare what amendments need to be made in the order, in accordance with the like rules as apply under section 3(4) above to the amendment under that section of a collective agreement, so as to remove that discrimination between men and women; and when the **Board** have declared the amendments needing to be so made, the Secretary of State may by order made by statutory instrument coming into operation not later than five months after the date of the **Board's** decision direct that (subject to any further wages regulation order) the order referred to the **Board** shall have effect subject to those amendments.

(2) A wages regulation order shall be referred to the Industrial **Arbitration Board** under this section if the Secretary of State is requested so to refer it either—

(*a*) by a member or members of the wages council concerned with the order who was or who were appointed as representing employers; or

(*b*) by a member or members of that wages council who was or who were appointed as representing workers;

or if in any case it appears to the Secretary of State that the order may be amendable under this section.

(3) Where by virtue of section 12(1) of the Wages Councils Act 1959 a contract between a worker and an employer is to have effect with modifications specified in section 12(1), then (without prejudice to the general saving in section 11(7) of that Act for rights conferred by or under other Acts) the contract as so modified shall have effect subject to any further term implied by virtue of section 1 above.

(4) In this section " wages regulation order " means an order made or having effect as if made under section 11 of the Wages Councils Act 1959.

Agricultural wages orders.

5.—(1) Where an agricultural wages order made before or after the commencement of this Act contains any provision applying specifically to men only or to women only, the order may be referred by the Secretary of State to the Industrial **Arbitration Board** to declare what amendments need to be made in the order, in accordance with the like rules as apply under section 3(4) above to the amendment under that section of a collective agreement, so as to remove that discrimination between men and women; and when the **Industrial Arbitration Board** have declared the amendments needing to be so made, it shall be the duty of the Agricultural Wages Board, by a further agricultural wages order coming into operation not later than five months after the date of the **Industrial Arbitration Board's** decision, either to make those amendments in the order referred to the **Industrial Arbitration Board** or otherwise to replace or amend that order so as to remove the discrimination.

(2) Where the Agricultural Wages Board certify that the effect of an agricultural wages order is only to make such amendments of a previous order as have under this section been declared by the Industrial **Arbitration Board** to be needed, or to make such amendments as aforesaid with minor modifications or modifications of limited application, or is only to revoke and reproduce with such amendments a previous order, then the **Agricultural Wages** Board may instead of complying with paragraphs 1 and 2 of Schedule 4, or in the case of Scotland paragraphs 1 and 2 of Schedule 3, to the Agricultural Wages Act give notice of the proposed order in such manner as appears to the **Agricultural Wages** Board expedient in the circumstances, and may make the order at any time after the expiration of seven days from the giving of the notice.

(3) An agricultural wages order shall be referred to the Industrial Arbitration Board under this section if the Secretary of State is requested so to refer it either—

(*a*) by a body for the time being entitled to nominate for membership of the Agricultural Wages Board persons representing employers (or, if provision is made for any of the persons representing employers to be elected instead of nominated, then by a member or members representing employers); or

(*b*) by a body for the time being entitled to nominate for membership of the Agricultural Wages Board persons representing workers (or, if provision is made for any of the persons representing workers to be elected instead of nominated, then by a member or members representing workers);

or if in any case it appears to the Secretary of State that the order may be amendable under this section.

(4) In this section " the Agricultural Wages Board " means the Agricultural Wages Board for England and Wales or the Scottish Agricultural Wages Board, " the Agricultural Wages Act " means the Agricultural Wages Act 1948 or the Agricultural Wages (Scotland) Act 1949 and " agricultural wages order " means an order of the Agricultural Wages Board under the Agricultural Wages Act.

Exclusion from ss. 1 to 5 of pensions etc.

6.—(1) Neither an equality clause nor the provisions of section 3(4) above shall operate in relation to terms—

(a) affected by compliance with the laws regulating the employment of women, or

(b) affording special treatment to women in connection with pregnancy or childbirth.

(1A) An equality clause and those provisions—

(a) shall operate in relation to terms relating to membership of an occupational pension scheme (within the meaning of the Social Security Pensions Act 1975) so far as those terms relate to any matter in respect of which the scheme has to conform with the equal access requirements of Part IV of that Act; but

(b) subject to this, shall not operate in relation to terms related to death or retirement, or to any provision made in connection with death or retirement.

(2) Any reference in this section to retirement includes retirement, whether voluntary or not, on grounds of age, length of service or incapacity.

Service pay.

7.—(1) The Secretary of State or Defence Council shall not

make, or recommend to Her Majesty the making of, any instrument relating to the terms and conditions of service of members of the naval, military or air forces of the Crown or of any women's service administered by the Defence Council, if the instrument has the effect of making a distinction, as regards pay, allowances or leave, between men and women who are members of those forces or of any such service, not being a distinction fairly attributable to differences between the obligations undertaken by men and those undertaken by women as such members as aforesaid.

(2) The Secretary of State or Defence Council may refer to the Industrial **Arbitration Board** for their advice any question whether a provision made or proposed to be made by any such instrument as is referred to in subsection (1) above ought to be regarded for purposes of this section as making a distinction not permitted by that subsection.

. . . .

Commencement.

9.—(1) . . . the foregoing provisions of this Act shall come into force on the 29th December 1975 and references in this Act to its commencement shall be construed as referring to the coming into force of those provisions on that date.

. . . .

Preliminary references to Industrial Arbitration Board.

10.—(1) A collective agreement, pay structure or order which after the commencement of this Act could under section 3, 4 or 5 of this Act be referred to the Industrial **Arbitration Board** to declare what amendments need to be made as mentioned in that section may at any time not earlier than one year before that commencement be referred to the **Board** under this section for their advice as to the amendments needing to be so made.

(2) A reference under this section may be made by any person authorised by section 3, 4 or 5, as the case may be, to make a corresponding reference under that section, but the Secretary of State shall not under this section refer an order to the Industrial **Arbitration Board** unless requested so to do as mentioned in section 4(2) or 5(3), as the case may be, nor be required to refer an order if so requested.

(3) A collective agreement, pay structure or order referred to the Industrial **Arbitration Board** under this section may after the commencement of this Act be again referred to the **Board** under section 3, 4 or 5; but at that commencement any reference under this section (if still pending) shall lapse.

. . . . .

Short title, interpretation and extent.

11.—(1) This Act may be cited at the Equal Pay Act 1970.

(2) In this Act the expressions " man " and " woman " shall be read as applying to persons of whatever age.

(3) This Act shall not extend to Northern Ireland.

Section 27.

SCHEDULE 2

TRANSITIONAL EXEMPTION ORDERS FOR EDUCATIONAL ADMISSIONS

Public sector (England and Wales)

1. Where under section 13 of the Education Act 1944 (as set out in Schedule 3 to the Education Act 1968) a responsible body submits to the Secretary of State, in accordance with subsection (1) or (2) of that section, proposals for an alteration in its admissions arrangements such as is mentioned in section 27(1) of this Act the submission of those proposals shall be treated as an application for the making by the Secretary of State of a transitional exemption order, and if he thinks fit the Secretary of State may make the order accordingly.

2. Regulations under section 33 of the Education Act 1944 may provide for the submission to the Secretary of State of an application for the making by him of a transitional exemption order in relation to a special school, and for the making by him of the order.

3. Regulations under section 100 of the Education Act 1944 may provide for the submission to the Secretary of State of an application for the making by him of a transitional exemption order in relation to an establishment—

(*a*) which is designated under section 24(1), and

(*b*) in respect of which grants are payable under subsection (1)(*b*) of the said section 100,

and for the making by him of the order.

4. Regulations under section 5(2) of the Local Government Act 1974 may provide for the submission to the Secretary of State of an application for the making by him of a transitional exemption order in relation to any educational establishment maintained by a local education authority and not falling within paragraphs 1 to 3, and for the making by him of the order.

Private sector (England and Wales)

5.—(1) In the case of an establishment in England or Wales not falling within paragraphs 1 to 4 the responsible body may submit to the Equal Opportunities Commission set up under Part VI an application for the making by the Commission of a transitional exemption order in relation to the establishment, and if they think fit the Commission may make the order accordingly.

(2) An application under this paragraph shall specify the transitional period proposed by the responsible body to be provided for in the order, the stages by which within that period the body proposes to move to the position where section 22(*b*) is complied with, and any other matters relevant to the terms and operation of the order applied for.

(3) The Commission shall not make an order on an application under this paragraph unless they are satisfied that the terms of the application are reasonable having regard to the nature of the premises at which the establishment is carried on, the accommodation, equipment and facilities available, and the financial resources of the responsible body.

Public and private sectors (Scotland)

6. Any application for a transitional exemption order made by the responsible body in relation to an establishment falling within paragraph 6 or 7 of the Table in section 22 shall be made to the Secretary of State, and in relation to an establishment falling within paragraphs 8, 9 and 10 of that Table shall be made to the Equal Opportunities Commission.

7. An application under paragraph 6 shall specify the transitional period proposed by the responsible body to be provided for in the order, the stages by which within that period the body proposes to move to the position where section 22(*b*) is complied with, and any other matters relevant to the terms and operation of the order applied for.

8. The Secretary of State on any application under paragraph 6 may make a transitional exemption order on such terms and conditions as he may think fit.

9. The Commission on any application under paragraph 6 may if they think fit make a transitional exemption order, but shall not make such an order unless they are satisfied that the terms of the application are reasonable having regard to the nature of the premises at which the establishment is carried on, the accommodation, equipment and facilities available, and the financial resources of the responsible body.

Section 53.

SCHEDULE 3

EQUAL OPPORTUNITIES COMMISSION

Incorporation and status

1. On the appointment by the Secretary of State of the first

Commissioners, the Commission shall come into existence as a body corporate with perpetual succession and a common seal.

2.—(1) The Commission is not an emanation of the Crown, and shall not act or be treated as the servant or agent of the Crown.

(2) Accordingly—

(*a*) neither the Commission nor a Commissioner or member of its staff as such is entitled to any status, immunity, privilege or exemption enjoyed by the Crown;

(*b*) the Commissioners and members of the staff of the Commission as such are not civil servants; and

(*c*) the Commission's property is not property of, or held on behalf of, the Crown.

Tenure of office of Commissioners

3.—(1) A Commissioner shall hold and vacate his office in accordance with the terms of his appointment.

(2) A person shall not be appointed a Commissioner for more than five years.

(3) With the consent of the Commissioner concerned, the Secretary of State may alter the terms of an appointment so as to make a full-time Commissioner into a part-time Commissioner or vice versa, or for any other purpose.

(4) A Commissioner may resign by notice to the Secretary of State.

(5) The Secretary of State may terminate the appointment of a Commissioner if satisfied that—

(*a*) without the consent of the Commission, he failed to attend the meetings of the Commission during a continuous period of six months beginning not earlier than nine months before the termination; or

(*b*) he is an undischarged bankrupt, or has made an arrangement with his creditors, or is insolvent within the meaning of paragraph 9(2) of Schedule 3 to the Conveyancing and Feudal Reform (Scotland) Act 1970; or

(*c*) he is by reason of physical or mental illness, or for any other reason, incapable of carrying out his duties.

(6) Past service as a Commissioner is no bar to re-appointment.

Tenure of office of chairman and deputy chairmen

4.—(1) The chairman and each deputy chairman shall hold and vacate his office in accordance with the terms of his appointment, and may resign by notice to the Secretary of State.

(2) The office of the chairman or a deputy chairman is vacated if he ceases to be a Commissioner.

(3) Past service as chairman or a deputy chairman is no bar to re-appointment.

Remuneration of Commissioners

5. The Secretary of State may pay, or make such payments towards the provision of, such remuneration, pensions, allowances or gratuities to or in respect of the Commissioners or any of them as, with the consent of the Minister for the Civil Service, he may determine.

6. Where a person ceases to be a Commissioner otherwise than on the expiry of his term of office, and it appears to the Secretary of State that there are special circumstances which make it right for that person to receive compensation, the Secretary of State may with the consent of the Minister for the Civil Service direct the Commission to make to that person a payment of such amount as, with the consent of that Minister, the Secretary of State may determine.

Additional Commissioners

7.—(1) Paragraphs 2(2), 3(1) and (6), and 6 shall apply to additional Commissioners appointed under section 57(2) as they apply to Commissioners.

(2) The Commission may pay, or make such payments towards the provision of, such remuneration, pensions, allowances or gratuities to or in respect of an additional Commissioner as the Secretary of State, with the consent of the Minister for the Civil Service, may determine.

(3) With the approval of the Secretary of State and the consent of the additional Commissioner concerned, the Commission may alter the terms of an appointment of an additional Commissioner so as to make a full-time additional Commissioner into a part-time additional Commissioner or vice versa, or for any other purpose.

(4) An additional Commissioner may resign by notice to the Commission.

(5) The Secretary of State, or the Commission acting with the approval of the Secretary of State, may terminate the appointment of an additional Commissioner if satisfied that—

(*a*) without reasonable excuse he failed to carry out the duties for which he was appointed during a continuous period of three months beginning not earlier than six months before the termination; or

(*b*) he is a person such as is mentioned in paragraph 3(5)(*b*); or

(*c*) he is by reason of physical or mental illness, or for any other reason, incapable of carrying out his duties.

(6) The appointment of an additional Commissioner shall terminate at the conclusion of the investigation for which he was appointed, if not sooner.

Staff

8. The Commission may, after consultation with the Secretary of State, appoint such officers and servants as they think fit, subject to the approval of the Minister for the Civil Service as to numbers and as to remuneration and other terms and conditions of service.

9.—(1) Employment with the Commission shall be included among the kinds of employment to which a superannuation scheme under section 1 of the Superannuation Act 1972 can apply, and accordingly in Schedule 1 to that Act (in which those kinds of employment are listed) the words " Equal Opportunities Commission " shall be inserted at the appropriate place in alphabetical order.

(2) Where a person who is employed by the Commission and is by reference to that employment a participant in a scheme under section 1 of the Superannuation Act 1972 becomes a Commissioner or an additional Commissioner, the Minister for the Civil Service may determine that his service as a Commissioner or additional Commissioner shall be treated for the purposes of the scheme as service as an employee of the Commission; and his rights under the scheme shall not be affected by paragraph 5 or 7(2).

10. The Employers' Liability (Compulsory Insurance) Act 1969 shall not require insurance to be effected by the Commission.

Proceedings and business

11.—(1) Subject to the provisions of this Act, the Commission may make arrangements for the regulation of their proceedings and business, and may vary or revoke those arrangements.

(2) The arrangements may, with the approval of the Secretary of State, provide for the discharge under the general direction of the Commission of any of the Commission's functions by a committee of the Commission, or by two or more Commissioners.

(3) Anything done by or in relation to a committee, or Commissioners, in the discharge of the Commission's functions shall have the same effect as if done by or in relation to the Commission.

12. The validity of any proceedings of the Commission shall not be affected by any vacancy among the members of the Commission or by any defect in the appointment of any Commissioner or additional Commissioner.

13. The quorum for meetings of the Commission shall in the first instance be determined by a meeting of the Commission attended by not less than five Commissioners.

Finance

14. The Secretary of State shall pay to the Commission expenses incurred or to be incurred by it under paragraphs 6, 7 and 8, and, with the consent of the Minister for the Civil Service and the Treasury, shall pay to the Commission such sums as the Secretary of State thinks fit for enabling the Commission to meet other expenses.

15.—(1) The Commission shall keep proper accounts of their income and expenditure, and shall prepare and send to the Secretary of State statements of account in relation to each financial year of the Commission.

(2) The financial year of the Commission shall be the twelve months ending on 31st March.

Disqualification Acts

16.—(1) In part II of Schedule 1 to the House of Commons Disqualification Act 1975 and Part II of Schedule 1 to the Northern Ireland Assembly Disqualification Act 1975 (bodies of which all members are disqualified under those Acts) there shall (at the appropriate place in alphabetical order) be inserted the following entry:—

" The Equal Opportunities Commission ".

(2) In part III of Schdeule 1 to each of those Acts of 1975 (other disqualifying offices) there shall (at the appropriate place in alphabetical order) be inserted the following entry:—

" Additional Commissioner of the Equal Opportunities Commission ".

Section 83.

SCHEDULE 4

Transitional Provisions

1. Section 12 does not apply, as respects any organisation,—
   (*a*) to contributions or other payments falling to be made to the organisation by its members or by persons seeking membership, or
   (*b*) to financial benefits accruing to members of the organisation by reason of their membership,

where the payment falls to be made, or the benefit accrues, before 1st January 1978 under rules of the organisation made before the passing of this Act.

2. Until 1st January 1978, section 12(2) does not apply to any organisation of members of the teaching profession where at the passing of this Act—

(*a*) the organisation is an incorporated company with articles of association, and

(*b*) the articles of association restrict membership to persons of one sex (disregarding any minor exceptions), and

(*c*) there exists another organisation within paragraphs (*a*) and (*b*) which is for persons of the opposite sex and has objects, as set out in the memorandum of association, which are substantially the same as those of the first mentioned organisation, subject only to differences consequential on the difference of sex.

3.—(1) Until a date specified by order made by the Secretary of State the courses of training to be undergone by men as a condition of the issue of certificates to them under the Midwives Act 1951 or the Midwives (Scotland) Act 1951 (as amended by section 20) must be courses approved in writing by or on behalf of the Secretary of State for the purposes of this paragraph.

(2) Until the date specified under sub-paragraph (1), section 9 of the Midwives Act 1951 and section 10 of the Midwives (Scotland) Act 1951 (regulation of persons other than certified midwives attending women in childbirth) shall have effect as if for the words from the beginning to (but not including) " attends a woman in childbirth " where they first occur there were substituted the words—

" If a person other than—

(*a*) a woman who is a certified midwife, or

(*b*) in a place approved in writing by or on behalf of the Secretary of State, a man who is a certified midwife ".

The amendment made by this sub-paragraph shall be read without regard to the sections 35A and 37A inserted in the said Acts of 1951 by section 20(4) and (5).

(3) On and after the said date the words to be substituted for those, in the said sections 9 and 10, mentioned in sub-paragraph (2) are—

" If a person who is not a certified midwife ".

(4) An order under this paragraph shall be laid in draft before each House of Parliament, and section 6(1) of the Statutory Instruments Act 1946 (Parliamentary control by negative resolution of draft instruments) shall apply accordingly.

4.—(1) If the responsible body for any educational establishment which (apart from this sub-paragraph) would be required to comply with the provisions of section 22(*b*), and of section 25 so far as they apply to acts to which section 22(*b*) relates, from the commencement of those provisions, is of the opinion that it would be impracticable for it to do so, it may before that commencement apply for an order authorising discriminatory admissions during the transitional period specified in the order.

(2) Section 27(2) to (5) and Schedule 2 shall apply for the purposes of sub-paragraph (1) as they apply in relation to transitional exemption orders.

5.—(1) Section 6 of the Equal Pay Act 1970 (as amended by paragraph 3 of Schedule 1 to this Act) shall apply as if the references to death or retirement in subsection (1A)(*b*) of the said section 6 included references to sums payable on marriage in pursuance of a contract of employment made before the passing of this Act, or the commutation, at any time, of the right to such sums.

(2) In relation to service within section 1(8) of the said Act of 1970 (service of the Crown) for the reference in this paragraph to a contract of employment made before the passing of this Act there shall be substituted a reference to terms of service entered into before the passing of this Act.

Section 83.

SCHEDULE 5

MINOR AND CONSEQUENTIAL AMENDMENTS

Factories Act 1961 (*c.* 34)

1. In section 15(2) (unfenced machinery: operations carried out by specified male persons) the word " male " shall be omitted.

The Registration of Births, Deaths and Marriages (Scotland) Act 1965 (*c.* 49)

2. In section 21(6) for the word " woman " there shall be substituted the word " person ".

Health and Safety at Work etc. Act 1974 (*c.* 37)

3. In Schedule 1, after the entry relating to the Emergency Laws (Miscellaneous Provisions) Act 1953, there is inserted the following—

1954 c. 57.	The Baking Industry (Hours of Work) Act 1954.	The whole Act.

Trade Union and Labour Relations Act 1974 (*c.* 52)

4. In Schedule 1, in paragraph 26(1), after " paragraph " there is inserted " and in section 64 of the Sex Discrimination Act 1975 ".

Section 83.

SCHEDULE 6

FURTHER REPEALS

Session and Chapter	Short Title	Extent of Repeal
7 & 8 Geo. 6. c. 31.	Education Act 1944.	Section 24(3).
14 & 15 Geo. 6. c. 53.	Midwives Act 1951.	In section 11(1), the words " or a male person ".
10 & 11 Eliz. 2. c. 47.	Education (Scotland) Act 1962.	Section 82(2).

Alphabetical Index

A

PAGE

Abandoning excess damages ... 40
Access to benefits or facilities, affording tenant ... 148
Access to public places ... 127
Access to training courses ... 54, 55
Accident insurance policy ... 13
Accommodation, Communal ... 108, 154, 155
employment necessitating ... 36
discrimination in ... 144, 149
discrimination in provision of ... 144, 146, 149
hotels, etc. ... 127
residential ... 36, 108, 152, 154
shared ... 146, 151, 152, 154
Accountant ... 63, 70, 79
" Accustomed to act "... 27, 60, 80
" Activities not carried on for profit " ... 130, 132
Acts extending over period ... 43, 87, 116, 159
Acts extending throughout contract ... 43, 87, 116, 159
" Act within the jurisdiction of an industrial tribunal " ... 51, 94, 124, 125, 168, 176
Actuarial data ... 13, 31
Additional Commissioner ... 45, 89, 179
Administration of political parties ... 132
Admissibility in evidence, information of ... 42, 86
Admissibility in evidence, questionnaires and replies ... 188
Admission as pupil to educational establishment ... 97, 109, 112
Admission to communal accommodation ... 57
Advertisement ... 28, 61, 81, 106, 142, 147, 148, 157, 171, 172, 173, 174, 176, 187
Advertisement for staff ... 28
Advertisement in connection with disposal of premises ... 147, 148
Advertiser ... 61, 142, 173, 174, 175
Advertising accommodation ... 147, 148
Advertising for employees ... 174
Advertising, forms of ... 172
" Affiliates of " political parties ... 132
Agency ... 128, 141
Agent ... 26, 27, 39, 59, 74, 79, 105, 141, 144, 149, 156

INDEX

PAGE

Agent, managing 149
Agent, for premises 144, 149, 156
Aiding to discriminate, knowingly 60, 79
Aircraft or hovercraft 137, 160
" Alice through the looking-glass " 1
Amending unreasonable requirement in non-discrimination notice 47, 121, 164
Amendment, educational trusts of 112
Annual report of Commission 190
Announcements 173
Annuity 13
Anti-victimisation provisions 8
Appeal, forms of 52, 125
Appeal procedures, statutory 74
Appeals against non-discrimination notices... ... ... 47, 91, 121
Application for modification of educational trust 112
Application for premises, refusing 145
Applications to industrial tribunals, time limits for 43
Application to industrial tribunals 39, 43, 74, 85
by Commission... ... ... 41, 43
Application to the Crown 26, 31, 48, 92, 107, 117, 123, 160, 165
Appointment to office or post by Minister 26
by government department 26
Approval 71
Armed forces 31, 107
Arrangements for offer of a partnership 75, 77
Arrangements for offer of employment 18
Assistance by Commission in relation to proceedings 189
in cases raising question of principle... 189
" Associated employers " 30
Associations, Business... ... 63, 64, 65, 66, 68, 82, 83, 84, 91, 93, 94, 95
Private 129, 130
Professional 63, 64, 65, 66, 68, 82, 83, 86, 91, 93, 94, 95
Associations of employers 54, 59, 64
Attorney-General 117, 160
Authorisation 70, 71, 72
Authority able to confer a qualification 71, 73
Authority, acts within agent's 26, 105
Average man 12
Average woman 12

B

Bank, provision of facilities or services by 23, 127, 135, 136
Banking and insurance, etc., facilities for 127, 135, 136
Barber 129
" Bedsitter ", letting for first time 148, 151
constitutes premises 148

INDEX

PAGE

Benefits consisting of payment of money 22
Benefits, facilities or services, provision by employer to public and employees 23, 26
Benefits, facilities or services, provision of to one-sex bodies ... 130, 131
Benefits or facilities, affording tenant access to 148
refusing tenant access to 148
Black list 9, 17
Boarder a licensee 148
Boarders... 108
Boarding houses 144, 148, 149, 151
Boarding schools 108, 109
Bodies, non-profit-making 110, 130, 131, 153
Bodies which confer professional qualifications 71, 73
control entry to professions, vocations, occupations, trades or businesses 71, 73
Bonuses, discretionary... 19
Breach of contract 39
British Medical Association 70
Brokerage 128
Building society, provision of facilities or services by 24, 127
Business associations 63, 64, 65, 66, 68, 82, 83, 86
Business purposes, premises for 145
Bungalows 149

C

Caption to illustration in advertisement 173
Caravans 149
Caretakers, resident 38
Cases raising question of principle, assistance in 189
Certification 70
Certiorari, order of 48, 52, 92, 95, 125, 169
Chambers of Commerce 63
Changes in practices 46, 90, 119, 163
Character, consideration of 73
Charge on costs receivable and property recovered 190
" Charitable instrument " 11, 111, 129
" Charitable purposes " 11
Charity 11, 12, 111, 129, 130
Chartered Accountants' Institute 63, 70
Civil proceedings, disclosure of information in 182
Civil Service 107
Clothing allowance 22
Clubs 129
member 130
Coal Mines Regulation Act 1908 33
Co-educational schools 108, 109
Commercial travellers 29

INDEX

PAGE

Commission, Equal Opportunities ... 41, 43, 45, 46, 48, 49, 50, 84, 86, 90, 92, 93, 94, 95, 118, 120, 122, 124, 125, 162, 163, 164, 165, 167, 168, 175, 176, 178 *et seq.*
charge on costs recovered, of 190
Commissioner 45, 89, 119, 178, 179, 183
Additional 45, 89, 119, 179, 183
Communal accommodation 154, 155
employment necessitating 36
training involving 57, 69
educational establishments in 108, 109
Comparison of cases 3, 9, 66, 73, 77, 99, 139
Compensation 17, 37, 40, 41, 50, 58, 69, 82, 83, 84, 94, 114, 158
Complainant, Industrial tribunal to 39, 82, 83
Complaint, to Industrial Tribunal 39, 43, 82, 86
Conciliation 42, 78, 86, 140
Conciliation officer 42, 78, 86
Condition, unjustifiable and detrimental 2, 4, 7
Conditions of employment 19, 39
Conditions of sale 128
Confederation of British Industry 63
" Confer " 70, 72
Conferences, women's, political parties of 133
Consent to assignment, landlord's 145
Conservative Party 133
Consideration of good character 73
Constituency parties 133
Constitution of political party 132
Construction sites 35
workers 29
Continues to reside on the premises 151, 152
Contract of employment 15, 16, 19, 21, 23, 24
Contract terms 23, 43, 62, 77, 87, 116, 140,
application to County Court *re* 78
Contract workers 25
Costs payable to complainant, charge on 190
County court ... 17, 39, 41, 47, 48, 50, 51, 83, 90, 92, 93, 94, 96, 103, 114, 115, 116, 120, 121, 124, 125, 126, 140, 158, 159, 163, 164, 165, 167, 168, 176, 182, 187
Courses of physical training 110
for teachers of physical training 110
Court of Appeal 122, 165
Court proceedings, bar on 39
Covert discrimination 2, 4, 6, 7, 16, 41, 84, 114, 158
" Crammers " 128
Creation of new lease 145
Creation of licence to occupy 145
Creation of tenancy 145

INDEX

PAGE

Creation of tenancy at will ... 145
Credit facilities ... 127, 128, 140
Criminal liability ... 28, 39, 42, 61, 80, 81, 86, 105, 107, 141, 175, 183, 184
Criminal proceedings, disclosure of information in ... 184
Crown, application of Act to ... 26, 31, 48, 92, 107, 117, 123, 160, 165
Crown Proceedings Act 1947 ... 48, 92, 117, 123, 165
Cubicles ... 134
Cutter ... 129

D

Damages ... 17, 39, 40, 41, 114, 158, 159
Death benefits ... 30, 66, 76
Decency or privacy, to preserve ... 34, 36, 108
Decision whether advertisement contravened Act ... 176
Declaratory order ... 17, 40, 50, 82, 85, 93, 187
" Deemed to aid " ... 79
Defence ... 26, 37, 58, 69, 105, 156, 174
Defence to proceedings ... 2, 79
Degrees conferred by universities ... 73
Delegation of Commission's functions ... 45, 89, 119, 179
Deliberate omission, time of ... 43, 87, 116
" Deliberately omitting " to provide goods, facilities or services ... 137, 138
" Demarcation provision " ... 21, 104
Designated educational establishment ... 101, 102
Detriment ... 2, 4, 7, 21, 25, 28, 33, 37, 58, 60, 65, 66, 70, 75, 80, 98, 100, 138, 149, 150
Detrimental requirement or condition ... 2
Disclaimer in advertisements ... 174
Disclosure of information obtained in formal investigations ... 183
Directions by Minister for Education ... 113
Discretionary bonuses ... 19
Discrimination ... 2, 6, 7, 8, 30, 70, 71, 137, 178
- overt ... 2, 3, 6, 8
- covert ... 2, 4, 6, 7, 64, 76
- by employee or agent ... 26, 39, 61, 80, 105
- against non-members ... 63

Discrimination against " person victimised " ... 8, 9
- positive ... 31, 55, 67

Discrimination, elimination of ... 178
Discrimination encouraged ... 31, 55, 67
Discrimination in the provision of goods, facilities and services ... 137
Discrimination in terms of employment ... 21, 22, 24
Discriminatory admissions, single-sex schools to ... 109, 111
Discriminatory advertisement ... 28, 106, 142, 171, 173
Discriminatory offer of employment ... 18, 19, 21, 24
Discriminatory practices ... 10
Discriminatory terms of employment ... 21, 23
Discriminatory training ... 55, 56

INDEX

PAGE

Disposal of premises 144, 147, 151
" Disposal " in connection with licence to assign 145
Dispose 145
Disposing of accommodation in " small dwellings " 151
Doctrines of religion 32, 110, 134, 150
Domestic responsibilities 56
Dormitories 36, 109, 154
Dramatic performances 34
Dressing-rooms... 134
Driving schools... 128

E

Education Act 1944 ... ... 101, 102, 113
Education Acts 1944 to 1975 101
Education authority 101, 105
Education, facilities for 97, 100, 101, 102, 103, 127
Minister for 113, 115, 116
personal services promoting 37
sanctions for discrimination in 113
Education, orders giving directions by Minister for 113
Educational activities by the Commission 178
Educational bodies 97, 105, 106
Educational establishments 73, 97, 98, 99, 100, 101, 102
Educational trusts 111, 112
Elected committees of organisations 68
Elimination of discrimination... 178
Employee of Commission 184
Employees, advertisements for 28, 173, 174
complaint to industrial tribunal by 39
" knowingly aiding " discrimination by employer ... 27, 105, 141, 156
liability for acts of 26, 39, 61, 78, 105, 155, 156
liability for own acts 27, 105, 141, 156
no right of action 39
suitable 34, 38
selecting 18, 19
Employers' associations 54, 60, 63
Employers' organisations 63
Employment Agencies 25, 56, 59, 70
Employment contract 15, 16, 19, 21, 23
Employment, exceptions for particular categories of 31
Employment for purpose of a private household 30
Employment necessitating communal accommodation 36
Employment, offer of 18, 19, 21, 39
Employment Service Agency 54, 56
Employment, terms of... ... ... 21, 22, 23, 24
Employment and Training Act 1973... ... ... 56, 57

INDEX

PAGE

Enforcement of statutory rights and duties 52
Enrolment 71
Entertainment 34
facilities for 127
Entry into professions 70
Entries in register of non-discrimination notices, certified copies of ... 185
Equal Opportunities Commission ... 41, 43, 45, 46, 48, 50, 51, 84, 86, 89, 90, 92, 93, 94, 95, 118, 120, 122, 124, 125, 162, 163, 164, 165, 167, 168, 175, 176, 178 *et seq.*
Equal Opportunities Commission, charge on costs of 190
Equal Pay Act 1970 ...9, 15, 17, 19, 21, 22, 24, 25, 28, 49, 51, 93, 95, 124, 125
Equality clause 15, 19, 21, 22, 125, 181
Equality of opportunity, promotion of 178
Equivocal replies to preliminary questionnaires 188
Establishment, nature or location of,... ... ... 35, 37
in Great Britain 28
Establishments for persons requiring special care, supervision or attention 110
Estate agent, services of 147, 149
Estate in premises, owner of 147
Evasive replies to preliminary questionnaires 188
Evicting tenant 148, 149, 150
Evidence, admissibility in 188
Exceptions for discriminatory training 55
Exceptions—general, unlawful discrimination to ... ... 10 *et seq.*
Exceptions to discrimination in provision of accommodation 150
Exemption order 109
" Extra-contractual " discrimination 16

F

Facilities... ... ... 127, 128, 135, 136, 138, 155
Facilities by way of banking or insurance 23, 135
Facilities for purpose outside Great Britain... 135
Facilties for training 31, 55, 56
Factories Acts 58
Failure " without reasonable excuse " to comply with court order 47, 91, 120
False allegation 9
False information 28, 42, 61, 81, 86, 106
Family responsibilities... 56
Female baby 4, 5
Filling a vacancy 34, 38
Films 173
" Final ", non-discrimination notice becoming 49, 124, 168
Finance, facilities for 127, 135
Financial benefits 22

INDEX

PAGE

Financial discrimination 16
Financial limits on county court jurisdiction ... 40, 41, 83, 114, 158, 159
Financial rewards, contractual 22, 23
non-contractual... ... ... 22, 23
Finding of unlawful discrimination 50, 51, 93, 94, 124, 125, 168, 187
First charge on costs to be paid to complainant 190
First charge on rights under compromise 190
Flat, constitutes " premises "... ... ... 147, 148, 149
Flat, furnished 149
Flat, letting for first time 148
Flat, " small premises " in 151
Foreign countries, acts done within the jurisdiction of 137
Foreign language schools 128
Foreign travel 111
Formal investigation 45, 46, 89, 90, 118, 162, 179, 181, 183, 184
terms of reference 45, 89, 119, 162, 179, 181, 186
Formal investigation naming person... ... ... 45, 89, 162, 181
Formal investigation to determine whether requirements of non-discrimination carried out 186
Freehold, owner of premises of 145, 149
Freehold, sale of 145, 147
Friend, tenant of 149
Fringe benefits 23
Furnished flats 149

G

Game 12
General duty in education 97, 102, 113
General Medical Council 74
" Genuine occupational qualification " 25, 33, 76
Good character, consideration of 73
Goods, facilities and services 127, 128, 135, 136
—" of the like quality " 137, 138
Governing bodies for professions and trades 70
Government department 26, 48, 92, 107, 117, 123, 160, 165
Governors, educational establishment of 100, 102, 115
Grants, facilities for 127
Great Britain, within 28, 55, 137, 144, 146
outside 111, 116, 136, 137, 160
Guarantees 128

H

High Court ... 39, 41, 48, 52, 84, 92, 96, 115, 117, 125, 126, 159, 165, 169
Hire purchase facilities 128, 140

INDEX

PAGE

Hospital facilities, exemption from S29. 134
Hotels 144, 148, 149, 151
Hotels, private 148, 151
House, constitutes " premises " 149
House, " similar establishment " 149
Households, small premises in 152
Housing and accommodation... 144
Housing associations 131
Hovercraft 137, 160
Hypothetical man 3, 15, 16
Hypothetical woman 3

I

Illustrations in advertisements 173
Independent schools 73, 100, 101, 103, 113
Inducing discrimination 28, 60, 80, 106, 142, 157, 187
Industrial Training Boards 54
Industrial tribunal, application to 39, 42, 74, 94, 187
Industrial tribunals ... 14, 17, 39, 40, 41, 42, 47, 50, 51, 52, 82, 83, 84,86, 91, 94, 96, 124, 126, 167, 168, 187, 188
time limit for applications to 43
Industry 127
Inferior courts, appeals from 52, 95, 96, 125, 126, 169
Information, affording to others 46, 90, 119, 120, 163
Information, non-admissibility in evidence 42
Information, notice requiring... ... ... 180, 181, 182, 183, 186
Injunction ... 17, 47, 48, 50, 51, 90, 92, 94, 114, 120, 122, 124, 164, 165, 167, 168, 187
Injury to feelings, compensation for 40, 83, 114, 158
Instructions to discriminate 27, 60, 106, 141, 156, 187
Insurance companies 31, 173
Insurance, facilities for 127, 135, 136
Intention to do an unlawful act 41, 84, 114, 158, 171, 173, 174
Interst in premises, owner of 147
Interpretation Act 1889 3
Investigation, formal ... 45, 46, 89, 90, 118, 119, 120, 162, 163, 179, 180, 181, 183, 185
Investment, premises for 145

J

Job description 174
Jockey Club 70
Jurisdiction of county courts, territorial 116, 160
financial 41, 83, 114, 159
" Justifiable " requirement or consideration 4, 5, 7, 66, 139

INDEX

K

PAGE

Knowingly aiding 27, 59, 61, 79, 105, 141, 156

L

Labour Party 133
Ladies' underwear, sale of 135
Landlady 148
Landlord, friend of 149
Landlords 144, 145, 148
Law Society 70, 74
Laws regulating the employment of women 38
Learned societies 130
Lease, sale of 145, 147
creation of new... 146
assignment of 146
" Less favourable " treatment 8, 9
Lessee 149, 152, 155
Lessor, licence to assign by 146
Licence to assign, landlord's 146
Licence to occupy 145
Licensing justices 70
Lfe assurance policy 13
Lighthouse 35
" Like manner as any other claim in tort "... ... ... 115, 122, 158, 166
Limit of compensation 17, 40, 41, 83
Limit on county court jurisdiction 41, 83, 115
Limited partnerships 75, 77
List, treatment of applicant for premises in relation to 145
Lived in, normally 35
Lloyds 63, 70
Loans, facilities for 127
Local authorities 59, 61, 70, 73, 100, 103, 144, 149, 155
services of 127
Local authority's Housing Department 149
Surveyor's Department 149
Local Education Authorities 59, 97, 100, 101, 115
Lodger a licensee 148
Lodgers, small premises in 153
Long lease, sale of 145, 147
" Looking-glass " provision 1, 15, 34, 64, 104, 134, 147
" Lump ", the 25

M

Magistrates' court 183
" Main object " of non-profit-making bodies 131, 132, 153
" Man " defined 5

INDEX

PAGE

" Man in the same employment " 15, 16, 20
Management of premises 144, 148, 149
accommodation 154
Manager, premises of 144, 149
Managers, school of 101, 102, 115
educational establishment of 101
Managing Agents 149
Mandamus, order of 48, 52, 92, 95, 96, 125, 126, 169
Manner of serving preliminary questionnaire and reply 189
Manpower Services Commission 54, 56, 58
Manufacturer's guarantees 128
credit facilities 128
Manufacturing trade 127, 128
Marital status 3, 6, 7, 14, 19, 21, 24, 33, 99, 100, 139, 144, 146, 158
" Marriage bar " 14
Married couple 38
Masseurs 135
" Material difference " between circumstances 20
" Materially different " 3
Members of relevant occupier's household, not 147, 151, 153
Membership 63, 65, 66, 110, 130, 131, 153
elected committees of organisations of 68
Midwife 32, 33
Mines and quarries 33
Minister for Education 113, 115, 116
Minister of the Crown... ... ... 26, 107
Misleading information 28, 61, 81, 86, 106
Modification of restrictions in educational trusts 112
Motive 2

N

" Near relative " 146, 151
New lease, creation of... 146
Non-contractual term for payment of money 19, 23
Non-disclosure, information obtained in formal ivestigations of... 183, 184
Non-discrimination notices ... 45, 46, 49, 88, 89, 90, 93, 118, 119, 121, 162, 163, 164, 165, 167, 185
procedure for 45, 88, 89, 118, 162
terms of 46, 89, 90, 119, 163
power of Commission to serve 45, 89, 90, 118, 162, 185
appeals against 47, 91, 121, 164, 185
appeals becoming final 49, 90, 93, 164, 185
register of 185, 186
amendment of 47, 91, 121, 164, 185
Non-profit making bodies 110, 130, 131, 153

INDEX

PAGE

" Normal in his case "... 138
Normal practice, exercising skills in accordance with 129
Notice of formal investigation 45, 89, 119, 179, 181, 182
Notice requiring information 180, 181, 182, 183, 186
order to comply with 182

O

Occupation of premises, terms of 148
Occupation, premises for 145
Occupational qualification, genuine ... ... 33 *et seq.*, 76
Occupier, relevant 146, 151, 152
" Occupying the premises " 148
Offer of employment 18, 19, 20, 21, 28
Offer of partnership, arrangements for 75, 77
Oil rig 35
Omission, deliberate ... 18, 21, 25, 43, 54, 58, 59, 64, 65, 71, 75, 77, 87, 97, 98, 100, 104, 116, 137, 138
Omission to reply to preliminary questionnaires 188
" One-sex " educational trusts 111, 112
" One-sex " religious sects 134
Opportunities for holding posts in organisation, encouraging 67
Opportunities for promotion, transfer or training 21
Order, declaratory 17, 40, 50, 82, 85, 93, 176
Order declaring educational body in default 113
Order for compensation 40
Order to comply with notice requiring information 182
Order to enforce compliance with non-discrimination notice ... 47, 120
Orders giving directions by Minister for Education 113
Orders of Certiorari, Mandamus and Prohibition ... 48, 52, 92, 95, 125, 169
Organisation of political party 132
Organisations of employers 63
Organisations of workers 63
Organised religion 32, 110, 134, 150
" Outworkers "... 25
Overt discrimination 2, 3, 6, 16
Owner-occupied boarding houses and hotels 151
Owner-occupiers, exception for 146, 147, 148, 151
Owner, of freehold 149
Owner, of premises 144, 146, 152, 155, 156

P

Pamphlets 173
Parliamentary candidates, promotion of 132
Particular courses of instruction 108
Particular skills exercised differently for men and women... 129

INDEX

PAGE

Partners, limited 75, 77
access to benefits, facilities or services 75, 77
Partnership contracts 78
Partnerships 75, 76, 77, 78, 82, 83, 84, 91, 93, 94
" Payment of money ", term for benefits consisting of 19, 20, 22
Permanent injunction 122, 165
" Persistent discrimination " 93, 124, 167
" Person "—defined 3
" Person holding statutory office " 26
Person specified in terms of reference, formal investigation for ... 45, 89, 119
Personal attributes 20
Personal services 37
Physical contact with men 34, 135, 151
Physical training courses 110
teachers, courses for 110
" Physiology ", reasons of 34
Pictures in advertisements 173
Place occupied or used for purposes of an organised religion 110
Political parties... ... ... 132, 133
Positive discrimination 31, 55, 67, 68
Postal tuition courses 128
Power to dispose 144, 145
Practices, changes in 46, 90, 120, 163
Preliminary applications by Commission 50, 93, 187
Preliminary issue of admissibility of questionnaires and replies 189
Preliminary questionnaires 188
Premises... ... ... 144, 145, 147, 148, 149
—disposal of 144, 145, 147
—management of 144, 149
—terms of offer of 145
Premises for residential purposes 145
business purposes 145
occupation 145
investment 145
treatment of applicant for in relation to list 145
Premises, small 146, 151, 152
Press advertisements 147
Primary education 101
Prior notice of non-discrimination notice 45, 89, 119
Prison 32, 37
Governors 32, 37
Officers 32, 37
Privacy, reasons of 35, 108
Private associations 129, 130, 150
Private hotels 151

INDEX

PAGE

Private household 30
Probation service 37, 38
Procedures for the settlement of grievances, other 42, 86
Proceedings, assistance by Commission *re* 189
Proceedings, questionnaires preliminary to 188
Procuring discrimination 27, 60, 80, 106, 142, 157
" Profession " 63, 70
services of any 127
Professional associations ... 63, 64, 65, 66, 67, 68, 69, 70, 82, 83, 93, 94
—elected committees of 68
Professional bodies 58, 63, 65, 66, 68, 70, 82, 83, 93, 94
—elected committees of 68
Prohibition, order of 48, 52, 92, 96, 125, 126, 169, 170
Promotion, opportunities for 21
Pronouns, job-descriptive 174
Property management firms 144
Property recovered by complainant, charge on 190
" Proportion of married women " 7, 139
" Proportion of women " 4
Proprietor, independent school of 100, 101
special school of 100, 102, 115
Protection against legislation 8
Protective legislation 38
Providing accommodation in " small dwellings " 151
Provision of accommodation, discrimination in ... 144, 145, 147, 149, 150, 151, 153, 154
Provision of benefits for one sex 110
Provision of same benefits, facilities or services to public 23
Public address system 173
Public authority 103, 127
Public bodies, appeals from 52, 74, 96, 126, 169
Public capacities, people in 129
Public houses, management of 38
" Public or a section of the public " 128, 129, 150
Publication of annual report 190
reports of formal investigations 180
Publisher 61, 81, 157, 171, 172, 174, 175
Pupil 97, 98, 100, 107, 108
Purchasers " personally introduced " 147

Q

Qualification 70, 71, 72
Qualifying bodies for professions and trades 71
" Quash " to 47, 52, 91, 95, 121, 164, 169
" Question of principle ", assistance in cases raising 189
Questionnaires preliminary to proceedings 188, 189

INDEX

R PAGE

Race Relations Board *v.* Edward Chater 129, 131
Radio 173
" Reasonable cause to believe " party will not comply with non-discrimination notice 47, 90, 120, 164, 182
" Reasonable excuse ", failure to comply with court order without ... 47, 91, 120, 164, 182
" Reasonably object ", physical contact to 135
Reception centre, exemption from S29. 134
Recognition 71
Recommendation to take certain action, Industrial Tribunals by ... 40, 41, 50, 83, 85, 94, 187
Recommendations for changes in law, Commission by 180
Recommendations for changes in policies or procedures, Commission by 180
Recreation, facilities for 127
Redressing an imbalance 67
Refreshment, facilities for 127
Refusing application for premises 145
" Right to occupy premises "... 145
Register of non-discrimination notices 185
certified copies of entries in 185
Registration 71
Relation, owner of premises of 144, 149
Relative, near 146, 151
Relevant circumstances 3, 72, 139
" Relevant occupier " 146, 151, 152
Religion 32, 110, 134, 150
Religious bodies 32, 73, 110
sects 135
Religious susceptibilities 32, 110, 134, 150
Remedies 41, 84, 115, 159, 166
Reparation for breach of statutory duty 114
Replies to questionnaires, Respondent by 188
Report for publication... 184
Report of findings of Commission in formal investigation ... 180, 183, 184
Request to conciliation officer 42, 85
Requirement in non-discrimination notice ... 46, 47, 48, 90, 91, 121, 164, 181, 185
formal investigation to determine whether carried out 186
Requirement—unfavourable 66, 72, 139
Requirement, unjustifiable and detrimental... ... ... 2, 4, 7, 73, 139
Research or educational activities by the Commission 178
Resident caretakers 38
Residential accommodation 35, 108, 152, 154
Residential purposes, premises for 145
Residing on the premises 146, 151, 152
Respondent, questionnaires to 188
Respondent, to complaint to Industrial Tribunal 40, 82

INDEX

PAGE

Responsibilities, domestic or family 56
" Responsible body " for educational establishment 97, 109, 111, 121, 125
of educational trusts 112
Restriction of membership of non-profit making bodies 130, 131, 153
Restrictions in educational trusts, modification of 112
Retail trade 127
Retirement pensions 30, 76
benefits 66, 67, 76
Review of statutory provisions, by Commission 178
" Risks wholly or mainly arising outside Great Britain " 136
Room, parting with possession of 148

S

Salary 22
Sale of freehold... 145
Sale of goods, contract for 140
Sale of lease 145
" Sanction " 122, 166
Sanctions for discrimination in employment 39
by business and professional associations, trade unions and partnerships 82
in the supply of goods, facilities and services 158
in education 113
in the provision of accommodation 158
Sanitary facilities 34, 35, 108, 154
appliances 135
School 101
Secondary education 101
Secretary of State ... 45, 56, 89, 103, 111, 113, 115, 117, 118, 188, 190
" Section of the public " 104, 128, 129, 130, 150
Section 7 exceptions ... ... 33 *et. seq.*
" Seeking training " 54
Selecting employees 18
Selection for training 55
" Serious embarrassment " to users of facilities or services ... 134, 151, 155
Service flats 149
Service of preliminary questionnaire and reply 188
Services 127, 128, 134, 135, 137, 138, 155
Settlement of dispute by conciliation officer 42, 85, 86
Sexual connotation to words in advertisements 174
Shared accommodation 146, 147, 151, 152, 154
Shared sleeping accommodation 154
Sheriff court 40, 176
Ships 35, 136, 160
Short lease, sale of 145

PAGE

Single-sex educational establishments 107, 108, 109
Single-sex non-profit making bodies 130, 131
Skills exercised differently for men and women 129
Sleeping accommodation shared 36, 108, 154
Small businesses 30
Small dwellings 151, 152
Small premises 146, 147, 151, 152
Soliciting additional members 67
Solicitors 71, 79
Special cases in employment 31
" Special consideration " for assisting applicant 189
Special school 100, 102
Specific disclaimer in advertisements... 174
Sport 12
" Squatter " 149
Staff, educational 106
" State of undress " 34, 134, 151
Statements made knowingly or recklessly ... 27, 28, 42, 105, 107, 156, 175, 183
reliance upon advertiser's 28, 175
Statutory appeal procedures 74
Statutory bodies 26
Statutory rights and duties, enforcement of... 52
Stock Exchange 63, 70
Suitable employees 34, 38

T

Tailor 129
Tailoring 135
Teachers of physical training, courses for 110
Teaching classes 108
Television 173
Temporary injunction 122, 165
Temporary staff 25
Tenancies created before passing of Act 146
" Tenancy " 146
Tenancy at will 145
Tenancy, creation or transfer of 145
Tenant 152
Tenant, evicting 148, 149
Tenant, friend of 149
Term for payment of money 19, 21
Terms of employment 21
Terms of offer of partnership, ... 75
Terms of offer of premises 145
Terms of occupation of premises 149

PAGE

Terms of reference for formal investigation... ... 45, 89, 119, 162, 179, 181
Territorial jurisdiction of county courts 116, 160
Territorial limits,—S29 for 135
Threatening 28, 60, 157
Time for appealing from non-discrimination notice 47, 91
Time for serving preliminary questionnaire... 189
Time limit for applications to industrial tribunals 43, 86
Time limits for proceedings in county courts ... 45, 95, 115, 116, 124, 159, 167
Tort 114, 122, 158, 166
Trade 70
facilities for any 127
authorisation for qualification which facilitates engagment in ... 70
Trade association 93
Trade organisations 63, 70
—elected committees of 68
Trade Union and Labour Relations Act 1974 ... ... 17, 40, 42, 83, 86
Trade unions 63, 64, 71, 82, 83, 86
—elected committees of 68
Training body 54, 55
Training courses 54
Training facilities for a minority sex... ... ... 24, 31, 67
for employment 21, 24, 25, 54, 55
Training involving communal accommodation 57, 69
Training Services Agency 54, 56, 58
Transfer of lease 145
Transfer of tenancy 145
Transfer, opportunities for 21
Transitional period, discriminatory admissions during 111
Transitional provisions—single-sex schools for 109, 111
Transport, facilities for 127
Travel agent 136
Travel allowance 22
Travel, foreign 111
facilities for 127
Treasury list of government departments for proceedings... ... 117, 160
Treasury Solicitor 117, 160
Treatment during occupation, tenant of 148
Tribunals 50, 82, 91, 96, 125, 168
Trustee, premises of 144, 155
Trustees of educational trusts... ... ... 111, 112
Trusts, educational 111, 112
Twenty-five years rule 112

U

" Undergoing training " 54
Undress, state of 34, 134, 151

INDEX

PAGE

Unfavourable requirement 2, 77, 99, 139
Unfavourable treatment 2, 6, 84, 99
Uni-sex seats on committees 68
United Kingdom, outside 38
within—*see* " Great Britain ".
Universities 73, 100, 101, 113
Unjustifiable requirement 2, 7, 77, 99, 139
Unlawful act, inference of 188
Unlawful advertisements 61, 171, 173, 174, 175
Unlawful discrimination ... 18, 25, 54, 56, 58, 59, 63, 65, 70, 75, 97, 101, 103, 128, 144, 146, 148
finding of 49, 51, 93, 124, 125, 167
Unreasonable for applicant to act unaided 189
Unreasonable requirement in non-discrimination notice 47, 121, 164

V

" Vacancies " an advertisement 148
Vacancy, filling a 34, 38
Vacant possession, sale with 147
Vendors of property 147
Vicarious liability 26, 60, 78, 140, 155
Victimisation 8, 18, 24, 30, 76, 98, 100
Vocation 63
Vocational training bodies 24, 54, 60, 61

W

Wages or salary 22
Welfare, personal service promoting... 37
Wholesale trade 127
" Wholly occupies " premises, owner who 147, 148
" Woman " defined 5
Woman owner of premises 147
Women members of political parties... 133
Women who have been away from work 56
Women's conferences, political parties of 133
Women's sections and committees, political parties of 133
Work " rated as equivalent "... 16
Workers hired-out with equipment 25
Workers, organisations of 63